D0205542

PRUITT CAMPUS LIBRARY
Indian River State College

The Social Sciences and Rationality

The Social Sciences and Rationality

Promise, Limits, and Problems

edited by
Axel van den Berg
Hudson Meadwell

Transaction Publishers
New Brunswick (U.S.A.) and London (U.K.)

Copyright © 2004 by Transaction Publishers, New Brunswick, New Jersey.

All rights reserved under International and Pan-American Copyright Conventions. No part of this book may be reproduced or transmitted in any form or by any means, electronic or mechanical, including photocopy, recording, or any information storage and retrieval system, without prior permission in writing from the publisher. All inquiries should be addressed to Transaction Publishers, Rutgers—The State University, 35 Berrue Circle, Piscataway, New Jersey 08854-8042.

This book is printed on acid-free paper that meets the American National Standard for Permanence of Paper for Printed Library Materials.

Library of Congress Catalog Number: 2004047895
ISBN: 0-7658-0232-5
Printed in Canada

Library of Congress Cataloging-in-Publication Data

The social sciences and rationality : promise, limits, and problems / Axel van den Berg and Hudson Meadwell, editors.
    p. cm.
    Papers presented at a conference held at McGill University in March 1999.
    Includes biographical references and index.
    ISBN 0-7658-0232-5 (alk. paper)
    1. Rational choice theory—Congresses. 2. Social sciences—Congresses.
I. Van den Berg, Axel. II. Meadwell, Hudson.

HM495.S63   2004
300'.1—dc22   2004047895

To Carman Miller,
for his initial idea and steady support

Contents

List of Tables, Figures, and Diagrams

Acknowledgements

The contributions to this volume originated at a conference held at McGill University in March 1999. Carman Miller, then Dean of the Faculty of Arts, proposed that we organize a conference around a theme of general interest to social scientists to showcase the range and excellence of the members of our faculty. He asked us jointly to take on the task of choosing the theme and organizing the conference as we were serving as Chairs of the Political Science and Sociology Departments at the time. The role of the notion of rationality in social science explanations seemed a natural choice to us, being capable of engaging many of our own immediate colleagues no less than those in the Economics and even Philosophy Departments. We also invited some well-known proponents of conflicting positions with respect to the theme to help us liven up the debate. In addition to the participants who presented actual papers at the conference, collected in this volume, a number of our colleagues and guests contributed extremely thoughtful comments on those papers. By all accounts, the conference was a resounding success. The participants came away, without exception, with a feeling that they had participated in an extraordinarily fruitful, collegial, and constructive dialogue, a rarity especially when an essentially contested concept like 'rationality' is at stake. The constructive tone of the conference owes a great deal to contributions by James Booth, Ian Jarvie, Anthony C. Masi, Alan Patten and Filippo Sabetti, and we hereby want to express our gratitude to them. We also wish to thank our students, Tolga Bölükbasi, Jeff Cormier and Jeff Osweiler, for their energetic assistance in organizing the conference and in helping to run things

xi

smoothly and efficiently. But most of all, we want to thank Carman Miller for having proposed the conference and for his vigorous moral and material support in getting it off the ground. The publication of this volume is yet another tribute to his years of wise and inspired leadership during one of the Faculty's most difficult periods.

Hudson Meadwell
Axel van den Berg
Montreal, September 2003

Introduction

The Social Sciences and Rationality: Promise, Limits and Problems

Axel van den Berg and Hudson Meadwell

The chapters of this book are the result of a most unusual conference that took place at McGill University in March 1999. As Ian Shapiro noted in his closing remarks to the conference, the debates about rational choice theory[1] have been characterized by a great deal of heat but remarkably little light. A major aim of the conference was to make a contribution towards rectifying this unhealthy state of affairs.

The conference was unique in at least two respects. First, it brought together (mild) critics and (moderate) advocates of rational choice theory to engage in real dialogue rather than the customary straw-manning and name-calling. In fact, the atmosphere and discussions at the conference proved to be unusually constructive, and fruitful far beyond what we could have hoped for. Second, we brought together scholars from the different social sciences and humanities, including economists, sociologists, political scientists and philosophers. Much of the debate over rational choice theory is conducted *within* the boundaries of the separate disciplines, which goes some way towards accounting for its enormously different reception among them: confidently dominant in economics, a major contender in political science, but marginal in both sociology and philosophy. A recurring complaint among sociologists, political scientists and philosophers is, moreover, that economists simply do not deign to take any serious notice of the criticisms leveled against their preferred approach coming from outside the circle of certified neoclassicists. What has become clear during this conference is that neither of these are necessarily the case. Participants from the different dis-

1

ciplines turned out to be surprisingly capable of arguing with each other about the supposed merits and flaws of rational choice theory and even fairly mainstream economists turned out to be remarkably willing to question the orthodox utility maximization model in quite fundamental ways.

Critics like Ian Shapiro have rightly denounced a kind of "verificationist" use of rational choice theory that is quite widespread. It consists of applying rational choice theory, more or less successfully, to some specific case and then saying: "see, another proof that people really *are* rational." Evidently, such rational choice theorists are committed to the fundamental assumptions of the model in some *ontological* sense. In his remarks Shapiro takes a stab at explaining why the debates over rational choice theory have been so heated. No doubt part of the explanation lies in the exaggerated and, indeed, arrogant claims made by the more enthusiastic champions of rational choice theory to be rigorously "scientific," as he claims. But another, in a sense deeper reason for all the heated debates about "rational peasants" (Popkin 1979; Scott 1977), the rationality of Captain Cook's killers (Obeyesekere 1997; Sahlins 1995; Hacking, 2000: 207-223), Azande magic (Winch 1964,1958; Dallmayr and McCarthy 1977: Part III; Okrent, 1984), and so on, is surely related to the ontological, verificationist tendency just mentioned. For many, commitment to the tenets of rational choice theory, *or* their rejection, is really a matter of belief, faith even, concerning such fundamentals as whether "deep down" people "really" are all the same or not, or whether such a claim to ultimate sameness is nothing but a covert claim to the superiority of *our own* conception of rationality or, to the contrary, an assertion of the basic dignity of all humans, and so on. These are inherently deeply held beliefs and it is profoundly disturbing when they are being questioned. But this kind of ontological rational choice theory is, consequently, more a matter of moral or ideological commitment than one that can be fruitfully debated and examined by scientific means. No cumulation of cases will ever suffice to show the skeptic that people really *are* rational everywhere, while no piling up of examples of seemingly "irrational" behavior will ever persuade the committed ontological rationalist that most people are, deep down, really *ir*rational. Yet much of the "debate" between the two sides has consisted of just this kind of competitive piling up of examples.[2]

The second and potentially much more fruitful use of rational choice theory is, by contrast, explicitly heuristic. It takes rational choice theory to be a convenient, *relatively* (compared to the nearest competitors) clearly worked-out explanatory recipe that can be used to attempt to explain some phenomenon or other. Sometimes, but by no means all of the time, this works fairly satisfactorily, as in the case of Chris Manfredi's chapter on why Canada's Supreme Court turned around completely in its interpretation of the role of the judiciary within a ten-year period. In such cases, rational choice theory apparently provides some significant part of the explanation for a hitherto unexplained phenomenon. At other times, the application of rational choice theory fails to explain the phenomenon in question. In such cases it is hoped that rational choice theory, due to its relative explicitness in defining its concepts and in specifying the empirical connections between them, will produce clear cues as to why and in which directions the model will have to be modified, or perhaps abandoned completely, so that we will be better able to account for the phenomenon we are trying to understand. Michael Smith's criticism of game theory as an explanation for relations of loyalty and trust between employers and employees is an excellent example of this kind of fruitful criticism of rational choice theory.

As opposed to an ontological commitment to the ultimate rationality of actors, this use of rational choice theory is strictly *methodological*. It rests on a pragmatic assessment of how one might best go about getting an initial explanatory handle on a problem, without expecting that this will provide the whole explanation or that it will always work. Most of those participating in this conference would endorse or at least accept this methodological use of rational choice theory. Of course, there is likely to be some elective affinity between the methodological and ontological assumptions: among those who are attracted to rational choice theory as a methodological, heuristic device there is no doubt a disproportionate number who *also* believe, deep down, that rational choice is valid in a more ontological sense. And this surely is one reason why there is so much slippage between strictly methodological and more moral-philosophical arguments in the ongoing debates. But at least in principle the two are distinct and in practice there is a great deal to be said for trying to keep them as clearly apart as we can. Only then can we hope to grapple effectively with the methodological promises *and* problems of the rational choice approach in the social sciences and humanities, in a spirit of mutual respect and cooperation between opposite camps.

This spirit is, we are happy to say, quite evident throughout the chapters that follow. In this volume, the defenders of rational choice theory and the critics are equally familiar with the arguments of their opponents and quite prepared to consider them seriously and thoroughly. This is what makes the tone of the discussions so remarkably constructive and these chapters such a satisfying read. Thus we have Michael Hechter, well-known for his forceful advocacy of rational choice theory in sociology, presenting a decidedly modest, pragmatic case for it. "Rational choice theorists gamble that social outcomes can be understood on the basis of admittedly incomplete models of individual action", he concedes. Moreover, he views it as something of a second-best approach: the simplifying assumptions of the type of rational choice theory that he espouses are most useful when we seek to explain the behaviour of actors about whose aims and motivations we have little independent information[3]. This means, among other things, that this kind of rational choice theory is most sensibly applied to the "strange" behaviors of actors who are the furthest removed from us in terms of space, time and culture.[4] This is the basis for Hechter's claim that rational choice theory is particularly suited for historical sociology, in stark contrast with much conventional wisdom among historical sociologists.[5]

By contrast, well-known philosopher Mario Bunge, staunch and persistent critic of rational choice theory and neoclassical economics alike (Bunge 1996: ch. 14; Bunge 1995; Bunge 1998: chs. 3 and 7), actually praises such famous purveyors of rational choice theory as James Coleman and Raymond Boudon for being "closet systemists" at worst. Bunge notes the rampant verificationism characterizing the debates between individualists and holists : "Each party parades a large collection of examples, without bothering about counterexamples." He also makes the important point that rational choice theorists, precisely because they make the deliberate simplifying assumptions about actors' aims and intentions that they make, are bound to let the structures and institutions within which actors find themselves do much of the explanatory work. Rational choice theory, in short, is much less of an individualist theory than it is claimed to be by advocates and opponents alike.

The confusion seems to be due at least in part to the close connection we generally tend to see between reason-based explanations and voluntarism. In a carefully reasoned exposition, philosopher Storrs McCall seeks to clarify the notion of rationality, which takes on a bewildering variety of meanings even among the relatively like-minded gathered here. In the process of unpacking the notion, McCall draws a sharp distinction between the deliberation reasons that precede an action and the explanation reasons that account for the action after the fact. This helps him make a case for an indeterministic, intentional conception of action.

Yet ironically, *both* proponents and opponents of rational choice theory have tended to extol their *own* approaches for their voluntarism while decrying those of their opponents as overly deterministic.[6] But surely one of the most attractive features of rational choice theory is the fact that, on one hand, it explicitly takes actors' intentions to be part of the explanation of their actions, while, on the other hand, it assumes a psychology of actors' intentions simple and possibly widespread enough to allow one to explain, however partially, the actions of large numbers of actors primarily by reference to externally observable pushes and pulls, costs and benefits, opportunities and constraints. This is what allows its advocates to extol its voluntaristic emphasis on choice where its critics only see passive, automaton-like responses to external stimuli. Arguments that incorporate intentionality in rational choice analysis are able to deal with choice under constraint. There is no commitment to full-blown voluntarism here. Yet as long as our purpose is to *explain* actors' behaviour causally, that is, in a way that goes beyond the hermeneutic goal of celebrating the actors' reasons *as* good reasons, then clearly "indeterminacy" is of not much help. Instead, we will need simplified but plausible psychological mechanisms. Rational choice offers up one type of mechanism.[7] Rather than denouncing the crude simplicity of its psychological assumptions, perhaps the critics ought to focus on developing alternative but equally plausible mechanisms (Chong, 1996) instead, *if*, that is, they *are* interested in advancing the cause of an explanatory social science.

No doubt the most spectacular evidence for the possibility of a constructive dialogue is provided by the two contributions of economists George Grantham and Robin Rowley. In a masterful historical tour d'horizon, Grantham shows how, in the discipline of economics, the original, relatively "weak" notion of rationality, involving piecemeal improvement rather than instant perfect maximization, was overtaken by the "strong," pure optimization model developed by the likes of Samuelson, Hicks, and Von Neumann and Morgenstern in what would come to be known as the "rational revolution" of the 1940s. This triggered a proliferation of ever more sophisticated optimization computation models, assuming hyperrational agents increasingly at variance with empirical reality.[8] As the unfavourable trade-off between ever-ascending generality and shrinking realism has become a matter of growing concern among economists, Grantham maintains, economic thinking has had to turn "back towards the weaker concepts of rationality." (p. 24). The weaker, Marshallian model of rationality, allowing for varying degrees of rationalization is acquiring a new appeal.

In an intriguingly parallel analysis, econometrician Robin Rowley criticizes the "rational expectations" assault on conventional ("Keynesian") econometrics for its ideologically inspired extremism. While granting many of the specific points of the so-called "Lucas critique," Rowley insists that these in no way justify a return to the utterly abstracted purity of "new classical theory" but, to the contrary, they should lead us towards much more serious efforts at improving the accuracy and realism of our models of economic behavior which will require taking seriously and incorporating the results of the other social science disciplines. In refreshing contrast to the plainly disingenuous calls for "interdisciplinarity" serving as a cover for economic "imperialism" denounced by Shapiro, Rowley's is a genuine call for an interdisciplinary approach, granting some room even for "economic sociology."[10]

Coming from almost the opposite end of the spectrum, so to speak, historical sociologist John A. Hall offers some reflections on Clausewitz's thinking on the role of "science" and "art" in warfare in order to arrive at a balanced view of the proper use of rational choice theory in the social science enterprise. Hall argues forcefully for the restricted *methodological* application of rational choice theory, as a research tool rather than as a complete description of the world. It cannot fully do justice to the real-world complexities facing actual decision-makers, he says, nor can it account for the emergence of preferences and the structural context that constitute the "games" analysed by game theory to begin with. Thus, scientistic overconfidence in the power of rational choice modeling is to be avoided.

Similarly, in his closely argued chapter, Michael Smith shows that the classic Prisoners' Dilemma game is inappropriate for modelling the kind of trust between employers and employees that according to the industrial relations literature has many beneficial consequences. An adequate conceptualization requires a richer, more sociological concept of trust. As noted, his paper is an excellent example of the heuristic uses that can be made of a relatively simple and clear model of behaviour based on rational choice theory in order to explore the *limits* of the theory.[11]

By contrast, Chris Manfredi shows in his chapter on the major shift of the Canadian Supreme Court from judicious caution in the 1988 *Morgentaler* case on abortion rights to an unprecedented judicial assertiveness in the 1998 *Vriend* case on discrimination on the basis of sexual preferences, that conceiving of the justices of the Supreme Court as strategic actors in an evolving arena of political forces provides a plausible explanation. But the demonstration of the *possibility* of applying such a rational choice explanation does not necessarily mean it is the only valid or best one, of course. To make the latter claim—which Manfredi carefully avoids, by the way—is to fall victim to precisely the kind of "verificationism" criticized by Bunge and Shapiro. With respect to Smith's paper, the converse point is also worth making: the inapplicability of *one* particular rational choice-based model need not disqualify all of them (see also Chai 2001: ch.2).

At first sight it may seem a bit odd to end a volume intended as a somewhat friendly contribution to thinking about the uses of rational choice theory with a comment by Ian Shapiro, one of the theory's best known and most persistent critics in recent years. But look again. To be sure, Shapiro begins his contribution by rehearsing his now well-known and much-discussed (see Friedman 1996) criticisms of rational choice theory's "pathologies." But this does not at all mean that Shapiro dismisses rational choice theory altogether. To the contrary, his commentary ends with a series of recommendations meant to *improve* rational choice theory rather than do away with it. In effect, Shapiro ends up giving quite a strong endorsement to the heuristic, methodological, rather than ontological, use of rational choice theory that we have advocated throughout this introduction.

It should be plain by now that the contributions to this volume form an unusually coherent whole, unusual especially in view of the variety of subject matters and the very different positions and disciplines that are represented here. In part this coherence is due to the fact that there are several themes and arguments that recur throughout. The advocacy of a heuristic, pragmatic use of rational choice theory is one of these. Another is a firm commitment to rational choice theory as an explanatory strategy, not a normative model of ideally rational behaviour to guide action. Some of the confusion in the debates about rational choice theory could be avoided simply by keeping these two possible uses of rational choice theory clearly separate. As several of the contributors to this volume point out, if rational choice theory is to be an explanatory strategy first and foremost, its main task will be to explain the behaviour of (in some sense) typical members of a large population which should not be confused with a prescriptive decision-making theory that can be used to rationalize the behavior of individuals (see the chapters by Hechter and Rowley). This means, among other things, that simple models based on relatively casual (in Grantham's terms "weak") levels of rationality are to be preferred over highly sophisticated models of hyperrationality.[12]

Although we have emphasised the civility of debate between the contributors to this volume, we do not want to end with a self-congratulatory pat on the back. Civil debate does not mean bland agreement. There remains plenty of productive controversy around rational choice theory even after the unproductive straw-manning and name-calling is put to one side, as it was in these pages. So another measure of the success of this colloquy should be whether our contributors clarify the issues at stake in the debate about rational choice theory and thus advance the larger discussion in the human sciences about rationality.

On this score, let us consider two important questions that came out of the discussion. First, what is distinctive about rational choice analysis and, second, what fuels some of the criticism of rational choice theory?

Before trying to address the first question directly, it may be worth our while identifying some of the respects in which rational choice theory is *not* as distinctive as sometimes claimed. *Pace* the many critics who denounce it for its 'atomistic' individualism, rational choice theory is *not* really a theory of *individual* action. As noted already, Mario Bunge and others have made the important point that structures and institutions rather than individuals do the actual explanatory work in rational choice theory (see also, e.g., Farmer 1992: 418, fn.2; also Goldthorpe 1998: 173; Latsis 1976; Hollis 1994: 185-6; England and Farkas 1988: 345). Their point clarifies an important feature of rational choice analysis. The latter is far less vulnerable to the charge that it presupposes atomised individuals than some of its critics realise. The position that persons are embedded in relations, networks, institutions and structures is a stepping-off point for rational choice analysis rather than a fatal objection to it. It is not going to separate rational choice analysis from approaches used by some of the critics of rational choice analysis.[13]

Nor does rational choice theory necessarily assume, as Hechter emphasizes in his contribution, that people are, always and everywhere, totally consumed by their immediate material interests. Quite to the contrary, his "Athin" variant of rational choice theory assumes very little about the nature of people's ultimate or even proximate aims and preferences. All he assumes is that people will not knowingly choose a way of realizing them that is manifestly more wasteful of valuable resources than is necessary. That is, most if not all actions involve the expenditure of resources, some of which, such as time, basic material resources, physical security and so on, are both significant across cultures and usually to some degree scarce. This simple set of assumptions, then, allows the social scientist to explain and/or predict at least the direction of movement of the "average" behavior among large numbers of people in response to changes in resource-relevant conditions in a remarkably wide variety of situations and societies, irrespective of the no doubt profound differences in ultimate goals and outlooks between them.[14]

While the degree of success of the explanation will vary from case to case, as Hechter admits freely, in most cases this approach will at least contribute *something* towards the explanation of the behavior of large populations. Now, it may well be that in this moderate garb rational choice theory simply reduces to fairly trivial common sense, as Mario Bunge has suggested. But it is a form of common sense that still allows us to do a lot more explaining with relatively little in the way of assumptions than appears to be the case for any of the alternative approaches currently on offer, as advocates of rational choice theory are fond of pointing out. As Hechter puts it, "This paucity of other methodologically and ethically attractive theoretical options helps account for the resilience of rational choice" (p. 8). It may also be resilient because theoretical common sense is more widespread than is usually believed. Macro theories of institutions and structures may use rational choice mechanisms (perhaps along with other mechanisms) more often than is advertised.

But, of course, all of this only renders our second question more pressing: if rational choice theory really is little more than common sense, what, then, accounts for the often heated, sometimes downright shrill criticisms of rational choice theory?[15] Moreover, this is not a recent phenomenon. The basic ideas on which rational choice theory rests were exceedingly controversial throughout the long history of their cumulative formulation (Hirschman 1977). Without question, some of their early formulations were quite explicitly meant as polemical weapons in a political campaign to debunk the exalted moral pretensions of traditional elites (see, e.g., Holmes 1990; Phillips, 1993), thus virtually *inviting* controversy. As a result, political and ideological considerations have never been far below the surface in the controversies they provoked. But the critics of rational choice theory and its philosophical ancestry have hardly been just apologists for pre-industrial elites. And quite apart from the often all too obvious political undertow[16] there is a distinctly *moral* flavor to much of the criticism of rational choice theory, then as now, sometimes quite explicitly so.[17] This suggests that more fundamental issues are at stake than mere politics.

What seems to provoke the greatest amount of moral outrage among the critics is the assumption they attribute to rational choice theorists, whether rightly or wrongly, to the effect that social order and community are possible on the basis of purely calculative, self-interested behavior of the individuals that make up the community. In the eyes of many of the critics, this particular notion, above all others, is both preposterous and deeply offensive. As the two predicates suggest, there are actually two distinct issues here that tend all too often to become confused in the heat of the debate. For the sake of clarifying what is and what is not necessarily in dispute, and how we might move past the current polemical impasse, it is very much worth our while, however, to try to keep them analytically separate. While one concerns, in principle at least, a matter of fact, the other is fundamentally evaluative. The first question is: is the kind of rational, calculative, and, especially, materialistic and selfish behavior supposed by rational choice theory a cross-cultural and cross-temporal universal or is it a peculiar feature of the *modern, Western* societies only? Second, is the prevalence of such behaviour a good thing or a bad one?

Much of the debate, however much couched in "technical" terms, is really about the second question, that is, about whether the spread of materialism, individualism and rationalism is an abomination or a blessing. This is, in fact, what much of the argument going under the heading of 'the problem of social order' (Parsons) is *really* about. The claim here is that if people really acted according to the assumptions of rational choice theory then a viable social order would be impossible, as it would disintegrate into a Hobbesian war of all against all. The issue is, of course, intimately linked to the "free rider problem" and the "tragedy of the commons," both of which have received a great deal of attention from rational choice theorists. But while it is often presented by the critics as a purely technical kind of 'impossibility theorem' demonstrating the absurdity of rational choice theory, the underlying idea of what exactly constitutes a *viable* social order is a notoriously slippery one. What ultimately seems to be at stake is not so much whether purely selfish and calculative behavior by all, or the absence of any normative commitments, would inevitably lead to utter chaos and disorder but whether it would be an order *worth having*. That is, do we really *want* such a dog-eat-dog world? Rational choice theorists, on the other hand, seem to have just as deep a moral commitment to the very desirability of this brave new world, one that *they* see as a true emancipation from the *Harmonielehren* of the Dark Ages with their moral indoctrination and hypocrisy (see Holmes 1990: 284). Many of the well-known debates referred to earlier seem to be about this. They those who feel that society without some sense of common purpose does not constitute a *community* against those who abhor precisely the kind of "community" that claims to represent some common purpose.

Clearly, one person's chaos may be another person's order. For many critics of rational choice theory, "true" communities have a communal *telos* and the economic and political activity of members of a true community is and should be subordinated to it. Their opponents, by contrast, are deeply suspicious of any such *telos* and would much rather live in a world where none exists. We rapidly reach ontological rock bottom here, or, if you prefer, quicksand. Matters of fact (to what extent *is* there a trade-off between liberty and equality and/or "order"?) and moral commitments (what kind of "order" do we *want*?) seem to get hopelessly entangled at this point and ultimately based on fundamental—in the sense of not really shakeable by logic or evidence—ontological assumptions about what humans are, deep down, *really* like.

Ultimately, of course, the very nature of modernity is at stake here. To be sure, there is tremendous ambivalence about modernity underlying the criticisms of rational choice analysis that draw on the kind of communitarian intuition suggested. And it produces some interesting ironies as well. *Some* of the time, the critics' major claim seems to be that the modern world is a profoundly corrupt and "inauthentic" place. Modern economies and polities—markets and states, materialism and power—have corrupted the ancient virtues. By implication, rational choice analysis is only suitable for a corrupted world. A position like this underlies many criticisms of rational choice analysis including Scott's arguments in the Popkin-Scott debate alluded to before. It is also central to hermeneutic criticisms of which the work of Charles Taylor is a good example. The hermeneutics of Heidegger (Ott, 1993; Wolin, 1993) and Gadamer (1974; Margolis, 1991: 175-179) is shot through with ambivalence about, if not hostility toward, the modern world and these were important sources in the work of Taylor (1978; 1993; 1985). Even Habermas, who has a stratified theory of action that includes strategic and instrumental action, treats the "lifeworld" as the only *true* community which in the modern world is in danger of being "colonized" by the "system" which, because it is steered by power and money, is a realm that is constituted by instrumental and strategic types of action (see Habermas 1984; 1987; cf. van den Berg 1990; Meadwell, 1994; 1995).

But if the true communities of yore have indeed been corrupted in the modern world, then this would seem to have the ironic implication that a pure hermeneutics is becoming irrelevant. Rather, for the analysis of *modern* societies at least, rational choice analysis would seem to be appropriate and adequate "all the way down," although the world may well be worse off for it.

Unsurprisingly, this is not the conclusion drawn by most of the hermeneutically inclined critics. Instead, their argument tends to slide over into quite a different claim, namely that the sway of modern rationalism and instrumentalism is exaggerated and that forces that lie outside the purview of rational choice analysis constitute decisive chunks of social life, in modern and other societies alike. Consequently, so the argument continues, the extension of rational choice analysis to these parts of life is a characteristic mistake of the modern attitude. Rational choice analysis, that is, is an intellectual expression of the hubris of modernity, *Western* modernity, to be exact. Some time ago, Polanyi drew his famous distinction between economics in the 'formal' and in the 'substantive' sense precisely in order to make this point. According to Polanyi (1958), mainstream economists have illegitimately extended the former to situations where only the latter was relevant. The calculative, resource-economizing attitude of formal economics was typically modern and Western, he argued, an attitude entirely foreign to the substantive economies of non-Western and traditional societies, and the West before the emergence of capitalism. That is, other societies are able to satisfy their material needs in ways that do *not* encourage a fierce competition of materialistic calculators but are based, instead, on moral principles of sharing and fair exchange. These societies have household economies that are organized around the needs of a community. This kind of argument has been vigorously revived by various versions of current anti-globalism, of course. And it is easy to see how much moral sustenance can be derived from the assurance that such alternative communal arrangements exist and are viable.

Yet unlike the first, evaluative issue, this is a matter that *can* be cast in factual terms. For surely the degree to which people actually do behave in a materialistic, calculative manner, whether in the satisfaction of their material needs or in other domains of life, is in principle *variable*. So then the question becomes, *are* people in modern, Western societies more inclined to pursue their materialistic interests in a calculative manner than elsewhere? Much of the fruitlessness of the debates about rational choice theory in the recent past has been due to the fact that both sides have tended to attribute to their opponents an extreme position on this issue that nobody subscribes to. No critic of rational choice theory, no matter how deeply disgusted he or she may be with the cold, calculative greed of *homo economicus*, would ever claim that considerations of resource economy *never* play a role *anywhere* in human behaviour, nor would even the most extreme advocate of rational choice theory insist that people are *everywhere* and *at all times* concerned *only* to maximize their material well-being. The *degree* to which material self-interest and cold calculation as opposed to moral commitment, emotion or habit prevail surely varies from place to place and time to time, and so will, consequently, the degree of success of rational choice theory in accounting for the resulting behavior. Further, the ways in which commitment and calculation might *interact* in particular places and times will never be brought into view if we do not agree from the start that this kind of interaction is possible *and* worthy of examination.[18]

Instead of pointing to the bankruptcy of either the rational choice approach or any of its theoretical rivals, these questions of *degree* and *interaction* would seem to open up a vast agenda for theory and research that *both* should be able to subscribe to. For the really fruitful questions turn out to revolve around *how* and *why* different social, economic and historical conditions engender different mixes of social behavior.

But acceptance of such a research agenda presupposes a commitment to a strictly *heuristic* use of rational choice theory. It treats rational choice theory as a *family* of "sometimes-true" models (Hernes 1992: 425-7) and no more. To be sure, no discipline can avoid thinking about the problem of rationality, as is quite evident from the contributions to this volume. At the same time, the sheer variety of arguments and approaches is striking and might have been much less apparent if we had not cast our net as widely as we did. But it remains an open question whether there is a unified theory that underpins all of the uses of rationality in the papers presented. Both users and critics of rational choice theory often seem to proceed as if there was. It would seem to be far more prudent to remain agnostic on this point for now.

But then, if we really are interested in making some progress in explaining the social world, rather than forcing it all unto our preferred Procrustean bed of rationality, perhaps the issue is not particularly pressing. It would seem more fruitful simply to accept that there is a whole array of rational choice models, ranging from near common sense to fairly far-fetched, with probably varying ability to account satisfactorily for the empirical phenomena we wish to explain, just as there is, or should be, a host of alternative models with equally varying promise. The task, then, would be to try and identify the conditions under which one rather than another model works and, eventually, to explain *why* they do.

Such a strategy does require an as yet unusual degree of common purpose among otherwise sharply divided scholars, however. One of the outstanding features of the chapters that follow is that they *do* seem to be inspired by something like such a common purpose. And it is not simply a matter of good will, since the Chapters build on some shared intellectual terrain. In an age of postmodern fragmentation it is truly heartening to see such a degree of philosophical common sense, in both senses of the term, among scholars of such diverse backgrounds. The resulting spirit of constructive dialogue, and the remarkably similar positions and recommendations that it appears to have produced, demonstrate another important and encouraging truth: that, given some minimal agreement on the basic purpose of our joint enterprise it *is* possible to make cumulative progress through critical but respectful examination of arguments and facts.

Notes

1. Goldthorpe (1998: 187, fn.3) prefers the term rational *action* theory on the grounds that we are concerned with action in general rather than with choice only. We take his point but use the more traditional term for the purely pragmatic reason that it might avoid at least one unnecessary terminological issue.
2. For a good example see the debate between James Coleman and the critics of his monumental *Foundations of Social Theory* (Coleman 1990) in the pages of *Theory and Society*, showing both very clearly what ontological commitments are at stake and how intemperate the "debate" tends to become as a result (see Alexander 1992; Coleman 1992; Sica 1992; Stinchcombe 1992; and Warfield Rawls 1992).
3. It does not follow, however, that as we know more about actors we are obliged to abandon rational choice theory, or that rational choice theory is most useful when what we know about actors asymptotically approaches zero! To argue this implies that actors are actually non-rational, and that we can believe otherwise only if we know little or nothing about them.
4. This may be seen as conceding critical ground to those, beginning with Winch (1958), who argued that western social science cannot understand other cultures from the inside. Their point of view is not without problems, however. Some of these arguments rest on a mistake made originally by Winch (1958)—that cultures are a form of private language. Wittgenstein, whom Winch used in support of his argument, actually showed the impossibility of a private language. Ironically, even Winch (1964) was led to argue for the importance of human constants across cultures: birth, death and sexual relations. However much ritual practice and meaning is invested in them, these constants are not cultural in the first instance; they are moments in the reproduction of the human species. Ritual practices around these moments are different practices of the same *kind*.
5. See also Kiser and Hechter (1998) and the reactions in Goldstone (1998) and Somers (1998). For some of the typical arguments *against* the applicability of rational choice theory to history, from an Eliassian perspective, see Goudsblom (1996) and de Swaan (1996), and van den Berg for a reply (1999). For recent applications of rational choice and game theory to a variety of historical issues and episodes, generating a spirited debate about its merits and shortcomings, see Bates et al. (1998), Elster (2000), Bates et al. (2000), and the Symposium (2000) in *Social Science History*.

6. For a brief discussion of this somewhat curious phenomenon, see van den Berg (1998: 444-5).
7. For a more thorough articulation of this argument, see Goldthorpe (1998).
8. Compare Conlisk (1996): 674-5) on the drift towards impossibly high standards of rationality due to the increasing sophistication of computational techniques among game theorists, producing ever more glaring anomalies.
9. This is the central argument in van den Berg (1998).
10. For a rather less sanguine view of economic sociology coming from an economist not particularly known for his orthodoxy—rendering his trenchant criticisms all the more painful—see Piore (1996).
11. Interestingly, Gary Miller, who is one of the main targets of Smith's critique, has himself argued that the major theoretical payoff of the introduction of Downsian rational choice theory, which is based on economic theory, into the analysis of politics has been to help identify those vast areas of political behavior which *cannot* be fully understood by analogies to economics (see Miller 1997)!
12. On this important point, see also Goldthorpe (1998).
13. As (Becker 1976, p. 5) notes, "In the economic approach, [prices and other market instruments] perform most, if not all, of the functions assigned to 'structure' in sociological theories." Interestingly, Smelser, the well-known sociologist with structural-functionalist leanings, presents this as a *flaw* of rational choice theory. "What strikes one as remarkable about this construction is how much is given (i.e., stable, parametric) and how little is variable. Actors' internal environments are regarded as stable and unvarying, and outcomes of exchanges are, in the last analysis, regarded as a product of variations in the availability of goods and services, their cost or price, and the capacity of economic actors to initiate exchanges for those goods or services. In this sense action is, paradoxically, based on free choice but is determined in the end by external factors" (Smelser , 1995: 78). There is this difference, however, to which we return in the Conclusion: Under perfect market competition, there are a large number of isolated agents, all price-takers, and there are no coalitions of agents. There is no analogue in the sociological analysis of structures to perfect competition and thus there is no sociological contradiction between social structures and social coalitions in the presence of large numbers of agents. However, outside of a private goods economy (that is, in the presence of public goods), which must be a characteristic of the perfectly competitive economy if the latter is to generate price-taking behavior, large numbers generate a market failure—the problem of free-riding—a problem that cannot arise in a perfectly competitive economic market of individual agents.
14. See Hechter and Kanazawa (1997), Goldthorpe (2000, 1998) and Little (1991) for more thorough parallel arguments along these lines.
15. Sometimes admittedly so. "The strident tone of this essay is a personal reaction to the unrelenting ascendancy of rational choice theory in the social sciences... I believe it is necessary as an antidote to the inflated claims of many rational choice theorists and to their condescending attitude towards alternative methods of political inquiry" (Petracca 1991: 188, n.3).
16. Compare Seidman (1991) who accuses rational choice advocates of being elitist and sexist anti-democrats, dismissed by Heckathorn (1997:15) as fairly typical of the "the hysterical attacks that have all too often marred debates on [rational choice]".
17. See, e.g., Etzioni (1988), MacIntyre (1984), Davidson and Davidson (1988), cf. Kirzner (1990), Zafirovski (2001), Lichbach (2003).
18. This position is nothing like a universal predilection. A plausible argument can be made that competing models should only be tested one against the other. For this kind of argument about the "paradox of voting," that seeks to test "pure" rational

choice arguments against competing arguments, see Blais (2001). However, there is no obvious reason why we need to proceed in one direction alone (Morton, 1999: 242-276).

References

Alexander, Jeffrey C. 1992. Shaky foundations: the presuppositions and internal contradictions of James Coleman's *Foundations of Social Theory. Theory and Society* 22: 203-217.

Bates, Robert, Avner Greif, Margaret Levi, Jean-Laurent Rosenthal, and Barry R. Weingast. 1998. *Analytic Narratives*. Princeton, NJ: Princeton University Press.

Bates, Robert H., Avner Greif, Margaret Levi, Jean-Laurent Rosenthal, and Barry R. Weingast. 2000. The analytic narrative project. *American Political Science Review* 94:696-702.

Becker, Gary. 1976. *The Economic Approach to Human Behavior*. Chicago: University of Chicago Press.

Blais, André. 2001. *To Vote or Not to Vote? The Merits and Limits of Rational Choice Theory*. Pittsburgh, PA: University of Pittsburgh Press.

Booth William, J. 1994. On the idea of the moral economy. *American Political Science Review* 88: 653-667.

Bunge, Mario. 1995. The poverty of rational choice theory, in I.C. Jarvie and N. Laor (eds.) *Critical Rationalism, Metaphysics and Science*. Dordrecht and Boston: Kluwer.

Bunge, Mario. 1996. *Finding Philosophy in Social Science*. New Haven, CT: Yale University Press.

Bunge, Mario. 1998. *Social Science Under Debate*. Toronto: University of Toronto Press.

Chai, Sun-ki. 2001. *Choosing an Identity: A General Model of Preference and Belief Formation*. Ann Arbor: The University of Michigan Press.

Chong, Dennis. 1996. Rational choice theory's mysterious rivals, in Jeffery Friedman (ed.) *The Rational Choice Controversy. Economic Models of Politics Reconsidered*. New Haven, CT and London: Yale University Press.

Coleman, James S. 1990. *Foundations of Social Theory*. Cambridge, MA: Harvard University Press.

Coleman, James S. 1992. The problematics of social theory. *Theory and Society* 21: 263-283.

Conlisk, John. 1996. Why bounded rationality? *Journal of Economic Literature* XXXIV: 669-700.

Dallmayr, Fred R. and Thomas A. McCarthy (eds.). 1977. *Understanding and Social Inquiry*. Notre Dame, IN: University of Notre Dame Press.

Davidson, Gregg, and Paul Davidson. 1988. *Economics for a Civilized Society*. New York: W. W. Norton.

de Swaan, Abram. 1996. Rational choice as process: the uses of formal theory for historical sociology. *The Netherlands' Journal of Social Sciences* 32 : 3-15.

Elster, Jon. 2000. Rational choice history: a case of excessive ambition. *American Political Science Review* 94:685-695.

England, Paula , and George Farkas. 1994. Economic and sociological views of industries, firms, and jobs. Chapter 14 in *Industries, Firms, and Jobs: Sociological and Economic Approaches*, expanded edition, edited by George Farkas and Paula England. New York: Aldine de Gruyter.

Etzioni, Amitai. 1988. *The Moral Dimension: Toward a New Economics*. New York: The Free Press.

Farmer, Mary K. 1992. On the need to make a better job of justifying rational choice theory. *Rationality and Society* 4: 411-420.

Friedman, Jeffrey (ed.). 1996. *The Rational Choice Controversy*. New Haven, CT: Yale University Press.

Gadamer, Hans-Georg. 1975. *Truth and Method* translation revised by Joel Weinsheimer and Donald G. Marshall. New York: Crossroad.

Goldstone, Jack A. 1998. Initial conditions, general laws, path dependence, and explanation in historical sociology (in Symposium on Historical Sociology and Rational Choice Theory), *American Journal of Sociology* 104: 829-845.

Goldthorpe, John. 2000. *On Sociology: Numbers, Narratives, and the Integration of Research and Theory*. Oxford: Oxford University Press.

Goldthorpe, John. 1998. Rational action theory for sociology. *British Journal of Sociology* 49: 167-192.

Goudsblom, Johan. 1996. Rational and other choices. Comments on the rational choice model. *The Netherlands Journal of Social Sciences* 32: 16-25.

Green, Donald P. and I. Shapiro. 1996. *Pathologies of Rational Choice Theory: A Critique of Applications in Political Science*. New Haven, CT: Yale University Press.

Habermas, Jürgen. 1984. *The Theory of Communicative Action, Vol. 1: Reason and the Rationalization of Society*. Boston: Beacon Press.

Habermas, Jürgen. 1987. *The Theory of Communicative Action, Vol. 2: Lifeworld and System: A Critique of Functionalist Reason*. Boston: Beacon Press.

Hacking, Ian. 2000. *The Social Construction of What?* Cambridge, MA: Harvard University Press.

Hechter, Michael, and Satoshi Kanazawa. 1997. Sociological rational choice theory. *Annual Review of Sociology* 23:191-214.

Heckathorn, Douglas D. 1997. Overview: the paradoxical relationship between sociology and rational choice. *American Sociologist* 28: 6-15.

Hernes, Gudmund. 1992. We are smarter than we think. *Rationality and Society* 4: 421-436.

Hirschman, Albert O. 1977. *The Passions and the Interests: Political Arguments for Capitalism before its Triumph*. Princeton, NJ: Princeton University Press.

Hollis, Martin. 1994. *The Philosophy of Social Science*. Cambridge: Cambridge University Press.

Holmes, Stephen. 1990. The secret history of self-interest in Jane J. Mansbridge (ed.) *Beyond Self-Interest*. Chicago: University of Chicago Press.

Kirzner, Israel M. 1990. Self-interest and the new bashing of economics: a fresh opportunity in the perennial debate. *Critical Review* 4: 27-40.

Kiser, Edgar, and Michael Hechter. 1998. The debate on historical sociology: rational choice theory and its critics. *American Journal of Sociology* 104: 785-816.

Latsis, Spiro J. 1976. A research programme in economics, in Spiro J. Lastis *Method and Appraisal in Economics*. Cambridge: Cambridge University Press .

Lichbach, Mark I. 2003. *Is Rational Choice Theory All of Social Science?* Ann Arbor: The University of Michigan Press.

Little, Daniel. 1991. *Varieties of Social Explanation: An Introduction to the Philosophy of Social Sciences*. Boulder, CO: Westview Press.

MacIntyre, Alasdair. 1984. *After Virtue: A Study in Moral Theory*. Notre Dame, IN: Notre Dame University Press.

Margolis, Joseph. 1991. *The Truth About Relativism*. Oxford and Cambridge: Blackwell.

Meadwell, Hudson. 1995. Post-marxism, no friend of civil society, in John A. Hall (ed.) *Civil Society*. Oxford: Polity Press.

Meadwell, Hudson. 1994 The foundations of Habermas's universal pragmatics. *Theory and Society* 23: 711-727.

Miller, Gary J. 1997. The impact of economics on contemporary political science. *Journal of Economic Literature* XXXV: 1173-1204.

Morton, Rebecca B. 1999. *Methods and Models.* Cambridge and New York: Cambridge University Press.

Obeyesekere, Gananath. 1997. *The Apotheosis of Captain Cook: European Mythmaking in the Pacific.* Princeton, NJ: Princeton University Press.

Okrent, Mark. 1984. Hermeneutics, transcendental philosophy and social science. *Inquiry* 27: 23-49.

Ott, Hugo. 1993. *Martin Heidegger A Political Life*, Allan Blunden (trans.) London: HarperCollins Publishers Ltd.

Petracca, Mark P. 1991. The rational actor approach to politics: science, self-interest, and normative democratic theory, in Kristen R. Monroe (ed.) *The Economic Approach to Politics: A Critical Reassessment of the Theory of Rational Action.* New York: HarperCollins Publishers.

Phillips, Derek L. 1993. *Looking Backward: A Critical Appraisal of Communitarian Thought.* Princeton, NJ: Princeton University Press.

Piore, Michael J. 1996. Review of the handbook of economic sociology. *Journal of Economic Literature* 34: 741-754.

Polanyi, Karl. 1958. *The Great Transformation.* Boston: Beacon Press.

Popkin, Samuel. 1979. *The Rational Peasant: The Political Economy of Rural Society in Vietnam.* Berkeley: University of California Press.

Sahlins, Marshall D. 1995. *How Natives Think: About Captain Cook, For Example.* Chicago: University of Chicago Press.

Scott, James C. 1977. *The Moral Economy of the Peasant: Rebellion and Subsistence in Southeast Asia.* New Haven, CT: Yale University Press.

Seidman, Steven. 1991. Postmodern anxiety: the politics of epistemology. *Sociological Theory* 9: 180-190.

Sica, Alan. 1992. The social world as countinghouse: Coleman's irrational worldview. *Theory and Society* 21(2): 243-262.

Smelser, Neil J. 1995. Economic rationality as a religious system, in Robert Wuthnow (ed.) *Rethinking Materialism: Perspectives on the Spiritual Dimension of Economic Behavior.* Grand Rapids, MI: William B. Eerdmans Publishing Company.

Somers, Margaret R. 1998. 'We're no angels': realism, rational choice, and relationality in social science (in Symposium on Historical Sociology and Rational Choice Theory), *American Journal of Sociology* 104: 722-784.

Stinchcombe, A. 1992. Simmel systematized. *Theory and Society* 21(2): 183-202.

Symposium. 2000. *Social Science History* 24: 653-696.

Taylor, Charles. 1993. Engaged agency and background in Heidegger in Charles B. Guignon (ed.) *The Cambridge Companion to Heidegger.* Cambridge: Cambridge University Press.

Taylor, Charles. 1985. *Human Agency and Language.* Cambridge: Cambridge University Press.

Taylor, Charles. 1975. *Hegel.* Cambridge: Cambridge University Press.

Taylor, Michael. 1996. When rationality fails, in Jeffrey Friedman (ed.) *The Rational Choice Controversy.* New Haven, CT: Yale University Press.

van den Berg, Axel. 1990. Habermas and modernity: a critique of the theory of communicative action. *Current Perspectives in Sociological Theory* 10:161-193.

van den Berg, Axel. 1998. Out of habit: notes toward a general theory of deliberate action. *Amsterdams Sociologisch Tijdschrift* 25: 429-463.

van den Berg, Axel. 1999. A note on rational choice theory, historical sociology and the *ceteris paribus* assumption. *The Netherlands Journal of Social Sciences* 35: 165-173.

Warfield Rawls, A. (1992). Can rational choice be a foundation for social theory. *Theory and Society* 21: 219-241.

Winch, Peter. 1964. Understanding a primitive society. *American Philosophical Quarterly* 307-324.

Winch, Peter. 1958. *The Idea of A Social Science*. London: Routledge and Kegan Paul.

Wolin, Richard. 1993. *The Heidegger Controversy: A Critical Reader*. Cambridge, MA: MIT Press.

Zafirovski, Milan. 2001. *Exchange, Action, and Social Structure: Elements of Economic Sociology*. Westport, CT: Greenwood Press.

Part 1

Rationality, Social and Economic

1

Towards a Sociological Rational Choice Theory

Michael Hechter

Introduction

This chapter discusses the utility of general theory in the social sciences, and of rational choice theory in particular. The first section of the chapter contrasts thin and thick versions of rational choice, and argues for the superiority of the latter approach. Some of the implications of thick rational choice theory for the practice of historical sociology, a field that recently has become notoriously skeptical of the charms of general theory, are developed in the second section. The final section concludes and summarizes the argument.

General Theory and Rationality in the Social Sciences

General theories in the social sciences attract scholars the way naked flames attract moths.[1] Freudianism, Marxism, and structural-functionalism seem to be dead, but new totalizing ambitions live on in rational choice theory. This has not done rational choice theory any favors. Is it doomed, too?

As its influence spread from its homeland in economics outward to politics, sociology, philosophy, and law, the theory has, of course, changed. Even so, it continues to inspire criticism by those who seek to slow or reverse its advances on their own disciplinary territory.

What are the main points of contention? The theory assumes that we calculate the expected consequences of our options and choose the best of them. Yet casual introspection apparently makes plain that we often act impulsively, emotionally, or merely by force of habit. Think how agonizing decisions about jobs, spouses, and children can be. Were we the calculating agents that rational choice theorists assume us to be, most such decisions would be cold-blooded and a cinch. But if the theory has so little superficial plausibility, why then has it gained so rapidly in fields distant from economics?

To understand its growing intellectual appeal, a common misconception first must be put to rest. Contrary to what many critics believe, rational choice theory does not try to explain what a rational person will do in a particular situation. This question lies firmly in the domain of decision theory. Genuine rational choices theories, by contrast, are concerned with *social* rather than with individual outcomes. Given that each individual acts rationally, will the aggregate outcome therefore be rational or desirable? Not necessarily. Regarded as stable equilibria, in which agents have no incentive to deviate from their course of action given others' behavior, social outcomes can be both unintended and undesirable. The overgrazing of the commons is a classic example of this dark side of Adam Smith's invisible hand (Ostrom 1990). Among other outcomes, rational choice theorists try to explain why people in industrial societies have fewer children than those in less developed countries (Becker 1981), or have any children at all (Friedman, Hechter and Kanazawa 1994); why the markets for rice and rubber differ (Popkin 1981); why Japan has less crime than the United States (Miller and Kanazawa 2000), or why nationalism is a creature of the modern rather than the ancient or medieval worlds (Hechter 2000).

Unlike decision theory, rational choice theory is inherently a multi-level enterprise (Coleman 1990: ch. 1). At the lower level its models contain arguments about individual values. At the higher level they specify agents' social and material context. Since elements such as norms are part of the social context, rational choice theories do not rest on premises pertaining exclusively to individuals. By the same token, the rational choice theorist's world is a great deal more complex than the decision theorist's. To reduce this complexity to more manageable limits, rational choice theorists assume some model of individual action, often one based on subjective expected utility theory. They disagree about the most appropriate model, however. And so rational choice is more a rubric or a family of theories than a single all-encompassing one.

Perhaps the most important division separates "thin" and "thick" models of individual action (Ferejohn 1991). "Thin" rational choice models are unconcerned with the particular values (or goals) which individuals pursue. These models are based on a small number of strong assumptions (Dawes 1988): for example, that whatever an individual's values may be, they must be stable and transitive (if someone prefers *a* to *b,* and *b* to *c,* they must prefer *a* to *c*). Rational choice theories based on thin models are highly universalistic and to that extent resemble theories in physics and biology concerning the optimal behaviour of atoms and organisms.

"Thick" models of individual action are substantively richer, for they countenance some aspects of intentionality. Since people have reasons for what they do, their behaviour is predictable only if we know what motivates them. Thick models therefore specify the individual's existing values and beliefs. There are several means of doing so, but the most popular strategy has been to assume that individuals seek maximum quantities of exchangeable private goods such as wealth and, arguably, power or prestige. Wealth is commonly valued because it can be exchanged for a multitude of other goods in the marketplace. Thick models allow that individuals also value non-exchangeable goods—that some people live for the music of Mozart, and others for the thrill of horse racing. Indeed, the models assume that for any given individual, idiosyncratic values of this sort can outweigh the common one. Hence, without knowing each person's unique value hierarchy, individual behaviour is unpredictable. As the size of groups increases, however, these idiosyncratic values tend to cancel each other out. In many circumstances the remaining common value permits quite accurate behavioral predictions at the collective level (Hechter 1994).

Thin models are substantively empty. They can be made consistent after the event, therefore, with nearly any kind of behavior. Thick ones—such as those postulating wealth-maximization—often are just plain wrong. To the degree that the idiosyncratic values are not distributed randomly in a population, explanations based on the pursuit of exchangeable private goods, such as wealth, power and prestige, will fail. Since outcomes may be partially a function of individual motivations, predictions made on the basis of thick models can be mutually inconsistent. Such inconsistencies can only be resolved on the basis of empirical evidence. That decision theorists can routinely invalidate subjective expected utility theory is also troubling, even if they have yet to formulate a superior alternative to it. All told, the mechanisms of individual action in rational choice theory are problematic.

Is a theory of higher-level outcomes invalidated by the inaccuracy of its lower-level mechanisms? The issue is controversial. Some, like Milton Friedman (1953), are content to judge theories by the adequacy of their predictions alone. One of the most sustained examples of this strategy is found in evolutionary biology. To animate his theory of biodiversity, Darwin proposed an individual-level mechanism of genetic transmission (based on blending) that subsequently was revealed to be inaccurate, rather than the accurate one (based on particulate inheritance). Darwin's use of the blending mechanism made it difficult to understand genetic variability: if blending were the proper mechanism, then genetic variance would be halved in every generation. To explain the high rates of diversity he observed, Darwin had to assume a mutation rate that was ten times higher than it actually is. The neo-Darwinian synthesis, which combined natural selection with Mendelian particulate inheritance, is superior to Darwin's theory (Fisher 1930). Yet Darwin's mistaken mechanism of genetic transmission did not keep him from devising a higher-level theory of natural selection that is currently the main unifying paradigm in biology. (That the idea for this higher-level theory originated with Malthus, a social scientist, may be yet more grist for this particular mill.)

A similar story can be told in physics. Boyle's Law and the other gas laws—relating the pressure, temperature and volume of a gas—were formulated before physicists understood mechanisms at the atomic level. These laws still hold, but they have nothing to say about the distribution of individual particles in space. To predict the dynamics of a gas—like forecasting the weather—requires complex nonlinear ("deterministic chaos") models that are highly sensitive to initial conditions. For some kinds of problems, nevertheless, outcomes at the higher level can be predicted independent of knowledge of lower-level mechanisms. For predicting other kinds of outcomes, however, accurate lower-level mechanisms are essential.

Physicists studying the collective behavior of individual particles using effective field theories have observed that the robustness of individual-level mechanisms increases with the number of dimensions in which particles can move. When particles can move in only one spatial dimension (say, length), individual differences in initial conditions have greater effects on collective outcomes than when particles can move in three dimensions. If social structures (such as the institutions of caste or slave societies) are conceived analogously as limiting individual action, then individual differences should loom larger in determining organizational than market outcomes, for organizations are more highly structured. This may explain why thin models of individual action are more popular for studying markets than hierarchies.

What kinds of social scientific problems should general theories attempt to answer? The social sciences have yet to produce a Linnaeus, let alone a Boyle. Skeptics, of whom there are many, doubt that they ever will. Rational choice theorists gamble that social outcomes can be understood on the basis of admittedly incomplete models of individual action. At the present time, explaining social equilibria (the social scientist's version of Boyle's problem) seems quite ambitious enough. Predicting the course of future social outcomes (analogous to the problem of weather prediction) is beyond our reach (Hechter 1995).

Are there any alternatives to rational choice? For many critics, social and political phenomena are too complex and historically contingent to be successfully captured by any conceivable general theory (Green and Shapiro 1994). They hold that there should be no search for alternatives since the enterprise itself is misguided. But these critics fail to recognize the possibility that general theories might account for social equilibria such as patterns of fertility, market structures and crime rates. And the standards they uphold for theory are so demanding that not even natural selection passes muster, on account of its presumed unfalsifiability. Interestingly, the debate on natural selection recapitulates many of these same arguments.[2] In lieu of general theory, these critics advocate more inductive research that aims to establish causal generalizations of limited scope. This surely is feasible, but what does it leave us with?

If abandoning general theory *tout court* is one option, adopting structural theory, the flavour of the month in sociology, is another (Bourdieu 1977; Giddens 1984; Sewell 1992). Although it is difficult to define their core beliefs, most structuralists deny the need for any model of individual action at all. Apart from other liabilities, this view has dubious ethical implications. Theories that have no place for agents cannot distinguish between individual and collective interests. This means that they afford no basis for evaluating the ethical desirability of existing social arrangements (Coleman 1990: 16-17). In reality, of course, most structural theories in sociology do rely implicitly on models of individual action. This makes them vulnerable to many of the same criticisms levelled at rational choice theories, however. This paucity of other methodologically and ethically attractive theoretical options helps account for the resilience of rational choice.

I believe that substantively richer models of individual action—based on rigorous independent measures of agents' values—can strengthen rational choice theory. Discovering the conditions in which particular values come to the fore thus is a crucial goal. Nonetheless, this incrementalist strategy of theoretical modification entails a risk illustrated in the history of astronomy by Thomas S. Kuhn (1970). To account for a growing number of unexpected empirical observations, Ptolemy's earth-centred theory of the planetary system had to be progressively modified by adding numerous epicycles. This only made the theory increasingly complex and obscure. Copernicus's elegant heliocentric model supplanted the clumsier Ptolemaic one because it provided a much more economical explanation of planetary movements. Thick models of individual action invariably complicate the simple core of rational choice theory.

Yet this added complexity does not necessarily vitiate the theory. In the remainder of this chapter, I illustrate how thick theory is being used by a small and brave group of historical sociologists.

Rationality and Historical Sociology

How should sociologists explain social outcomes and events? Good sociological explanations must consist of separate arguments pertaining, first, to the *motives* of individual actors and, second, to *models* of the contexts within which their action takes place. Good explanations in historical sociology are no different, save in one crucial respect. It is far more difficult to explain outcomes and events in societies distant in time and space than in our own.

All complete social explanations must include an analysis of individual motives and actions (Coleman 1986; Hechter 1983). For sociological purposes, individuals are the elementary units of analysis, for they cannot be divided into smaller acting units. If outcomes and events ultimately are the products of the actions of individuals, just how are these phenomena to be explained? What accounts for individual action? Since understanding the reasons why people act as they do is essential to explaining outcomes and events, we must employ a different methodology than that of the natural sciences.

Motives may be usefully divided into two elements, *orientations* to and *goals* of action.[3] Whereas goals are practically infinite in their variety, orientations to action are either instrumental or not. Instrumental action is consequentialist. People are motivated instrumentally whenever they choose a course of action which they believe is the most effective means of attaining their goals in a given situation. Instrumental action implies nothing at all about the nature of these goals, however: they can be materialist or idealist, conventional or wildly idiosyncratic. The wealth-maximizing capitalist and the salvation-seeking cleric are both instrumentally motivated.

Sometimes, however, orientations to action are non-instrumental. For instance, action may be determined by a conscious belief that a given ethical, aesthetic, or religious behavior must be taken because of duty, right, or merely for its own sake, regardless of its consequences. This is value-oriented action. Emotional action, which is determined by the actor's specific affects and feeling states, is likewise nonconsequentialist. Emotional action is carried out in the heat of the moment and without forethought—"crimes of passion" are a classic example. Finally, action can be purely habitual—determined by reflex rather than calculation or impulse.

Do instrumental orientations to action provide the best basis for explaining social outcomes and events? Ultimately, this is an empirical question. Often, however, direct and reliable evidence about orientations to action is difficult to come by. When, due to a lack of evidence, it is necessary to make assumptions about action orientations, explanations should proceed by assuming that actors are instrumentally oriented. Instrumental action is least ambiguous and therefore most understandable to the analyst, who may not share an emic perspective with her subjects. Hence, by assuming an instrumental orientation, the analyst can most easily derive models that yield empirical implications for any set of circumstances. Substantively, how could people or cultures whose action is predominantly non-consequentialist ever successfully compete against instrumental actors?

Since instrumental action is intentional rather than random or unconscious, it implies goals. If we do not understand the actor's goals, then we cannot deduce how an instrumentally motivated person would go about realizing them. To understand an action we must know the goals people hope to attain by undertaking that particular action, and the information available to them, including their beliefs.

Whereas actual behavior may be public, the mechanisms generating it—that is, intentional action based on goals—are internal states that can only be seen through a glass darkly (Hechter 1992b; Hechter, Nadel and Michod 1993). If an instrumental explanation of outcomes and events requires specification of actors' goals, doesn't the difficulty of discerning these goals mitigate our attempts at explaining outcomes?

Goals can be imputed at different levels of abstraction, and on this account with more or less realism. Most realistically, we can attempt to ascertain the actual goal in the given case of a particular actor (Hechter et al. 1999), or the average and approximate goal attributable to a given group of actors. Alternatively, we can assume that hypothetical actors are motivated to pursue given goals on the basis of theoretical considerations. Clearly, we would always prefer to employ the most realistic motivations in our explanations, but our ability to do so is limited by the availability of appropriate evidence. The greater the availability of evidence, the less we need to employ motivational assumptions to explain social outcomes. For example, to explain contemporary events we can exploit our knowledge of the relevant circumstances that we share with the actors in question as members of the same society. Even so, it is unlikely that we will be very knowledgeable about the precise nature of the actors' goals and circumstances. Since contemporary actors are, in principle, available for us to study, we can employ a battery of different data collection techniques ranging from sample surveys, to intensive interviews, to participant observation methods to elicit their goals and circumstances.

Unfortunately, however, we usually know much less about the goals and circumstances of individuals in societies that are distant in time or space than we do of those closer at hand.[4] On this account, historical sociologists must place greater reliance on motivational *assumptions* in their explanations. Therefore they must be sophisticated about deriving models from assumptions about goals and instrumental action.

Since the number of possible goals is astronomical, what kinds of assumptions should be made? Analysts should begin by assuming individual goals such as the pursuit of wealth, power, and prestige. These particular goals are fungible—they can serve as means to the attainment of a plethora of individual ends. Unlike non-fungible goals, which are more likely to be idiosyncratically distributed in any society, everyone can be relied on to prefer outcomes that promise them greater wealth, power and prestige to those promising less (Hechter 1994). Further, these goals also have straightforward behavioral implications, making it feasible to construct testable models.

Sociologists inspired by rational choice have been able to construct precise and detailed explanations using these simple microfoundations. A notable example is Brustein (1996). In sharp contrast to the prevailing wisdom that the rise of the Nazi party was due primarily to anti-Semitism, Brustein begins with the simple assumption that Germans chose to affiliate with the party whose platform best served their material interests. Brustein analyzed political party platforms in detail and collected "the most systematic and comprehensive database of Nazi membership files that exists today" (Anheier 1997) to test his arguments. The propositions generated by his theory and supported by the historical data are precise: he explains why livestock workers, import-oriented blue collar workers, and skilled laborers joined the Nazis much more frequently than grain growers, export-oriented blue collar workers, and unskilled laborers. Clearly this is no case of post hoc redescription of findings that others have already discovered, but a systematic analysis guided by general theory that produced a novel and complex understanding of an important historical event.[5]

The last element to be considered is the contexts that individuals face which limit or enhance their ability to attain their goals. These contexts can be analyzed either in concrete empirical terms (attempting to specify the particular constraints faced by actors in all of their historical detail), or in relation to abstract theoretical models of major types of contexts. The latter choice is preferable, on several counts.[6] As in the case of motives, abstract models of contexts serve to reveal anomalies and foster the cumulation of knowledge. They permit comparisons across cases (even those in very different places and times), and across substantive topics. Most fundamental, they are useful in generating testable hypotheses. One of the major advantages of abstract models over the use of classification schemes or orienting concepts is that they specify the interrelations between factors. As Rodney Stark (1996:26) puts it, "The difference here is that between a parts catalog and a working diagram of an engine ... a model explains why and how things fit together and function."

What sorts of contextual models should be constructed? Since an instrumental orientation to action and egoistic motivations have been assumed at the micro level, the answer is models that are consistent with these premises. Building these is one of the principal activities of rational choice theorists, who have developed a number of endogenous models of context from agency theory, game theory and group solidarity theory.[7] However, the analysis need not be limited to models developed on the basis of rational choice. Several other types of models are consistent with these microfoundations, including models of economic structure and group conflict derived from Marxism (Elster 1985; Przeworski 1991; Roemer 1986), models of social relations from network theory (Burt 1992; Coleman 1990) and Weberian ([1922] 1978) ideal-types of organizational forms and political systems.

The abstract scope conditions of rational choice theory render these explanations generalizable; this, in turn, increases their testability and contemporary relevance. For example, Stark's (1996) use of general theory in his analysis of the rise of Christianity allows him to compare the conditions that facilitated its rapid growth in the contemporary case of the Mormons. Moreover, Kiser and Schneider (1994) use agency theory to argue that when communications, transportation, and record-keeping technologies are inadequate, particular types of monitoring problems will arise in the collection of indirect taxes that are best mitigated by using tax farming (privatized tax collection) instead of salaried state administrators. Although the argument was first tested in the context of early modern states, since its scope was abstract—applying to conditions in which technologies of communication, transportation, and record-keeping are poor—it has also been used to explain forms of tax administration in contemporary less developed countries.

Rational choice theorists have often focused on ways that temporal sequence in which causal factors occur affects outcomes.[8] One set of rational choice models that can incorporate temporality come from game theory, especially extensive form games (Kreps 1990 13). These models explain outcomes as the consequence of temporally ordered strategic interaction—sequences of action and reaction. Abell's (1987) integration of game theory into narrative analysis is the most well-developed attempt to incorporate sequentiality in a theoretical manner, but there are other prominent examples. Lindenberg (1989) outlines an ordered sequence of game structures that are likely to unfold as a revolutionary situation moves toward revolution—and then employs them to construct brief narratives of the French and Russian revolutions. Heckathorn (1990; 1989) uses game theory to demonstrate the importance of collective sanctions in maintaining social control within groups. Brown and Boswell (1995) analyze past strike outcomes combining narrative, game theory, and qualitative comparative analysis—the sequence of "moves" by workers and unions is a critical determinant of the outcome.[9]

One feature of recent applications of game theory that increases its compatibility with historical sociology is the incorporation of the effects of institutions and even particular events. Formal game theory models often do not produce precise predictions of outcomes. The models yield multiple equilibria and cannot predict which of these will occur in a given situation (Hechter 1992a). At their best, these formal models reveal the outcomes that cannot occur—those that are off the equilibrium path. To make their explanations more precise, game theorists increasingly have attempted to integrate formal game theoretic models with particular features of the historical cases they study—since only these particular features can tell them why one of many possible equilibrium outcomes in fact occurred. The classic example of this strategy is found in Schelling's (1960) discussion of focal points.[10] Rational choice is also helpful in explaining the conditions under which path dependence will be strong or weak.

The testability of an explanation depends on the nature of available evidence and on the characteristics of the theoretical ideas. In historical research, evidence is often sparse and fragmentary. In such circumstances, only certain kinds of theories can be testable. To be testable, a theory must yield propositions. Further, the more general and fruitful the theory (the greater the number and diversity of its empirical implications), the easier it is to test. General theory entails all of these features.

Whether a test confirms the empirical implications of theoretical models built on the assumption of instrumental action is always an open question. If the evidence is roughly consistent with the model's expectations, then the analyst may presume to have explained the outcome or event, especially if alternative explanations are less consistent with empirical observations. If the explanations are at variance with empirical findings, however, then the search for an adequate explanation must continue. How should the resulting anomalies be resolved? Anomalous findings can be due either to the analyst's misspecification of the context in which action occurs, to misperception of the actors' goals, to misspecification of action orientations, or to the inadequacy of the theory. Modifications of the explanation should be made first in the least central aspects of the theory, with consideration of successively more central elements if that tack fails. Thus, if a given model comes up short, first change the model of social structural constraints. For example, if group solidarity theory is used, have any types of monitoring or sanctioning been neglected? Perhaps an inappropriate model has been used to explain the phenomenon. Perhaps the case is really a repeated game as opposed to a one-shot game, or maybe it's a chicken game instead of a prisoners' dilemma. Only if all such modifications fail to improve the fit, should one reassess the microfoundational assumptions (Popper 1994: 177).

Consider the specification of the actors' goals. This is one of the most difficult things to determine, and no doubt is the source of many of the incorrect predictions in historical explanations. If all else fails, perhaps the assumption of instrumental action is incorrect, and some other form of action should be employed in the explanation. The outcome of this process of successive, staged revision invariably improves the models and better specifies their scope, thereby advancing our understanding of the given event or social outcome.

Conclusion

Debates on historical methodology have been taking place for ages. If anything, the disciplinary scope of these debates has widened in recent years. Conflicts once confined to the human sciences now encompass critiques of the natural and physical sciences, as well. The thrust of many objections to rational choice rests on epistemological presuppositions. But epistemological differences are notoriously difficult to resolve. The advocates of rival views do not share enough common ground to engage in reasoned debate. Shouting matches are the usual result, but these are notoriously uninformative. My argument derives from a standard form of realism that undergirds, at least implicitly, most empirical research that is conducted in the social sciences. In contrast, many critics of rational choice (Somers 1998) argue for a new, idiosyncratic epistemology that has yet to withstand the critical scrutiny of most philosophers. *Caveat emptor.*

The debate over historical methodology will not be resolved by philosophers. Nor should it be. Presumably, the point of the debate is to improve the quality of research in historical sociology. Why then is an approach based on general theory to be preferred? For at least five reasons. If all historical analyses dwell on some facts at the expense of others, what guides this selection process? General theories suggest those facts that ought to be relevant and those that can be safely ignored. Without explicit theoretical guidelines, implicit biases are likely to creep into the set of facts deemed relevant. Precisely because all observation is theory-laden, the pretense to pure inductivism is at best self-delusory. Inductivism therefore relies on implicit rather than explicit theories; but surely social science is better off with explicit rather than implicit theories.

Second, such theories offer a source of generalizable causal mechanisms that suggest how and why given causes produce given effects. Third, general theories facilitate the cumulation of knowledge across substantive domains. Because their models and mechanisms are generalizable, within abstract scope conditions, this increases links between substantive domains as well as between the past and the present. Fourth, general theories are useful precisely because they do *not* provide perfect explanations. The anomalies they highlight are major sources of new ideas for research.

Last—and most important—research based on general theories provides the seeds of these theories' ultimate destruction. I advocate a sociological version of rational choice not because the theory is either true or beautiful; it just seems to be the best general theory currently on offer (Abell 1992). I'll be surprised and disappointed if it is possible to make the same assessment a few decades hence.

Therefore I can readily join those who criticize the adequacy of rational choice theory. I disagree, however, with most skeptics about the conditions for its eventual demise. Many critics seem to think that rational choice theory will go away if it is shunned. Quite the contrary. Rational choice will disappear only when it is supplanted by a superior general theory. Kenneth Shepsle's First Law of Wing Walking (Shepsle 1995: 217) puts the matter well: "Don't let go of something unless you have something else to hold onto."

Notes

1. This part of the chapter draws on Hechter (1996). My understanding of micro-macro relations in evolutionary biology and condensed matter physics owes much to conversations with Richard Dawkins and Robin Stinchcombe, respectively.
2. Compare Rosenberg's (1994) critique of neo-Darwinian biology with Dennett's (1995) spirited defence. Even so, one suspects that social scientists would get more respect, to say nothing of external funding, were their findings as compelling as those generated by evolutionary biologists.
3. This part of the argument draws on Kiser and Hechter (1991 and 1998), both of which are inspired by the methodological tenets enunciated in Part I of Max Weber's *Economy and Society* (Weber 1978).
4. Weber (1978: 5-6) notes that "[m]any ultimate ends or values toward which experience shows that human action may be oriented, often cannot be understood completely, though sometimes we are able to grasp them intellectually. The more radically they differ from our own ultimate values, however, the more difficult it is for us to understand them empathetically." Tilly (1975: 9) also comments on the "difficulty of verifying arguments emphasizing attitudes and intentions with this sort of [historical] documentation."
5. For a discussion of other empirical applications of sociological rational choice theory, see Hechter and Kanazawa (1997).
6. Strictly speaking, the first choice is impossible—to fully describe the context of an action would take longer than the life expectancy of most scholars. All of us have to choose to focus on some elements of the context to the exclusion of others.
7. See Becker (1976), Friedman and Hechter (1988) and Schelling (1978) for more detailed discussions of several of the models developed in rational choice theory.
8. Temporality is also important at a more micro level. Rational choice research on discount rates (the rate at which actors discount future costs and benefits relative to current ones) has contributed to our understanding of this process. Most economists assume that discount rates are normally distributed in the populations they study, a reasonable assumption if one does not know what causes discount rates to vary. More sociological rational choice models have been attempting to discover the structural determinants of variations in discount rates. For example, Levi (1988) shows that discount rates increase with the insecurity of rule.
9. Game theory is not the only means of incorporating temporality into rational choice explanations. Brinton (1993) shows that differences in the timing of human capital investments in Japan and the U.S. result in different levels of gender stratification. Barzel and Kiser (1997) demonstrate that the timing of factors affecting the insecurity of rule determines their effects on voting institutions—the Hundred Years War disrupted the development of voting institutions in France more than in England because their prior development (and thus the ability to withstand shocks) was greater in the latter. Rational choice work on agenda setting also incorporates temporality, generally by demonstrating how moving first allows certain actors to shape outcomes (see Weingast and Moran (1983) on congressional committees, and Mueller (1989: ch. 14) on bureaus proposing budgets).
10. More recently, game theorists have been integrating formal rational choice models with detailed narrative stories that incorporate initial conditions (Abell 1987; Bates, De Figueiredo Jr. and Weingast 1998; Bueno de Mesquita 1996; Weingast 1996). Ermakoff's (1997) analysis of the shift in medieval marriage norms is a case in point. Using Levi's (1988) notion of quasi-voluntary compliance, a game theoretic

model of bargaining between aristocrats and Roman prelates, and a detailed analysis of the historical evidence, he shows why late eleventh-century nobles decided to obey church norms about divorce and endogamy (marrying cousins). These models provide a way of constructing explanations that combine the general and the particular, while maintaining a clear distinction between the two.

References

Abell, Peter. 1987. *The Syntax of Social Life.* Oxford: Clarendon Press.

Abell, Peter. 1992. Is rational choice theory a rational choice of theory? in James S. Coleman and Thomas Fararo (eds.) *Rational Choice Theory: Advocacy and Critique.* Newbury Park, CA: Sage.

Anheier, Helmut. 1997. Studying the Nazi Party: "Clean models" versus "dirty hands," *American Journal of Sociology* 103:199-221.

Barzel, Yoram, and Edgar Kiser. 1997. The development and decline of medieval voting institutions: A comparison of England and France, *Economic Inquiry* 35:244-260.

Bates, Robert H., Rui De Figueiredo Jr., J. P. , and Barry R. Weingast. 1998. The politics of interpretation: rationality, culture, and transition, *Politics & Society* 26:221-257.

Becker, Gary S. 1976. *The Economic Approach to Human Behavior.* Chicago: University of Chicago Press.

Becker, Gary S. 1981. *A Treatise on the Family.* Cambridge, MA: Harvard University Press.

Bourdieu, Pierre. 1977. *Outline of a Theory of Practice.* Cambridge; New York: Cambridge University Press.

Brinton, Mary C. 1993. *Women and the Economic Miracle: Gender and Work in Postwar Japan.* Berkeley: University of California Press.

Brown, Cliff, and Terry Boswell. 1995. Strikebreaking or solidarity in the great steel strike of 1919: A split labor market, game-theoretic, and QCA analysis, *American Journal of Sociology* 94:1479-1519.

Brustein, William. 1996. *The Logic of Evil.* New Haven, CT: Yale University Press.

Bueno de Mesquita, Bruce. 1996. Counterfactuals in international affairs: Some insights from game theory, in Phillip Tetlock and Aaron Belkin (eds.) *Counterfactuals in International Relations.* Princeton, N.J: Princeton: Princeton University Press.

Burt, Ronald S. 1992. *Structural Holes: The Social Structure of Competition.* Cambridge, MA: Harvard University Press.

Coleman, James S. 1986. Social theory, social research, and a theory of action, *American Journal of Sociology* 91:1309-1335.

Coleman, James S. 1990. *Foundations of Social Theory.* Cambridge, MA: The Belknap Press of Harvard University Press.

Dawes, Robyn M. 1988. *Rational Choice in an Uncertain World.* San Diego, CA: Harcourt Brace and Jovanovich.

Elster, Jon. 1985. *Making Sense of Marx.* Cambridge: Cambridge University Press.

Ermakoff, Ivan. 1997. Prelates and princes: Aristocratic marriages, canon law prohibitions, and shifts in norms and patterns of domination in the central Middle Ages, *American Sociological Review* 62:405-422.

Ferejohn, John. 1991. Rationality and interpretation: parliamentary elections in early Stuart England, in Kristin Renwick Monroe (ed.) *The Economic Approach to Politics: A Critical Reassessment of the Theory of Rational Action.* New York: Harper Collins.

Fisher, Ronald A. 1930. *The Genetical Theory of Natural Selection.* Oxford: Clarendon Press.

Friedman, Debra, and Michael Hechter. 1988. The contribution of rational choice theory to macrosociological research, *Sociological Theory* 6:201-218.

Friedman, Debra, Michael Hechter, and Satoshi Kanazawa. 1994. A theory of the value of children, *Demography* 31:375-401.

Friedman, Milton. 1953. *The Methodology of Positive Economics*. Chicago: University of Chicago Press.

Giddens, Anthony. 1984. *The Constitution of Society: Outline of the Theory of Structuration*. Cambridge Cambridgeshire: Polity Press.

Green, Donald P., and Ian Shapiro. 1994. *Pathologies of Rational Choice Theory: A Critique of Applications in Political Science*. New Haven, CT: Yale University Press.

Hechter, Michael (ed.). 1983. *The Microfoundations of Macrosociology*. Philadelphia, PA: Temple University Press.

Hechter, Michael. 1992a. The insufficiency of game theory for the resolution of real-world collective action problems, *Rationality and Society* 4:33-40.

Hechter, Michael. 1992b. Should values be written out of the social scientist's lexicon? *Sociological Theory* 10:215-231.

Hechter, Michael. 1994. The role of values in rational choice theory, *Rationality and Society* 6:318-33.

Hechter, Michael. 1995. Introduction: Reflections on historical prophecy in the social sciences, *American Journal of Sociology* 100:1520-1527.

Hechter, Michael. 1996. Through thick and thin: How far can theory predict behavior? *Times Literary Supplement* 4852:15.

Hechter, Michael. 2000. *Containing Nationalism*. Oxford; New York: Oxford University Press.

Hechter, Michael, and Satoshi Kanazawa. 1997. Sociological rational choice theory, *Annual Review of Sociology* 23:191-214.

Hechter, Michael, Lynn Nadel, and Richard Michod (eds.). 1993. *The Origin of Values*. New York: Aldine de Gruyter.

Hechter, Michael, James Ranger-Moore, Guillermina Jasso, and Christine Horne. 1999. Do values matter? An analysis of advance directives for medical treatment, *European Sociological Review* 15:405-430.

Heckathorn, Douglas. 1990. Collective sanctions and compliance norms: A formal theory of group-mediated control, *American Sociological Review* 55:366-384.

Heckathorn, Douglas D. 1989. Collective action and the second order free rider problem, *Rationality and Society* 1:78-100.

Kiser, Edgar, and Michael Hechter. 1991. The role of general theory in comparative-historical sociology, *American Journal of Sociology* 97:1-30.

Kiser, Edgar, and Michael Hechter. 1998. The debate on historical sociology: Rational choice theory and its critics, *American Journal of Sociology* 104:785-816.

Kiser, Edgar, and Joachim Schneider. 1994. Bureaucracy and efficiency: An analysis of taxation in early modern Prussia, *American Sociological Review* 59:187-204.

Kreps, David. 1990. *Game Theory and Economic Modelling*. Oxford: Clarendon Press.

Kuhn, Thomas S. 1970. *The Structure of Scientific Revolutions*. Chicago: University of Chicago Press.

Levi, Margaret. 1988. *Of Rule and Revenue*. Berkeley: University of California Press.

Lindenberg, Siegwart. 1989. Social production functions, deficits, and revolutions: Prerevolutionary France and Russia, *Rationality and Society* 1:50-76.

Miller, Alan S., and Satoshi Kanazawa. 2000. *Order by Accident: The Origins and Consequences of Conformity in Contemporary Japan*. Boulder, CO and Oxford: Westview Press.

Mueller, Dennis C. 1989. *Public Choice II*. Cambridge; New York: Cambridge University Press.

Ostrom, Elinor. 1990. *Governing the Commons.* Cambridge: Cambridge University Press.

Popkin, Samuel. 1981. Public choice and rural development—Free riders, lemons, and institutional design, in Clifford S. Russell and Norman K. Nicholson (eds.) *Public Choice and Rural Development. Wa*shington, DC: Resources for the Future.

Popper, Karl R. 1994. *The Myth of the Framework: In Defence of Science and Rationality.* London: Routledge.

Przeworski, Adam. 1991. *Democracy and the Market: Political and Economic Reforms in Eastern Europe and Latin America.* Cambridge; New York: Cambridge University Press.

Roemer, John E. 1986. *Analytical Marxism.* Cambridge; New York: Cambridge University Press.

Rosenberg, Alexander. 1994. *Instrumental Biology or the Disunity of Science.* Chicago: University of Chicago Press.

Schelling, Thomas. 1960. *The Strategy of Conflict.* Cambridge, MA: Harvard University Press.

Schelling, Thomas C. 1978. *Micromotives and Macrobehavior.* New York: W. W. Norton.

Sewell, William. 1992. A theory of structure: Duality, agency, and transformation, *American Journal of Sociology* 98:1-29.

Shepsle, Kenneth A. 1995. Statistical political philosophy and positive political theory, *Critical Review* 9:213-222.

Somers, Margaret R. 1998. "We're no angels": Realism, rational choice, and relationality in social science, *American Journal of Sociology* 104:722-784.

Stark, Rodney. 1996. *The Rise of Christianity.* Princeton, NJ: Princeton University Press.

Tilly, Charles (ed.). 1975. *The Formation of National States in Western Europe.* Princeton, NJ: Princeton University Press.

Weber, Max. 1978. *Economy and Society.* Berkeley: University of California Press.

Weingast, Barry. 1996. Off-the-path behavior: A game-theoretic approach to counterfactuals and its implications for political and historical analysis, in Phillip Tetlock and Aaron Belkin (eds.) *Counterfactuals in International Relations.* Princeton, NJ: Princeton University Press.

Weingast, Barry, and Mark J. Moran. 1983. Bureaucratic discretion or Congressional control? Regulatory policymaking by the Federal Trade Commission, *Journal of Political Economy* 91:765-800.

2

Rationality Revised:
The Evolution of an Axiom in Economics

George Grantham

Introduction

The discipline of economics originated in two related problems connected to the concept of economic rationality that briefly claimed the attention of the ancient Greeks. The first was how best to manage a family estate (*oikos*), from which term economics acquired its name (*oikovoyia*); the second addressed ethical issues arising in the marketplace. Both focused on the relation between means and ends. In Xenophon's *Oeconomicus*, the problem addressed is how to maximize the value of an estate by an appropriate choice of means; in Aristotle's *Nicomachean Ethics,* the question, what is justice in the market place, opens an enquiry into how persons engaging in the mutual exchange of goods and services can be expected to act in defined contexts. The two problems are related, because people usually act in ways intended to advance their ends, making their actions predictable; but they are not identical. The first led to an absolute criterion of rational action: to choose the best means to an end; the second admitted a range of possible actions compatible with informed self-interest other than that which necessarily maximized it.

The two relations may be called "strong" and "weak" rationality, respectively. The distinction is that strong rationality proposes that agents optimize over the whole space of theoretically accessible alternatives, of which they are deemed to be aware; by contrast weak rationality requires merely choosing among alternatives that are immediately discernible and salient. The difference between them is cognitive. Strong rationality assumes a perfect cognitive capacity to perceive relations between means and ends, and to correctly calculate subjective value in terms of self-interest; weak rationality possesses less foresight, and reflects a smaller range of perceptible alternatives. In theoretical economics, the strong version has long been preferred because of the logical necessity of optimal solutions to real or stylized decision problems, which gives them the semblance of an absolute truth. Yet most economic actions can be explained by the comparative strategies of weak rationality; examples include migration, entry and exit of firms to and from industries, the movement of people between occupations, purchasing more of an object when its price falls, and rebalancing investment portfolios in response to changing rates of return. To assert that people respond to economic incentives is to assert at least this much rationality. They may not achieve the best of all possible worlds, but they expect their choices to put them in a state that is better, or at least no worse. The two types of economic rationality—one computational, one contextual—have long been a source of fruitful tension in economic thought. In the twentieth century the strong concept came close to obliterating the weak through the "mathematization" of the discourse of professional economics. Intended to clarify that discourse and to set it on secure logical foundations, the rationality of optimization eliminated the patina of cognitive realism that had informed the weaker and supposedly looser forms of economic thought. In so doing the proponents of strong rationality imagined agents whose cognitive abilities had greatly to surpass those of the ordinary people whose economic choices were being modeled. This essay briefly surveys the evolution of the two approaches to economic rationality, and considers some implications of recent advances in cognitive science for them.

The Rational Revolution

The triumph of strong rationality dates to the 1930s. The seminal works were *Value and Capital* (1939) by John Hicks, whose epigram is from *Paradise Lost* ("Reason also is choice") *Foundations of Economic Analysis* (1947) by Paul Samuelson, whose epigram is "Mathematics is a language," and *The Theory of Games and Economic Behaviour* (1944) by John von Neumann and Oskar Morgenstern's, which they had provisionally titled *Theory of Rational Behaviour*.[1] The quintessence of all three books was the use of advanced mathematics to determine optimal values of functions characterizing an economic situation.[2] The conflation of economic rationality with mathematical deduction is clearly stated in programmatic statements. Hicks wrote:

> I believe I have written a book. The basis for this claim lies not in unity of subject but in unity of method. I believe I have had the fortune to come upon a method of analysis which is applicable to a wide variety of economic problems.

Samuelson introduced his work in a similar vein:

> An economist of very keen intuition would perhaps have suspected that seemingly diverse fields—production economics, consumer's behavior, international trade, public finance, business cycles, income analysis—possess striking formal similarities, and that economy of effort would result from analyzing these common elements. ... Only after laborious work in each of these fields did the realization dawn upon me that essentially the same inequalities and theorems appeared again and again, and that I was simply proving the same theorems a wasteful number of times.[3]

Von Neumann and Morgenstern asserted the connection between rationality and the truth-tested language of modern mathematics.

> The purpose of this book is to present a discussion of some fundamental questions of economic theory which ... have their origin in the attempts to find an exact description of the endeavor of the individual to obtain a maximum of utility, or, in the case of the entrepreneur, a maximum of profit. ...[I]t may safely be stated that there exists, at present, no satisfactory treatment of the question of rational behavior....The chief reason for this lies, no doubt, in the failure to develop and apply suitable mathematical methods to the problem; this would have revealed that the maximum problem which is supposed to correspond to the notion of rationality is not at all formulated in an unambiguous way...This kind of problem is nowhere dealt with in classical mathematics.[4]

Mathematics powered a quantum leap in the centrality of strong rationality in economic reasoning for two main reasons. The first was practical. By modeling individual decisions as explicit optimizations economists could restrict the number of solutions to a set small enough to possess predictive power. Empirical testing was not, however, the primary focus, which was demonstrating the logical existence of general competitive equilibrium, and determining its connection with necessary and sufficient conditions for an efficient allocation of resources.[5] The second reason was aesthetic. Von Neumann and Morgenstern proudly asserted that

> We have even avoided giving names to the mathematical concepts introduced ... in order to establish no correlation with any meaning which the verbal associations of names may suggest. In this absolute "purity" these concepts can be the objects of an exact mathematical investigation.... The application to intuitively given subjects follows afterwards, when the exact analysis has been completed.[6]

From being originally a heuristic device, perfect optimization has been elevated to a defining axiom. Kreps approvingly sets out the conventional justification for mathematizing the concept of economic rationality.

> Economics and economic theorists have been disciplined to some extent by empirical testing, but as much or more by adherence to a tight paradigm that begins with rational behaviour by individual actors and moves on the equilibrium analysis given by that behaviour. If we permit *ad hoc* models of boundedly rational behaviour, we surely lose some of the discipline afforded by the economic paradigm.[7]

Rationality is thus a fundamental axiom of scientific economic reasoning, and therefore not subject to empirical control. The obvious empirical controls come from cognitive science, but in economics the cognitive aspects of rationality were long overshadowed by computational paradigms. As economists learned to compute increasingly complex optimizations, however, doubts arose when the assumed cognitive ability exceeded the human inheritance, and when optimizing solutions on finer and finer margins of decision revealed anomalies inconsistent with the axiom of perfect rationality. These developments have redirected economic thinking back towards the weaker concepts of rationality. To understand this redirecting it is useful to survey the intellectual history out of which it grows.

Economic Rationality and the Just Price

Although Xenophon's dialogue on "optimal" estate management is the earliest writing to contain a modicum of "economics," the science takes its true starting point from a comment on distributive justice in Book V of the *Nicomachean Ethics*, where Aristotle observes that an unjust man is one "who takes more than his share." [V: 1130a] Distributive justice requires that honors and public responsibility be allotted according to a person's status; by contrast, in the market place the law considers persons to have equal status, and "ask[s] only whether one has done and the other suffered wrong, and whether one has done and the other has suffered damage."[V: 1132a]. The context is judicial. A judge must decide whether a disputed transaction has been tainted by fraud, duress, or willful misinformation. The practical question is: What if any damages should be granted and on what grounds? This depends on the terms a reasonable person would have offered or accepted in the stated circumstances. Following this line of reasoning classical judges developed, and Aristotle stated, the concept of a "just" price that resulted from voluntary agreement among legal equals endowed with similar capacity to rationally evaluate consequences of their action. The paradigm of the "just" price conflated two distinct matters of enquiry: the first concerns the computational logic of goal-directed acts when means and ends are known; the second concerns the extent to which agents can correctly identify the means, and understand the specific connection between them and their consequences. Classical and medieval glossators on Aristotle's writings generally ignored the second cognitive question, preferring instead to elaborate the logic of choosing. This logic led them down two tracks. The first stressed the rationality of buyers; the other that of sellers. Together the two logics produced key fragments of an economic analysis of price determination based on the weakly rational mechanism of entry and exit to industries and occupations by suppliers.

The logic of the buyer was embedded in the Roman law of contract, which held that a freely negotiated price measures the worth of the purchased object to the purchaser.[8] Medieval commentators elaborated this precocious notion of "revealed preference" into a doctrine of the utility of goods. The logic of the supplier was nevertheless more immediately fruitful. It was based on the cost of supply. That logic requires that as a matter of justice no seller should be forced to accept a price that fails to cover his cost. The costs that justified a price were gradually extended to include storage, risk, and income forgone by lending one's capital rather than employing it directly. It was an obvious implication and a matter of common observation, that when price falls below cost suppliers exit the market, and when it rises above cost, they enter. Scholastic economists, however, were chiefly concerned with whether a given price was "justified" by circumstances; it was not before the second half of the seventeenth century that the entry and exit were understood to be the operative mechanism of price determination. While the individual cognitive ability that was required to drive that mechanism was not great, the assertion of a necessary equilibrium implied that non-perfect rationality might be economically unsustainable. From here it was a short logical, though temporally protracted, step to the proposition that economic agents are always fully rational.

Natural Price and the Law of One Price

The first person to construct a workable model of price determination based on an atomistic mechanics of entry and exit was

William Petty, who served for a time as amanuensis to Thomas
Hobbes.[9] In *A Treatise of Taxes and Contributions* (1662) Petty argued that the only set of prices compatible with market equilibrium
is that which makes the return to each input equal in all its employ-
ments. Any other set of prices will induce exit of labor and capital
from occupations generating an inferior return, and entry to those
generating a superior return. The equilibrating mechanism depends
on the inverse correlation between supply and market price, which
ensures that the flows from industry to industry eventually cease.
The cognitive demands of Petty's price-determining mechanism were
minimal. Suppliers had only to compare alternatives and choose the
better one. He did not consider how they learned about those alternatives and the returns to them. The theory of the natural price was
a theory of price in the long run, for it was only in the long run that
the relevant information revealed itself and the decisions resulting
from that information affected prices. The Natural Price was thus not
so much a matter of observation, but of implication. Given a minimal degree of economic rationality, it was the only possible price.

The Law of One Price decrees that at one time in the same market, one price must rule. Its most fruitful application is in the realm
of high finance, where the cost of simultaneously buying and selling securities is low enough for it to be continuously enforced by
arbitrage. The unique price defines equilibrium, since by definition
to be out of equilibrium means there is an opportunity for profitable
arbitrage. The law is thus a strict form of natural price. The law's
analytical power rests on its status as a logically necessary condition for equilibrium, which makes it a convenient shorthand for
working out final states resulting from what are often quite complex interactions. The propositions it helped to develop include
Hume's specie-flow theory of the balance of payments and international price level; Adam Smith's principle of compensating
wage differentials, which can be applied generally to interpret
price differentials in any commodity characterized by observable variation in quality; Ricardo's theory of rent; and his proof
that relative prices are not uniquely determined by labor inputs.[10]
To prove these theorems does not require explaining how equilibrium is attained. It is enough to know that rational agents presented
with two prices for the same item will sell the one and buy the other
to gain riskless profit. As Ricardo put it,

This restless desire on the part of all the employers to quit a less profitable for a more advantageous business has a strong tendency to equalise the rate of profits of all, or to fix them in such proportions as may, in the estimation of the parties, compensate for any advantage which one may have, or may appear to have, over the other. *It is perhaps very difficult to trace the steps by which this change is effected.*[11] (Italics added)

In fact, most economists did not think it was necessary to trace the steps. The law of one price reinforced an incipient tendency to forgo sustained enquiry into the way the equilibrium was achieved in order to study the properties of equilibrium. From here it was but a short step to suppose that, since economic agents are forced in the end to conform to equilibrium conditions, their decisions may be modeled as if they were continuously subject to those conditions, so that the thinking they do can be inferred by backward induction from the logic of equilibrium. That conflation implies a significant capability on the part of agents to compute the equilibrium and draw the necessary conclusions from it. The analysis of equilibrium, so necessary to the understanding of markets, was pushing the discipline towards greater and greater reliance on the assumption that economic agents are perfectly rational. That assumption would be powerfully assisted by the introduction of mathematical reasoning to economics.

Mathematical Rationality

Neither the algorithm of entry and exit nor the law of one price provide an obvious explanation of how price is determined when there is no entry or exit, or where a single seller charges more than one price for the same item. Treating these problems requires an explicit model of how prices and output are set by a unique seller as a consequence of profit maximization. The first work successfully to address this problem was Cournot's *Recherches sur les principes mathématiques de la théorie des richesses* [The Mathematical Principles of the Theory of Wealth (1838)]. A gifted professional mathematician, Cournot understood that the point of maximum profit for a monopolist is determined analytically by setting the first derivative of the profit function with respect to output equal to zero, and solving the resulting equation for the level of output.[12] To determine profit-maximizing supply, however, a monopolist must know exactly how price varies with quantity supplied. But how is this vital information acquired? Changing supply (and price) of a monopolized commodity affects demand (and supply) of other commodities, which in turn affect the demand for the monopolized good by those feedbacks that Ricardo noted are so difficult to trace, and the complexity of the interactions mounts exponentially with the number of feedbacks. What was trivial as mathematics was non-trivial as cognition.

The cognitive obstacles to optimization are even more pronounced in Cournot's celebrated generalization of his monopoly model to the case of n suppliers. Cournot demonstrated that if each firm determines its profit-maximizing supply on the rational assumption that other firms are doing the same thing, the interactions among them produce an equilibrium state defined by the condition that each firm maximizes its profit subject to the condition that all other firms are simultaneously maximizing theirs. The solution is determinate. More than a century later John Nash put this insight on the firm footing of mathematical generality in a one-page existence proof of a finite solution to an n-person non-cooperative game.[13] The optimizing algorithm, however, demands that in order to solve their optimum strategy, agents have simultaneously to solve the optimal strategies of all their competitors, and therefore need to know the constraints to which they are subject as well as their own constraints, and they need to work through the logic of all the interactions. The powerful formalism of Cournot's mathematical approach to economic rationality ushered in hyper-rational agents whose powers of reasoning were on a par with those of a grand master in chess. The cognitive implications of his mathematical modeling of strong rationality did not become evident until its widespread use in the latter part of the twentieth century made them inescapable.[14] For more than a hundred years following his construction economists employed a softer, but no less problematic, approach based on the homely example of a rational consumer.

Rational Hedonism

That production and exchange are motivated by wants (*bedürfniss*) and that the purpose of rational administration is to maximize their satisfaction was a staple of early nineteenth-century German economics,[15] but it was not until 1853 that an obscure Prussian bureaucrat stated the equi-marginal principle of constrained utility maximization ("the last atom of money creates the same pleasure in each pleasurable use"), therein revealing the connection between marginal utility and demand price.[16] On the surface Gossen's construction epitomizes consumer rationality. Yet his controlling social vision contained seeds of irrationality born of the search for maximum pleasure. God, Gossen argued, caused man to take diminishing pleasure from goods in order to force him into profitable intercourse with his fellows; puritanical constraints on individual pleasure seeking frustrated this intention, and to thwart the Puritans God had instilled an irrepressible urge to seek satisfaction in material things.

> He gave this force such an extraordinary strength that all human resistance can only weaken, but not paralyze it. And no matter how man may try to suppress this force in one of its manifestations, it will always reappear with increased strength in an unexpected and unforeseen new manifestation. ... **Man! Explore the laws of My creation and act in accordance with these laws!**[17] [Bold in the original]

In view of the above and like italicized and boldface utterances, it is hardly surprising that Gossen's contemporaries considered him to be a crank and ignored his work.

The mathematical findings, however, could not be long delayed, and Gossen's principle was rediscovered on at least four occasions between 1855 and 1870.[18] The marginal principle quickly became the cornerstone of economic reasoning about rational choice. The equivalence between its equi-marginal rule and the first-order conditions for a maximum in differential calculus was quickly uncovered, giving new impetus to the shift of attention away from the cognitive issues raised by the definition of utility as a psychological phenomenon in real time, to the purely computational aspects of utility maximization. In one area, however, the cognitive issues could not be avoided. This was the problem raised by optimal intertemporal choice.

Formally, the problem of optimally allocating a fixed endowment of resources over different periods of time is identical to that of optimally allocating resources among different uses at a single point in time. By the equi-marginal rule utility maximization requires that saving, lending, borrowing, and dissaving should be scheduled to equalize the marginal utility of consumption in each period. The problem was how to conceive the utility of events that have not yet happened. When balancing present against future consumption, did the agent maximize a utility function that sums the pleasure of present consumption and the present pleasure of anticipating future consumption, or did he maximize the expected utility of present and future consumption?

The difference is subtle but crucial. The urgency of the issue stemmed from the role of intertemporal optimization in explaining why interest rates are typically positive. That investments earn a positive rate of return is not a sufficient reason, because it does not explain why investment is not carried on until the net return is zero. The solution came with the recognition that the saving required to finance investment is at the cost of reduced present consumption, which means that the amount of savings must be determined by balancing benefits in the future against present cost, both of which are expressible in units of utility. On this logic, positive interest can be explained by positing a positive preference for present over future consumption, which implies a premium of extra future consumption - i.e., interest - to compensate the sacrifice of more highly valued present enjoyments. This phenomenon is known as time preference. On the hypothesis that all utility is currently experienced, the phenomenon of positive time preference is attributed to the lesser subjective pleasure of anticipated consumption as compared to that of actual consumption.[19] On the hypothesis that what is maximized is a mathematical expectation of pleasures to be experienced over a lifetime, the phenomenon is attributed to a failure by agents to accurately imagine the intensity of the future enjoyment, which the Austrian economist Böhm-Bawerk termed myopia. He further supposed that this infirmity of the imagination was constant across all future periods, so that the myopic rate of time discount connecting the subjective value of future consumption in years 19 and 20, was identical to that connecting the value of consumption in years 1 and 2. The proposition conforms to the law of one price with respect to the term structure of interest rates, which requires the net expected rate of return to investment over a defined period of time to be independent of the date at which the investment is made. Following Samuelson[20] the economics profession has adopted Böhm-Bawerk's hypothesis of constant time preference, which permits an unambiguous ranking of alternative intertemporal allocations.[21]

Mathematical tractability cannot be the sole criterion for assessing a psychological proposition, however, and the hypothesis of time-invariant time preference has turned out to be refuted by experimental and non-experimental evidence: Events that are close to the present are commonly discounted at higher rates than events that are further off in time. It is well known that individuals commonly fail to stick to diet and exercise programs they know to be in their best long-run interest; another common example is impulse buying at the checkout line. Such apparent irrationality also applies to more considered decisions. For example, American consumers in the 1970s and 1980s were generally prepared to assume high operating costs of inexpensive air conditioners rather than borrow from banks at 10 percent to purchase the more expensive efficient systems whose energy savings earned implicit returns exceeding 85 percent.[22] The use of credit cards as instruments of indebtedness carrying high interest charges instead of borrowing on lines of credit or liquidating financial assets with low implicit returns is another widespread example of irrationality, and one that has provided extremely profitable arbitrage for financial institutions who borrow from their depositors at low rates in order to lend back to them at higher ones. What accounts for the apparently hyperbolic path of time preference? One plausible answer is that the immediate context has the power to generate emotional responses that the future lacks, and that the emotions override the cautious counsel of rationality.[23] Choice with respect to future events is more than just a calculation.

Walras: The Algebra of General Equilibrium and the Algorithm of "Groping"

Calculation is at the heart of the other major development in economic theory that resulted from the introduction of utility maximization as a principle of economic thinking. Like the other marginal utility theorists, Walras showed that the diminishing marginal utility of goods to individuals implies a downward sloping demand curve. He also realized, however, that the equi-marginal condition implied by the budget constraint $[MU_i/P_i = MU_j/P_j]$ made the demand for any particular good a function of the prices of all goods. Solving the equilibrium price for any one thus required knowing the equilibrium price of all other goods. Since markets in equilibrium are defined by the condition that quantity supplied equals quantity demanded, a general equilibrium can be expressed as a set of simultaneous equations, one for each commodity. Walras' insight was to realize that because the number of prices equals the number of markets determining them the general equilibrium for an economy with n goods could in principle be solved as the solution set of a system of n-1 simultaneous equations.[24] A purely mathematical demonstration of the existence of general equilibrium, however, was not enough.

The problem was that the mathematics of simultaneous equations requires everything to happen at once, and this is obviously not the way things occur in real life. To circumvent the difficulty posed by the mathematical structure of his model, Walras proposed the fiction of the economy as an auction in which prices are cried out by an auctioneer, who tallies up the offers and bids, and adjusts the current price of each good upward or downward according as its net demand is positive or negative. By a succession of prices the market eventually converged to a set of prices that makes the net demand for each commodity zero. This is the solution of a simultaneous system of equations. Walras termed the iterative crying out of prices *tâtonnement*, or "groping," and proposed that no sales actually take place until it was over, so that bids and offers were purely provisional. The latter assumption is imposed by implacable logic of simultaneous equations, which requires exchange to take place at the equilibrium price set. If this were not the case, transactions completed prior to the closing of the auction alter the distribution of wealth among market participants, thereby changing the constraints that define the equation system. *Tâtonnement* was thus a metaphor for a computational algorithm that solves a simultaneous system of equations;[25] it disguised the essential timelessness of Walras' model where nothing real happens until the equilibrium is attained by rational calculations that reflect the endowments and technical constraints.

The calculations involved agents determining their optimal bids and offers at each price cried out by the auctioneer. To accomplish this feat of cognition, they have to know the price of every good in the market at every moment in market time. Since the formal model can only solve for equilibrium, however, time does not matter. *Tâtonnement* exists in a timeless world of pure calculation, where decision-making requires no special effort. Walras deliberately expunged the ephemera of real economic life to elucidate the logical structure of market economies in what he thought, on analogy with the fictions of physics, was a "pure" economics. The drawback was that in the real world the ephemera matter, and unlike the platonic world of Walras' auction, it is peopled by agents who make mistakes that can only be corrected, if at all, by the passage of real time at a real cost.

"But nothing of this is true in the world in which we live."

"The element of time," writes Alfred Marshall, "is a chief cause of those difficulties in economic investigations which make it necessary for man with his limited powers to go step by step."[26] On a superficial reading Marshall's homely parables celebrate the utilitarian calculus: a boy who stops picking berries at the point where the effort of picking just equals the utility of the last berry he eats, a housewife calculating how best to allocate the annual supply of knitting yarn between socks and vests, a clerk who ponders whether to ride the omnibus or walk to work in order to buy himself "a little indulgence." Yet, when one digs a little deeper, the principle of rational choice is everywhere qualified by impediments to its realization. The impediments arise from the fact that current decisions have to be made with an eye to their future implications, and events in the future are not perfectly predictable. Nowhere was this more evident than in the factors affecting the supply of human skills, which involve a time horizon that extends over a generation.

> Perfect competition requires perfect knowledge of the state of the market; and though no great departure from the actual facts of life is involved in assuming this knowledge on the part of dealers when we are considering the course of business in Lombard Street, the Stock Exchange, or in a wholesale Produce Market; it would be an altogether unreasonable assumption to make when we are examining the causes that govern the supply of labour in any of the lower grades of industry. For if a man had sufficient ability to know everything about the market for his labour, he would have too much to remain long in a low grade. (Marshall 1966 [1920] p. 449)

Anyone with the cognitive ability to cipher the future state of demand and supply for anything can do better by marketing that ability to others than by restricting it to the management of his own resources. That degree of rationality is a scarce resource.

Marshall fully understood the mathematical logic of general equilibrium,[27] but he did not think the method of simultaneous equations describes how markets actually achieve an equilibrium of supply and demand, nor did he believe that the general equilibrium necessarily represents an optimal state. "The theory of stable equilibrium," he wrote, "helps indeed to give definiteness to our ideas; and in its elementary stages it does not diverge from the actual facts of life....but when pushed to its more remote and intricate logical consequences, it slips away from the conditions of real life" (Ibid. pp. 381-82). One inescapable condition of real life is the unknowable future. For equilibrium to be general the current stock of capital has to be adjusted to the point where the return to each type of capital equals the marginal subjective cost of saving. For this to be true at any point in time, the suppliers of capital in the past must have correctly predicted the future that is now; otherwise, some types of human and physical capital would be in excess supply or demand, and thus earn less or more than a normal rate of return. The general equilibrium is conditional on suppliers having correct expectations. But how are flawed expectations corrected? By learning from mistakes, and learning takes time. The only state that can support a general equilibrium, therefore, is one in which enough time has passed during which the underlying conditions of technology and tastes have remained constant to permit the expectations of suppliers to conform to that constant reality. Marshall termed such an equilibrium a Stationary State. In it "no fundamental difference between the immediate and later effects of economic causes" could ever exist.[28]

"But nothing of this is true in the world in which we live."[29] To Marshall the economy never achieves the stationary state because nothing stays still long enough for expectations and the supply responses they elicit to produce it. In the real world agents are always adjusting to novelty, and novelty never ceases. Even if it did, a stationary state would be difficult to achieve by individual responses alone, because market supply is a joint product of decisions taken by many suppliers, and is affected by what Marshall termed external economies that make the average cost of production depend on the joint output of all suppliers rather than the cost attributable to them individually. Such external economies are subtle and quantitatively unpredictable, and are revealed after the fact, when they can no longer enter the *ex ante* rational calculation of cost and benefit that determines the supply of individual firms. It is only in the stationary state that the knowledge of them is known and exploited. Marshall's stationary state was more than a metaphor of general equilibrium; it captured the impossibility of agents fully knowing things in advance of their actually happening. The mathematical possibility of a rationally generated full equilibrium was not a possibility afforded by the real world.

Rationality and Mathematical Economics

Marshall's aversion to pursuing the pure logic of optimization into its more extreme recesses passed by osmosis to his student John Maynard Keynes. Trained in mathematics and author of a work on the logical foundations of probability,[30] Keynes resisted the project of using the principle of rationality to make economics over in the image of mathematics. Writing to Roy Harrod in 1938, he observed,

I also want to emphasise strongly the point about economics being a moral science. I mentioned before that it deals with introspection and values. I might have added that it deals with motives, expectations, psychological uncertainties. One has to be constantly on guard against treating the material as constant and homogeneous. It is as though the fall of the apple to the ground depended on the apple's motives.[31]

Economics, he noted in the same letter,

is a science of thinking in terms of models joined to the art of choosing models which are relevant to the contemporary world. It is compelled to be this, because unlike the typical natural science, the material to which it is applied is, in too many respects, not homogeneous through time.[33]

This comment may be usefully contrasted with that made by Oscar Morgenstern to his diary a few years later.

Economists simply don't know what science means. I am disgusted with all of this rubbish. – I am more and more of the opinion that Keynes is a scientific charlatan, and his followers not even that.[33]

Morgenstern's benchmark for pure science was axiomatic mathematics, and the axiom on which a science of economics was to be founded was the axiom of rationality.

The rise of mathematical economics can be traced to efforts by a group of mathematicians at the start of the twentieth century to reconstruct mathematics on the basis of independent axioms governing the properties of sets from which all valid mathematical propositions could be derived by definition or deduction.[34] The attempt to strip mathematics of empirical content constituted the leading edge of the tectonic shift from historical to structural explanation in spheres as diverse as mathematical physics, linguistics, anthropology, criticism, and economics that marked the first half of the twentieth century.[35] Truth was a matter of formal consistency, not intuitive plausibility, to be verified by establishing the independence of the axioms and the consistency of the logic linking them to the theorems.[36] Pascal had set out the purposes of mathematical argument more than two centuries earlier: "Such, then, is the whole art of... convincing...to define all notations used, and to prove everything by replacing mentally the defined terms by their notations."[37]

The axiomatic program achieved its initial successes in quantum mechanics and the theory of kinetic gases, where the higher mathematics of sets provided precise mathematical description of physical states.[38] It also provided a new way of describing economic states.[39] The new techniques were carried into economic reasoning in the 1920s and early 1930s by a few gifted mathematicians who were attracted to the field by its intellectual opportunities, and by a desire to apply mathematical logic to the pressing social problem of mass unemployment and the question of the relative efficiency of market versus socialist economies.[40] The first generation of mathematician-economists thus found their privileged sphere of enquiry in the theory of general equilibrium, whose mathematical foundations were notoriously unsound.[41] The mathematical contribution to this theory was to give a concise and logically consistent language for expressing economic propositions in a way that made it possible to determine whether they are logically true or false.[42] According to Koopmans, mathematical analysis of economic matters held ontological priority over merely empirical considerations.

The test of mathematical existence of an object of analysis postulated in a model is in the first instance a check on the absence of contradictions among the assumptions made. If we assume that not all members of a body of contradictory statements can have empirical relevance, this logical test has to be passed before any question of the application of a model to some aspect of reality can seriously be raised.[43]

Koopmans admitted that in fields like physics scientists often bypassed the question of mathematical existence in the rush to explore the physical properties of phenomena; "[b]ut the fruits of such studies are like predated checks until the non-contradictory character of their premises has been established" (p. 58). In short, what is real is necessarily logical and what is logical is necessarily real. Since mathematical truth is independent of empirical contingencies, the investigations of mathematical economists were neither preceded nor accompanied by an attempt to acquire a working understanding of actual economic behavior.[44] The mathematics was interesting enough in itself.

Rationality was central to the mathematical enterprise in economics because it supplied a rule for restricting the set of feasible outcomes to a subset that could be interpreted as an economic equilibrium. In keeping with axiomatic methodology, the mathematical economists defined utility as an ordering of economic outcomes characterized by the set-theoretic properties of equivalence, transitivity and completeness. The psychological connotations of the rationality assumption were stripped away, leaving a set of formal rules defining permissible operations on sets of real numbers. As economic reasoning became more and more rigorous and general, the agents whose behavior it modeled became psychologically less and less plausible.

They were also becoming more proficient calculators of self-interest. The urgent need to allocate strategic resources efficiently during the Second World War stimulated a search for numerical algorithms to find optimal solutions to problems characterized by multiple dynamic constraints.[45] The discovery of new optimization techniques greatly extended the range of optimal solutions that could be attributed to the ratiocinations of rational economic agents, although in practice most required the computational assistance of digital computers. The work also revealed the deep mathematical congruence of game theory, linear programming and activity analysis, which carried intimations of universal mathematical and therefore scientific Order. A solution to any of these problems was by definition one that would be chosen by a rational agent. By the 1950s the axiomatic approach was turning the intuitively plausible agents of conventional economics into disembodied personifications of mathematical algorithms. The revolution in method made economics a highly mathematized discipline on par with mathematical physics. A poll of economists conducted in the mid-1980s revealed that 98 percent considered proficiency in mathematics to be the most important factor in determining professional success. Only 22 percent thought that knowledge of the economy was even moderately important to professional success, and 68 percent considered it unimportant.[46]

Rationality Redux

The four decades following the publication of Samuelson's *Foundations* (1947) were the imperial age of strong rationality. Constrained optimization found applications across the whole range of conventional economic analysis, and from the late 1950s the hypotheses it generated could be implemented using the high-speed computational capacity of electronic computers. This confluence of analytical and computational technique produced a standardized research methodology in which an optimizing outcome was identified analytically and then tested for statistically using observable proxies for the theoretical variables analyzed in the analytical exercise. Considerable effort was dedicated to demonstrating the plausibility of the rationality assumption. This typically meant calculating the theoretical outcomes implied by agent optimization and comparing them with those observed. If they were similar, the similarity confirmed the axiom of rationality. Such tests rarely failed. Optimization was an axiom, empirical refutation of its implications simply stimulated further search for new constraints that would make the theoretical outcome conform to what was observed; failure to come up with appropriate constraints was not evidence that the rationality assumption was not valid in a particular context, but a sign of the investigator's lack of imagination and technical competence. The axiom was no longer a tool of analysis; it had become a censoring device.

The power of the new methods of finding optimal solutions to complex problems opened the way to employing economic analysis outside its traditional sphere of market behavior. The main effort was directed at reinterpreting social institutions as equilibrium outcomes generated by the interactions of rational agents. As in economics, the tests typically consisted in establishing congruence between observed outcomes and those theoretically predicted, and as in economics, the predictions could be made to conform to outcomes by multiplying the theoretical constraints. The limiting case of this approach was achieved in evolutionary biology, where evolution of specific traits was interpreted in terms of a repeated strategic game played by "as if" rational genes.[47] Rationality no longer even implied consciousness.

The rationality hypothesis was in fact most imperialistic in transforming macroeconomics, a field originally conceived in terms of the financial interactions between economic aggregates like consumption, investment, the price level, the foreign balance, and the government deficit. It was generally conceded that the decisions generating the aggregates had to conform to a rationality postulate, but the early Keynesians doubted that investigating the economy at this level of detail could yield much practical insight into the problems created by large short-term fluctuations in intersectoral flows of funds that appeared to be the source of the protracted Great Depression. The eroding of this pragmatic attitude began in the 1950s with efforts to understand household saving in terms of the theory of intertemporal choice.[48] That analysis indicated that fiscal policy designed to manipulate current household spending by altering personal disposable income would be defeated by offsetting changes in household saving. This proposition rested explicitly on the strongly rational assumption that people understand the economic connection between the present and future deficits and act on that understanding by saving part of the extra income from a present tax cut in order to finance the logically necessary future tax increase. This reasoning received a powerful fillip in the 1970s with the invention of the "overlapping generations" model, which proposed that agents have a target bequest that is logically projected through all future time by target bequests of successive generations of their heirs. By constraining future generations to be as rational with respect to their futures as the present generation is with its future, the model achieved perfect offsetting of fiscal policy by changes in household spending.

The most influential attack on Keynesian macroeconomics, came in the form of Lucas' concept of "rational" expectations.[49] Lucas argued that agents optimally adjust their model of the economy to perceived changes in the policy environment, making it impossible for governments systematically to affect aggregate demand by manipulating the supply of money or the size of the government debt.[50] The process of adjusting expectations of the policy regime, however, required agents to solve a stochastic dynamic programming problem, pushing theory further down the road of hyper-rationality. The terminus was the theory of the "real business cycle," which held that observed short-term fluctuations in economic activity are uniquely caused by optimizing labor supply responses by workers to exogenous productivity shocks. When productivity is above trend, workers work longer in response to the temporarily increased demand for labor; since interest rates tend to rise in booms, they save more in order to finance the withdrawal of their labor when the productivity shock is negative. The model thus proposes a smoothing of the lifetime supply of labor in a manner analogous to lifetime smoothing of consumption by households. Unemployment is never involuntary. The denial that the labor market can generate involuntary unemployment was the result of taking the axiom of rationality to its logical limit. It nevertheless rests on auxiliary assumptions that the axiom required to make the analysis mathematically tractable. They include (a) an economy that produces a single homogeneous good; (b) technology shocks as the sole source of variation to which agents have to respond; (c) infinitely lived identical agents whose menu of choice is restricted to deciding how to allocate their life time between work and leisure; (d) agents who know the timing and size of future productivity shocks with perfect certainty.[51] Keynes, practical macroeconomics had morphed into a mathematical algorithm.

We leave the real business cycle theory by citing two statements summarizing the tension created by the demand for a fully "rational" explanation of macroeconomic fluctuations. The first is by one of its inventors; the second by a Neo-Keynesian critic.

> The essential flaw in the Keynesian interpretation of macroeconomic phenomenon [sic] was the absence of a consistent foundation based on the choice theoretic framework of microeconomics.[52]
>
> The choice between alternative theories of the business cycle—in particular between real business cycle and new Keynesian theory—is partly a choice between internal and external consistency. ...New Keynesian theory, in its attempt to mimic the world more accurately, relies on nominal rigidities that are observed but only little understood. Indeed New Keynesians sometimes suggest that to understand the business cycle, it may be necessary to reject the axiom of rational, optimizing individuals, an act that for economists would be the ultimate abandonment of internal consistency.[53]

The Revolution Eats Its Own

Revolutions sometimes turn on their makers; so it was with the rational revolution in economics. The hyper-development of economic models peopled by hyper-rational agents exposed puzzles and anomalies that grew increasingly troubling as the twentieth century drew to a close. The final section of this essay briefly reviews some of these developments.

Puzzles and anomalies surfaced in three areas. The first was pure theory, where the theories of repeated games and optimal control revealed pervasive multiple equilibria, and where the analysis of dynamic non-linear systems revealed high sensitivity of equilibrium paths to minute perturbations in initial conditions.[54] Since strong rationality requires decision-makers to make judgments based on the likely consequences of their actions, the finding that a given set of initial conditions can generate multiple equilibria, and that imperceptible variations in initial conditions can produce wildly diverging outcomes was unsettling. The second sphere was management studies, where students of decision-making uncovered significant deviations from the precepts of profit maximization in large firms. The third area was experimental economics, where experiments designed to test the expected utility hypothesis and the consistency of individual preferences revealed systematic violations of rationality by subjects. In addition a growing body of non-experimental evidence cast doubt on the twinned postulates of strong rationality and market clearing,[55] and repeated econometric tests of standard propositions failed to sustain consistent findings across new data sets and new estimation techniques.[56] Finally, there was mounting evidence of large-scale irrational investment decisions in housing and equity markets.[57] The anomalies, puzzles and contrary results were too numerous to be written off as incidental curiosities. Their common element was the effect of limited human decision-making capacity. The economics of strong rationality assumed that outcomes could be predicted from external constraints because optimizing agents would place themselves on the boundaries defined by those constraints. If agents were incapable of calculating the optimum, however, the observable constraints no longer provided an infallible guide to the analysis of equilibrium.

Pure Theory

To theorists the finding that agent rationality and market-clearing do not guarantee predictable outcomes from a specified set of *ex ante* conditions was deeply troubling. Because equilibrium theory required that agents act as though they knew what the equilibrium was, a multiplicity of them weakened the case for supposing that by sheer deductive reasoning alone a representative agent could make the necessary decision that sustains equilibrium. Multiple equilibrium was to be sure a fundamental feature of Keynesian macroeconomics, but because the condition resulted from inflexible nominal wages "pure" theorists regarded Keynes' finding to be no more than the trivial consequence of abandoning the conventional market-clearing mechanism of flexible prices and of renouncing the principle of rationality with respect to workers' labor supply decisions. Keynes, who ridiculed the supposed rationality of professional investors,[58] had in fact given plausible reasons why workers might refuse a to take a cut in real income caused by a reduction in the money wage that they would accept were it to result from the combination of stable money wages and higher prices.[59] Those arguments, however, were buried by the rational expectations insistence on continuously full equilibrium as the only defensible methodological stance for scientific economics. By the 1990s, rational expectations methodology had shown that full rationality does not rule out self-fulfilling expectations that can generate equilibrium states on the basis of expectations with no empirical controls.[60] What one believed might be empirically untrue, but it was logically rational to act as if it were. In the one area where multiple equilibria really matter for policy, the debate had come full circle.

The paradox in microeconomics was a by-product of the increasing ability of mathematical economists to describe optimal decisions in complex settings. The theory of repeated games produced a veritable combinatorial explosion of outcomes that agents had to consider when deciding an optimal strategy; dynamic optimizations were described by differential equations whose state variables are solvable only by numerical algorithms that might take weeks for high-speed computers to complete.[61] The notion that ordinary people made such calculations when they decided how much to save or how much labor to supply was less and less plausible. By the 1980s the computational complexity had reached a point where economists could no longer plausibly presume that the benefits of perfect rationality were necessarily worth its cognitive costs. Kenneth Arrow observed that an economics based on the deductive implications of the rationality axiom alone is plausible only under "very ideal conditions."

When these conditions cease to hold, the rationality assumptions become strained and possibly even self-contradictory. They certainly imply an ability at information processing that is far beyond the feasible, and that cannot well be justified as the result of learning and adaptation.[62]

The paradigm of economic rational choice was in a blind alley.

Behavioral Economics

The "behaviorist" critique of the rationality axiom grew out of the finding that managers do not invariably maximize the net worth of the firm, raising the question why they systematically fail to do what they are so well paid to do, and why competition does not weed out suboptimal performance. One answer is that the underperformance occurred mainly in non-competitive industries, where weeding by market forces is lethargic, but this hypothesis is refuted by the proven ability of entrepreneurs to engineer profitable hostile takeovers financed by running the captured firms more efficiently. A second possibility is that the constraints on managerial choices or the firm's objective were incorrectly specified, in which case any discrepancy between theoretically optimal and observed performance can be as a consequence of poor theorizing.[63] This approach amounts to explaining away the evidence. The alternative was to rethink the limits to managerial cognitive capacity. Few business decisions have simple consequences; most open the door to outcomes that lead to other outcomes, so that the number of consequences grows exponentially with the number of conditioning events. In principle the expected value of any decision can be computed as a mathematical expectation, but even structurally simple situations generate impossibly large numbers of outcomes to compare and evaluate.[64] If cognitive capability is a scarce resource, then businessmen will optimize on that constraint as well as the external constraints defined by the availability of conventional inputs. This was the approach adopted by H. A. Simon, who called the practice of using routine rules of thumb that worked well but possibly not optimally "satisficing," and the condition of limited cognitive capacity that gave rise to it "bounded" rationality.[65]

Simon defined satisficing as using rules of thumb that work well enough to warrant not adopting more efficient rules. The rules are thus a rational response to the high cost of identifying and evaluating alternative courses of action in dynamic environments. The question remains whether the notion of optimal sub-optimization creates an infinite regress of optimizing that requires choosing rules of thumb for choosing rules of thumb, etc. Nelson and Winter proposed an evolutionary solution to this problem by arguing that the market tends to select those firms for growth and survival that have better (though by no means the theoretical best) rules of thumb.[66] Yet just as "good" species are occasionally eliminated by exogenous ecological shocks, so firms carrying the "gene" of a good rule of thumb can be eliminated by negative economic shocks. If the future could be known with certainty, the cognitive cost of computing an optimal rule would be covered by the present value of its benefits. But, as Marshall observed, this is not the world we live in.

> Were the context static or predictable, the organizational aspects could be solved "once and for all".... The costs of making this once-and-for-all analysis might not loom large when they are amortized over the time horizon of the economic system; arguably, the differences between organizational structures regarding these costs would not be particularly important.... In reality, the nature and magnitude of the organizational problem is intimately connected with the degree of economic flux.[67]

The only context in which natural selection by markets ensures full optimality is Marshall's stationary state. The theory of "bounded rationality" thus restored real time as part of the analysis of rational economic action.

Experimental Economics and Cognitive Psychology

Understanding how people make decisions generally requires knowing something about the psychology of decision-making. The study of human cognition has a long and checkered history.[68] But while psychologists continue to debate the meaning of intelligence, there is general agreement that the mind's capacity to perceive, classify, categorize, and manipulate information is limited, especially when the time allowed for taking decisions is short.[69] According to the paradigm of artificial intelligence, thinking is like the symbolic transformations performed by a Turing machine.[70] It begins with a signal inputting information from an external source or from long-term memory to a central processor; the processor carries out neural transformations of that information, the results of which are transmitted to the motor system or stored in memory. Like artificial computers, the mind can handle a limited amount of data and complexity, so people in their thinking as in their computer programs simplify the mental algorithms by ignoring some of the complexity. The metaphor of the mind as a computer thus provided the core argument for bounded rationality.[71]

In recent years the mechanistic metaphor of mind as a computing machine has been challenged by an alternative vision of cognition that locates the neural mechanics of the mind in the sensorimotor system. The challenge to the computer model was partly inspired by experimental findings of apparent irrationality in situations not complex enough to stress normal cognitive ability.[72] In experimental settings subjects regularly violated the transitivity property of consistent choice; they reversed declared preferences depending on how alternatives were presented or "framed"; as between substantively identical alternatives they preferred those artificially presented as the "status quo"; they preferred gambles presented as a chance of "winning" to identical gambles described in terms of "losing." They commonly miscalculated simple expected values, mistook random for patterned data (and vice versa), falsely inferred causal relations from casual observations, preferred confirming to disconfirming evidence, although the latter is decisive whereas the former is not; took sunk costs as mattering even when they are economically irrelevant; and objects that should be treated as alternatives subject to a common budget constraint were evaluated as if they had been placed in non-intersecting mental accounts.[73] In short, they behaved as though they were not totally rational. These findings are supported by a large body of research on the human capacity to process complex information. According to Lohman's survey subjects typically show flagrant biases in solving such problems as a function of the emotionality of the premise, subjects' agreement with the content of the premises, abstractedness of the content, and even the form in which the problems are presented. This suggests that, although such problems may be interesting candidates for research, they are probably not good candidates for assessments of individual differences in reasoning abilities.[74]

In brief, certain types of error in perception and reasoning are so common they must be considered normal.

In the economic sphere both experimental and non-experimental evidence reveals significant deviations from the predictions of conventional microeconomic rationality. We have already noted that people tend to discount imminent events at a higher rate than events in a distant future. Similar time-inconsistency has been detected in financial markets: the difference between closing stock prices on Friday and opening prices on Monday does not reflect the implicit interest cost of carrying the assets through the weekend; covered international interest rate differentials do not accurately predict future movement in exchange rates.[75] What is odd about these findings is that they occur in markets with the best facilities for arbitrageurs to profit from such deviations. Other examples from finance include the deviation in the value of index funds from the mean value of their component stocks, and the "irrational exuberance" that supported the Internet bubble from 1997 to early 2000.[76] In auctions successful bidders regularly inflict a "winner's curse" on themselves by bidding more than the item is worth to them.[77]

Although the puzzles and anomalies do not add up to a full indictment of the axiom of strong rationality, they raise the question why people so often act inconsistently when the returns to logical consistency are significant. The observed deviations from rationality transcend the metaphor of scarce computational capacity posited by theorists of bounded rationality; in many cases the context of decision is simple, making it unlikely that an erroneous choice was made because the alternatives were too difficult to compare with accuracy. Many common decisions seem fundamentally perverse. Why should emotion and pride stand in the way of rational decisions when all the facts are known? Why should people engage in risky sexual behavior or experiment with highly addictive substances when they really know better? Why do people pre-commit to involuntary saving plans when they can achieve a more efficient intertemporal allocation costlessly and with greater flexibility by following a standard period-by-period optimization program?[78]

Some social theorists have suggested that these and similar depar-
tures from rationality are a consequence of people having "multiple
selves," distinct centers of willpower resident in the same person.[79]
They argue that the several "selves" play strategic games with each
other to determine the conduct of the person whose behavior they
desire to control. The idea behind the gaming metaphor is that self-
control imposes an immediate psychological cost that can only be
offset by mental strategies that actualize its long-term benefits.[80]
The internal gaming by multiple selves is itself a rational, though
possibly sub-conscious strategy for optimization.

Embodied Rationality

A more radical approach to the paradox of apparently irrational
action has been proposed by cognitive scientists who conceive perception and reasoning as jointly integrated dynamic processes unfolding in real time.[81] The paradigm has important, but as yet
unexploited, implications for economics. According to it mind is
not a disembodied computing machine that processes information
from the outside using pre-assigned logical programs that have
evolved to map a transcendentally logical universe; instead the mind
thinks with preexisting neurological circuits that have evolved to
manage sense perceptions and feedbacks from bodily movement.
The vision rests on the proposition that there is no fundamental distinction between the neurology of perception, motor response and
"thinking." It is based on a growing body of evidence, much of it
assembled by cognitive linguists, indicating that the transmission of
sensorimotor information is subject to a "pipeline" constraint that
requires additional neurological circuitry in order to reduce the sensory data to packets small enough to traverse the synaptic connection from the sensory receptors to "dense ensembles of neurons" in
the brain.[82] The same probably holds for synaptic connections between "dense ensembles" within the brain. This reducing circuitry
categorizes information in ways that present themselves naturally
to the sensory apparatus. For example, positional categories of "front"
or "back" are a natural circuitry for beings with eyes that point in
one direction, those of "up" and "down" are natural to a being subjected to gravitational force. The abstraction notion of a class is
natural to beings familiar with containers. Because the operations
performed by such circuits are unconscious, the reasoning they support is inherently non-propositional, metaphorical, and contextual.

According to this line of argument the circuitry evolved to handle information generated by external stimuli and feedbacks from bodily movement is employed by the brain to code the information it "processes." If so, the categories of reason are not those of abstract logical truth, but represent evolutionary contingencies of man's perceptual interaction with his environment.[83]

If the sensorimotor and cognitive neural systems constitute an interacting dynamic system continuously in contact with the environment, then the state variables of that system will generate attractors reflecting temporary goal-oriented categories of thought and action, some of which survive by repetition and duration to become strong attracting mental categories for reasoning and other cognitive activity. The categories are therefore not hard-wired by logical necessity, but "softly assembled by individuals through dynamical patterns of activity that arise as a function of the intended task at hand."[84] In the language of modern economics, the machinery of cognition is path dependent. The reason our cognitive structures are so alike is because we have similarly formed bodies and confront common features of the environment. The stability of the categories reflects the stability of the forms of interaction.[85]

Research on the development of hand-eye coordination in infants provides strong evidence for the embodied approach to cognition. Infants learn successfully to reach for things in consequence of the development of neurological circuits that signal the strength of the forces generated by their limbs and bodies to their mind. The history of the imprinting is unique to each child, and is determined by its initial random movements and by the interaction of those movements with changes in the mass and strength of the limbs, which determine which muscles can be exercised at each point in time.[86] Since the child's successive movements are conditioned by the neural circuitry created by previous signals, the development of the circuitry controlling its hand-eye coordination is innately contextual. Nothing in the experimental evidence suggests that a child's ability to perceive and grasp objects in space is a product of an independently developing "mind" that comes to "know" the abstract logic of things located in three-dimensional space as a transcendental category.[87] The "logic" of spatial relations is a sensorimotor neural circuit with a developmental history, and therefore embodied.

The body constructs cognitive categories to achieve goals. Some of the categories are directly inferred from the gross properties of things, like "dog," "cat," or "tree," all of which can be easily distinguished by persons endowed with ordinary faculties of perception; they are also strongly imprinted on neural networks because they are frequently perceived.[88] As an evolutionary adaptation, the selective advantage conferred by the ability to receive, compare, and coordinate multiple sensory stimuli consists in enhanced ability to deal with unexpected events. If the environment were perfectly constant, natural selection would produce organisms wholly and unconsciously adapted to it, which is the case for all but about 14,000 (out of 50,000) species of mammal.[89] Intelligence means storing cases in memory, creating categories to group them, and identifying properties to compare them with new phenomena. Most of the categorizing in human beings—and presumably all of it in the other intelligent species—is performed unconsciously by neural circuitry that evolved to handle signals generated by the senses and events internal to the body.[90] Most thinking is carried out subconsciously using the primary categories. Rational choice covers only that small part of mental activity that surfaces as consciousness. If this is true, it explains why so much ordinary thinking appears to be conducted by analogy and metaphor, and why judgments seem so often to be contrary to the logic of rationality.

Primary categories are the source of metaphorical mappings in the mind. These mappings are part of neural circuitry because they are strongly imprinted by repeated experience. Other categories are not so strongly held because they are created for particular purposes. In economics the category "firm" was developed to provide a maximizing agent in order to analyze supply responses. Most people, however, would be hard put to find what is common about a corner barber and General Electric, just as they would find it hard to recognize themselves in the "representative agent" of abstract macroeconomics, which is a special-purpose analytical construct that has no meaning outside the limited world of professional economics. To take a more abstruse example: the set of all sets that do not contain themselves is a category with but one purpose: to demonstrate the impossibility of a universally applicable theory of sets. Goal-oriented categories arise in the course of action; if the actions giving rise to them are repeated the categories get reinforced in memory and may become the reference point for further mappings.

The dynamic model of cognition has been employed to restudy the anomaly of miscalculated expected utilities in gambles by

Townsend and Buseymeyer.[91] The anomaly occurs when subjects prefer a bet that yields $4.00 with 99 percent probability and $0.00 with one percent probability to a bet yielding $12 with a probability of 33 percent and $0.00 with probability 67 percent, yet when given the opportunity to sell the bets they charge a higher price for the second gamble. Tversky and Kahneman hypothesized that subjects assigned separate weights to the probability and value dimensions of the gambles, and that when asked to choose, they put more weight on the probability dimension in the first case, and more weight on the value dimension in the second. This is an example of "framing."[92] Townsend and Busemeyer argue that framing is not the cause of the paradox and looked instead at the presence of strong attractors that develop while the subjects are deliberating. The idea is that when deliberating their reservation price for a gamble, subjects imagine a price and then make a judgment whether it is too high or too low relative to the as yet unknown price that makes them indifferent between selling the bet and holding it. In actions that generate gains or losses, they worry about the strength of the connection between an action and its consequences, which they conceive alternatively as losses or gains; sometimes they worry more about the gains; other times they worry more about the potential losses. As they worry or deliberate, their subjective assessment of the strength of the link between the act and its consequences changes, which in turn changes the expected pay-offs. It is this well-documented "learning effect" that generates path-dependent choice. Since the indifference price is initially unknown to the decision-maker, it is a subjectively random variable, which means that the difference between the agent's initial hypothesized reservation price and the indifference reference point is also a random variable.

A common starting point for deliberating is the mid-point of the range as determined by the highest and lowest outcome of the gamble. When subjects select this initial reservation price, they systematically overestimate their true reservation price. This is easy to see for the 99:1 percent gamble because the variance of outcomes is so low, which causes the convergence to the actuarial value of the bet to occur rapidly. It is harder in the case of the 33:67 percent gamble with the same expected return, because the variance in the return is wider. In the second case the low level of discriminability generates a slower downward drift in the reservation price, which may not converge to the actuarial value before a decision about which gamble to accept has to be made. The result is that the reservation price of the second gamble will generally exceed its "true" indifference price when the indifference price for the first bet has been determined. When asked to choose the price at which they are willing to sell the bet at that point in time, agents will thus put a higher price on the high-variance gamble than a low-variance gamble having the same expected return.[93] The anomaly thus reflects dynamically adjusting differences in perception.

In certain contexts, then, systematic bias in reasoning may reflect the form of the primary metaphors that arise from the subconscious experience of daily life. We pay more attention to losses than to gains because in ordinary experience, some losses are life threatening. A metaphorical mapping from life-threatening loss to financial loss, however, is not accurate when the financial loss reproduces the state that would be achieved by an alternative event that yields a gain. This is what happens in the "framing" experiments. In conscious discourse the higher levels of abstraction coordinate primary concepts that arise at the level of the human body's interaction with its environment. But this coordination is not "natural" in the way that unconscious coordinating stimuli from sound waves, chemical substances in the atmosphere and the visible spectrum of electromagnetic radiation to determine the presence or absence of an object is natural. Nothing in our evolutionary history has required us to master the notion of negative, "irrational," or transfinite numbers. They are not intuitive in the sense that the number of countable apples in a bag is intuitive. For the same reason the optimizing choice that defines economic rationality is not a survival trait. We simply do not know whether or to what degree the evolution of the human mind was conditioned by a scarcity of resources so binding that it affected the development of neural circuitry. As Thaler observes, violations of the choice axioms of transitivity and stochastic dominance are rarely life threatening.[94] If people's choices are affected by emotion, aversion to loss, atypical but salient (i.e., attention-claiming) examples, or the status quo, it must be because the metaphorical structure of their thought overrides the logical structure. Some would argue that this metaphorical structure is the basis of logical structure.

The above anomalies can be viewed as a consequence of the way the neural system codes information. Psychological tests indicate that people presented with a complex problem of classifying new information do not exhaustively encode the terms to be classified and compared as a way of determining an appropriate analogy for reasoning, but instead scan the alternatives for clues to possible relationships.[95] By relying more on intuitive than on syllogistic principles to establish heuristic categories of thought relevant to new situations, they open themselves to error. This tendency is reinforced by the fact that the categories of intuition have been established and maintained for specific purposes, and thus are context or path-dependent.[96] What one sees is often determined by where one comes from. Simon reports an experiment in which a group of twenty-three executives enrolled in a business-training program were asked to analyze a real-world policy problem. Most of the sales executives identified the problem with sales; the production managers identified it with the internal organization of the company; the human resources, public relations and medical professionals identified it with human relations.[97]

The theory of embodied intelligence suggests that the empirical foundations of the rationality hypothesis are more unstable than has been thought to be the case. Whether they are so unstable as to place the edifice of economics in danger is not clear. Theoretical economists have begun to incorporate bounded rationality into their models, usually by assuming some kind of meta-optimizing to select the optimal means of making decisions.[98] Others have attempted to determine empirically whether agents devise a relatively stable decision rule when confronted with a complex decision tree.[99] Where this theorizing will go is not yet clear. Economic theory remains rooted in the principle of strong rationality and market clearing. The stock-flow relations that govern the supply of economists (and teachers of economists) make it likely that the strong rationality paradigm will continue to reign for a long time.

Conclusion

Economics is a European cultural product. It is hardly surprising, therefore, that the history of its central concept tracks the history of European thought. From its recorded beginnings in Greek philosophy the idea of rationality as a timeless and decontextualized intelligence identified with the Good constituted the core of western social and metaphysical thought. From Plato to Piaget the great tradition asserted a mind-body dualism which holds that mind "understands" the world through the agency of propositional logic embedded in computational structures of mathematical logic. In economics the notion of rationality was embodied in two kinds of Reason. The first was a reason of perfection: if we can rank outcomes by better or worse, the idea of a limit implies there is one that is best, and Reason commands us to do all in our power to find it and cleave to it. The second was the reason of common sense: when one chooses among alternatives, one does not knowingly choose one that is demonstrably inferior.

The crucial term is "knowing." Reason means seeking the best action in the degree that we know what it is. Born of the practical exigencies of commercial jurisprudence and penitential casuistry, economic reasoning developed on the axis of weak rationality. By the last quarter of the eighteenth century the paradigm of weakly rational choice had come to be embedded in the theory of price determination, where it provided the motivation for movement of labor and capital between industries and occupations that displayed the regularity of a natural law. That weakly rational economics sustained a sophisticated and largely accurate cost-based theory of long-run price. In the second half of the nineteenth century it was supplanted by a paradigm inspired by the logic of scarcity. That logic implied that rational men will choose in ways that make the most of their limited means, as they are determined by their income, their resources, technology and the constraints imposed by the optimizing actions of others. It also implied that in equilibrium what was chosen would be the best of all possible worlds subject to the constraints in question, and since it was the best, it was the world that policy should be designed to achieve. What had begun as a behavioral proposition was now a moral one.

By the early twentieth century, the success of mathematical expression in accurately describing one class of physical phenomena after another aroused the ancient belief in a mathematical order that determines the structure of the universe. That belief had especially strong resonance in mathematical economics, where mathematical game theory seemed to provide proof positive that seemingly intractable problems of social interaction could be successfully analyzed by logical deduction from the axiom of rationality. As the century developed, cracks in the axiomatic approach to the universe began to appear. It happened first in mathematics, where the case for a universal abstract truth had long been the ultimate goal. In other fields, and especially in economics, the belief in a transcendental order was maintained into the 1970s, when it began to be eroded by findings in neurology, cognitive linguistics and the chaotic dynamics of non-linear systems. Recent developments in cognitive science suggest that the traditional dualism that has sustained philosophical thought and economic analysis for over two millennia does not have a physical basis in neural circuitry. How these findings will eventually shape the form of a future economics is impossible to say. The effects are likely to be seen first in normative economics, which depend strongly on the proposition that people's values are manifested in what they choose. If the embodied mind hypothesis is true, then what people choose may not always be what they "rationally" want.

The concept of reason holds the central ground in western thought. It is the intellectual underpinning of civil liberty, representative government and private property rights. It sustains the structure of informal and formal economic reasoning, and it is our primary weapon against debilitating myth. Rationality also associated the Real with the Good. The religious connotation gave the concept of logical, legal and moral consistency staying power, to our everlasting benefit. In economics reason as consistency and reason as good fused the theory of price and the definition of economic optimum. At the turn of the twentieth century, however, it is evident that the canonical model of rational behavior is inconsistent with the findings of cognitive science. If most reasoning is unconscious, how important for actual conduct are the consciously constructed categories and syllogisms of formal rationality? In economics the doubts surfaced as anomalies with respect to the precepts of rational choice and as deviations from the predictions of general equilibrium. But similar anomalies abound in other spheres of social and personal life. The challenge for social thinkers in the next generation will be to construct an intellectual edifice that protects the civil liberty and social understanding won under the banner of human reason while incorporating what will come to be known about the makeup of the human mind.

Notes

1. Morgenstern (1976: 813).
2. Von Neumann and Morgenstern had in part to invent a new mathematics. 'Our static analysis alone necessitated the creation of a conceptual and formal mechanism which is very different from anything used, for instance, in mathematical physics.... [T]he conventional view of a solution as a uniquely defined number or aggregate of numbers was seen to be too narrow for our purposes, in spite of its success in other fields.' On the mathematics see Lennard (1995).

3.   Samuelson (1947: 3).
4.   Von Neumann and Morgenstern (1963 [1944]: 1, 9, 11).
5.   Koopmans (1957); Weintraub (1983).
6.   Von Neumann and Morgenstern (1963: 74); Cited in Lennard (1995: 756).
7.   Kreps (1998: 171).
8.   Langholm (1992).
9.   Letwin (1965).
10. The proof is based on the law of a one price with respect to the return to capital. Of two commodities produced with the same amount of direct and indirect labor, the one that takes longer to produce must sell at a higher price in order to cover the extra interest cost associated with the delay. If this premium were not secured by the selling price, the annualized rate of return would differ as between slow and rapid transformation of inputs into outputs, which is inconsistent with the law of one price.
11. Ricardo (1911[1821]: 48).
12. For simplicity of exposition Cournot assumed zero cost. He also solved the more general case of positive marginal cost.
13. Lennard (1994).
14. Arrow (1987; 1996).
15. Streissler (1990).
16. Gossen (1983 [1853]).
17. Ibid. pp. 4-6.
18. Menger (1871); Jevons (1871); Walras (1874) and Marshall (1966). Marshall did not publish his discovery until later. Stigler (1965: 84).
19. Unlike Proust's Narrator, for whom pleasures were always more intense in anticipation (and retrospect) than in the actual event.
20. Samuelson (1937).
21. The canonical form for consumption stream x(t) is $\int_0^T u\{x(t)\}e^{-rt}$ where r is the constant discount rate.
22. Ainslie and Haslam (1992).
23. Visceral emotions like anger, fear, and sexual impulse are clearly evolutionary traits that help ensure survival and quick response to emergencies. Loewenstein (2000).
24. Because of the budget constraint one supply-demand equation is redundant (if all but one market is in equilibrium, the last one must be by definition). Because the price of one commodity is arbitrary, the system is not underdetermined.
25. Jaffé (1987).
26. Marshall (1966):p. 304.
27. Marshall matriculated at Cambridge on a mathematics scholarship, where he was Second Wrangler, an honor shared by Clerk Maxwell and Lord Kelvin. Footnote xx in Appendix H of his *Principles* set out the entire Walrasian system of equations in half a page.
28. Marshall (1966: 305).
29. Marshall (1966: 306).
30. Keynes (1921).
31. Keynes (1973: 300).
32. Ibid. p. 296.
33. Cited in Lennard (1995: 730).
34. Weyl (1949: 18-23).
35. See Lennard (1995) and references cited there.
36. Weyl (1949: 18-23).

37. Cited in Weyl (1949: 19).
38. The mathematics includes combinatorial topology, the topology of real linear space, Hermitian forms, and matrix algebra, all of which passed into general use by way of quantum mechanics (Bell 1992: 205-206, 211). John Von Neumann (1932) and Tjalling Koopmans (doctoral dissertation, reprinted in Koopmans 1970) made fundamental contributions to this mathematics.
39. Mirowski (1991).
40. Contingencies of personal history also mattered. Abraham Wald's inability to obtain a university appointment in mathematics at Vienna because of anti-Semitism is a case in point (Weintraub 1983).
41. Weintraub (1983).
42. Koopmans (1957).
43. Koopmans (1957: 55).
44. In this respect it is interesting to contrast them with the English mathematical physicist Clerk Maxwell, who writes in the preface to his *Treatise on electricity and magnetism*, the importance of which is on the same order as Newton's *Principia*, "... before I began the study of electricity I resolved to read no mathematics on the subject till I had first read through Faraday's *Experimental researches on electricity*." (Cited in Holton and Roller 1958: 531).
45. The Office of Naval Research funded much of this work, which was supported after the war by the RAND corporation, a research subcontractor for the Defense Department. For an accessible description of the optimization techniques, see Scarf (1973: chapter 1).
46. Colander and Klamer (1987).
47. Maynard Smith (1982).
48. The seminal works are Modigliani and Brumberg (1954) and Friedman (1957).
49. Lucas (1972)
50. Lucas (1976).
51. Plosser (1989).
52. Plosser (1989: 51).
53. Mankiw (1989: 89).
54. Arthur (1989).
55. Conlisk (1996)
56. Goldfarb (1997)
57. Shiller (2000).
58. He likened short-term investing strategies to a guessing game, in which investors spend their energy trying to guess what other investors think the future price of an equity will be.
59. Keynes (1936); Tobin (1947).
60. Farmer (1999).
61. Most differential equations cannot be solved exactly by mathematical formulas, but must be approximated by numerical methods. In a recent seminar in the McGill Economics department a doctoral candidate at a major University reported that his optimization program took two weeks to converge to a solution.
62. Arrow (1987: 69).
63. For a review and analysis of this literature see Nelson and Winter (1982) and Winter (1986).
64. The (finite) number of possible strategies in chess is on the same order of magnitude as the number of molecules in the universe (Conlisk 1996: 679). By contrast the number of objects that humans (and other higher animals) can simultaneously perceive and distinguish is about six (Lakoff and Nuñez 1997: 33-34).

65.   Simon (1955; 1987).
66.   Nelson and Winter (1982).
67.   Quoted in Nelson and Winter (1982: 360).
68.   Gould (1981).
69.   Davidson and Downing (2000); Lohman (2000).
70.   Simon (1964).
71.   See Macleod (2000) for an example of how the internal cognitive constraint can be assimilated to the strong rationality paradigm as an optimal rule for learning by doing.
72.   Conlisk (1996).
73.   Thaler and Shefrin (1981); Thaler (1985).
74.   Lohmann (2000) p. 316.
75.   Thaler (1987a, 1987b); Froot and Thaler (1990). If capital is internationally mobile national interest rates adjusted for expected changes in the exchange rate should be identical.
76.   Shiller (2000).
77.   The phenomenon of the winner's curse was discovered in a review showing that the net return to successful bids for the right to explore for oil and gas in the Gulf of Mexico in the 1970s was *minus* $192,128 (Thaler 1988: 197).
78.   Frank (1992).
79.   Elster (1987); Shefrin and Thaler (1992).
80.   Schelling (1992); Ainslie and Haslam (1992).
81.   Van Gelder and Porter (1995); Lakoff and Johnson (1999).
82.   For example, the retina contains approximately 100 million light-sensing cells which are connected to the brain by only one million fibers. For information to pass from the retina to the brain there has to be a neural circuitry that condenses the information by an order of 10. Such condensation is necessarily categorical (Lakoff and Johnson 1999: 23-26).
83.   Lakoff and Johnson (1999); Lakoff and Nuñez (1997).
84.   Thelen (1995: 76).
85.   Lakoff and Johnson (1999).
86.   Thelen (1995).
87.   Thelen's work thus represents a major revision of Piaget's developmental theory, which holds that intelligence emerges when the child's mind outgrows context-bound perceptions and begins to think about the world with the abstract structures of logical thought.
88.   Baralou (1983).
89.   Jerison (2000).
90.   Lakoff and Johnson (1999).
91.   Townsend and Busemeyer (1995).
92.   Tversky and Kahneman (1981; 1987).
93.   Townsend and Busemeyer (1992: 114-115).
94.   Thaler (1987), p. 159.
95.   Lohman (2000).
96.   Baralou (1983).
97.   Simon (1997: 64).
98.   Macleod (2000).
99.   Gabaix and Laibson (2000).

References

Ainslie, George and Nick Haslam. 1992. Self-control, in George Loewenstein and Jon Elster (eds.), *Choice Over Time*. New York: Russell Sage Foundation.

Arrow, Kenneth J. 1987. Economic theory and the hypothesis of rationality, in John Eatwell, Murry Milgate and Peter Newman (eds.). *The New Palgrave: A Dictionary of Economics*. London: Macmillan.

Arrow, Kenneth J. 1996. Rationality of self and others in an economic system, in Hogarth and Reder.

Arthur, Brian W. 1989. Competing technologies, increasing returns, and lock-in by historical events, *Economic Journal* 99:116-31.

Baralou, Lawrence W. 1983. Ad hoc categories, *Memory and Cognition* 11:211-27.

Bell, E. T. 1992. *The Development of Mathematics*. New York: Dover Publications.

Colander, David and Arjo Klamer. 1987. The making of an economist, *Journal of Economic Perspectives* 1:95-111.

Conlisk, John. 1996. Why bounded rationality? *Journal of Economic Literature* 34:669-700.

Cournot, Augustin. 1963. *The Mathematical Principles of the Theory of Wealth*. Homewood, IL: Richard D. Irwin.

Davidson, Janet E. and C. L. Downing. 2000. Contemporary models of intelligence, in Robert J. Sternberg (ed.), *Handbook of Intelligence*. Cambridge: Cambridge University Press.

Elster, Jon (ed.). 1987. *The Multiple Self*. Cambridge: Cambridge University Press.

Farmer, Roger E. A. 1999. *The Macroeconomics of Self-Fulfilling Prophecies*. Cambridge: MA and London: MIT Press.

Friedman, Milton. 1957. *A Theory of the Consumption Function*. National Bureau of Economic Research. Princeton, NJ: Princeton University Press.

Froot, Kenneth A. and Richard H. Thaler. 1990. Anomalies: Foreign exchange, *Journal of Economic Perspectives* 4:179-192.

Gabaix, Xavier and David Laibson. 2000. A boundedly rational decision algorithm, *American Economic Review*. 90:433-438.

Goldfarb, Robert S. 1997. Now you see it, now you don't: emerging contrary results in economics, *Journal of Economic Methodology* 4:221-224.

Gossen, Hermann Heinrich. 1983. *The Laws of Human Relations and the Rules of Human Action Derived Therefrom*. Trans. Rudolph C. Blitz. Cambridge, MA: MIT Press.

Gould, Stephen Jay. 1981. *The Mismeasure of Man*. New York: W. W. Norton.

Hicks, J. R. 1939. *Value and Capital*. Oxford: Clarendon.

Hogarth, Robin M. and Melvin W. Reder. 1987. *Rational Choice: The Contrast between Economics and Psychology*. Chicago: University of Chicago Press.

Jerison, Harry J. 2000. The evolution of intelligence, in Robert J. Sternberg (ed.). *Handbook of Intelligence*. Cambridge: Cambridge University Press.

Jevons, William Stanley. 1871. *The Theory of Political Economy*. London: Macmillan.

Holton, Gerald and Duane H. D. Roller. 1958. *Foundations of Modern Physical Science*. Reading, MA and London: Addison-Wesley.

Keynes, John Maynard. 1973. *The Collected Writings of John Maynard Keynes*, vol. XIV. Donald Moggride (ed.). London: Macmillan.

Keynes, John Maynard. 1921. *A Treatise on Probability*. London: Macmillan.

Koopmans, Tjalling C. 1957. *Three Essays on the State of Economic Science*. New York: McGraw-Hill.

Koopmans, Tjalling C. 1970. *Scientific Papers of Tjalling C. Koopmans*. Berlin and New York: Springer-Verlag.

Kreps, David. 1998. Bounded rationality, in Peter Newman (ed.). *The New Palgrave's Dictionary of Economics and Law*. London: Macmillan, pp. 168-73.

Lakoff, George and Mark Johnson. 1999. *Philosophy in the Flesh. The Embodied Mind and its Challenge to Western Thought*. New York: Basic Books.

Lakoff, George and Rafael E. Nuñez. 1997. The metaphorical structure of mathematics: Sketching out cognitive foundations for a mind-based mathematics, in Lynn D. English (ed.). *Mathematical Reasoning: Analogies, Metaphors and Images*. Mahwah, NJ: Lawrence Erlbaum Associates.

Langholm, Odd. 1992. *Economics in the Medieval Schools. Wealth, Exchange, Value, Money and Usury According to the Paris Theological Tradition 1200-1350*. Leiden, New York, Köln: E. J. Brill.

Langholm, Odd. 1998. The medieval schoolmen, in S. Todd Lowry and Barry Gordon (eds.) *Ancient and Medieval Economic Ideas and Concepts of Social Justice*. Leiden, New York and Köln: Brill, pp. 439-502.

Lennard, Robert J. 1994. Reading Cournot, reading Nash: The creation and stabilization of Nash equilibrium, *Economic Journal* 104:492-511.

Lennard, Robert J. 1995. From parlor games to social science: von Neumann, Morgenstern, and the creation of game theory 1928-1944, *Journal of Economic Literature* 33: 730-61.

Letwin, William. 1965. *The Origins of Scientific Economics*. Garden City, NY: Anchor Books.

Lohman, David F. 2000. Complex information processing and intelligence, in Robert J. Sternberg (ed.), *Handbook of Intelligence*. Cambridge: Cambridge University Press.

Lucas, Robert E. 1972. Expectations and the neutrality of money, *Journal of Monetary Economics* 4:103-24.

——. 1976. Econometric policy evaluation: a critique, *Carnegie-Rochester Conference Series on Public Policy* 1 (1976), pp. 19-46.

Macleod, W. Bentley. 2000. Cognition and the theory of learning by doing, Department of Economics and the Law School of the University of Southern California. McGill University Seminar Paper October 20, 2000.

Mankiw, N. Gregory. 1989. Real business cycles: a new Keynesian perspective, *Journal of Economic Perspectives* 3:79-90.

Marshall, Alfred. 1966. *Principles of Economics*. 8th Edition. London: Macmillan.

Maynard Smith, J. 1982. *Evolution and the Theory of Games*. Cambridge: Cambridge University Press.

Menger, Carl. 1976. *Principles of Economics*. Trans. J. Dingwall and B. Hoselitz. New York and London: NYU Press.

Mirowski, Philip. 1991. The when, the how and the why of mathematical expression in the history of economic analysis, *Journal of Economic Perspectives* 5:145-57.

Modigliano, Franco and Richard Brumberg. 1954. Utility analysis and the consumption function: an interpretation of cross-section data, in Kenneth K. Kurihara (ed.), *Post-Keynesian Economics*. New Brunswick, NJ: Rutgers University Press.

Nelson, Richard R. and Sidney G. Winter. 1982. *An Evolutionary Theory of Economic Change*. Cambridge, MA and London: Belknap Press.

Petty, Sir William 1963-64[1662]. *The Economic Writings of Sir William Petty, Together With Observations upon the Bills of Mortality*. C. H. Hull. (ed.), New York: A. M. Kelley.

Plosser, Charles. 1989. Understanding real business cycles, *Journal of Economic Perspectives* 3:59-70.

Ricardo, David. 1911. *Principles of Political Economy and Taxation*. Everyman's Library. London: Dent, and New York: Dutton.

Samuelson, P. A. 1947. *Foundations of Economic Analysis*. Cambridge, MA: Harvard University Press.

Scarf, Herbert. 1973. *The Computation of Economic Equilibrium*. New Haven, CT and London: Yale University Press.

Shefrin, Hersh M. and Richard H. Thaler. 1992. Mental accounting and self-control, in George Loewenstein and Jon Elster (eds.), *Choice Over Time*. New York: Russell Sage Foundation.

Shiller Robert J. 2000. *Irrational Exuberance*. Princeton, NJ: Princeton University Press.

Simon, Herbert A. 1955. A behavioral model of rational choice, *Quarterly Journal of Economics* 69:99-118.

Simon , Herbert A. 1992 [1964]. Information processing in computer and man, in Herbert Simon, et al. 1992. *Economics, Bounded Rationality and the Cognitive Revolution*. Aldershot, UK and Brookfield, VT: Edward Elgar.

Simon, Herbert A. 1987. Satisficing, in John Eatwell, Murry Milgate and Peter Newman (eds.), *The New Palgrave: A Dictionary of Economics*. London: Macmillan.

Simon, Herbert A. 1997. *An Empirically Based Microeconomics*. The Raffaeie Mattioli Lectures. Cambridge: Cambridge University Press.

Thaler, Richard H. 1985. Mental accounting and consumer choice, in Richard H. Thaler, *Quasi-Rational Economics*. New York: Russell Sage Foundation.

—— 1987a. Anomalies: the January effect, *Journal of EconomicPperspectives* 1:197-201.

—— 1987b. Anomalies: Seasonal movements in security prices II; Weekend, holiday, turn of the month and intraday effects, *Journal of Economic Perspectives* 1:169-77.

—— 1987c. The psychology of choice and the assumptions of economics, in Alvin Roth, *Laboratory Experiments in Economics: Six Points of View*. New York: Cambridge University Press, reprinted in Richard Thaler, 1991, *Quasi-Rational Economics*. New York: Russell Sage Foundation.

——. 1989. Anomalies: Inter-industry wage differentials, *Journal of Economic Perspectives* 3:189-93.

——. 1992. *The Winner's Curse: Paradoxes and Anomalies of Economic Life*. New York: Free Press.

Thaler, Richard H. and H. M. Shefrin. 1981. An economic theory of self-control, *Journal of Political Economy* 39:392-406.

Thelen, Esther. 1995. Time-scale dynamics and the development of an embodied cognition, in Robert F. Port and Timothy van Gelder (eds.), *Mind as Motion: Explorations in the Dynamics of Cognition*. Cambridge, MA: MIT Press.

Tobin, James. 1947. Money wage rates and unemployment, in Seymour Harris (ed.), *The New Economics: Keynes' Influence on Theory and Public Policy*. New York: Alfred A. Knopf.

Tversky, Amos and Daniel Kahneman. 1981. The framing of decisions and the psychology of choice, *Science* 211:435-58.

Tversky, Amos and Daniel Kahneman. 1987. Rational choice and the framing of decisions, in Robert M. Hogarth and Melvin W. Reder (eds.), *Rational Choice. The Contrast Between Economics and Psychology*. Chicago and London: University of Chicago Press.

Van Gelder, Timothy and Robert F. Port. 1995. It's about time: an overview of the dynamical approach to cognition, in Robert F. Port and Timothy van Gelder (eds.), *Mind as Motion: Explorations in the Dynamics of Cognition*. Cambridge, MA: MIT Press.

Von Neumann, John and Oskar Morgenstern. 1963. *Theory of Games and Economic Behavior*. New York: John Wiley and Sons.

Walras, Léon. 1874. *Éléments d'économie politique pure*. 1ˢᵗ ed. Lausanne: L. Corbaz.

Walras, Léon. 1954. *Elements of Pure Economics*. Trans. W. Jaffé. Homewood, IL: Richard D. Irwin.

Weyl, Hermann. 1949. *Philoophy of Mathematics and Natural Science*. Princeton, NJ: Princeton University Press.

Weintraub, E. Roy. 1983. On the existence of a competitive equilibrium: 1930-1954, *Journal of Economic Literature* 21:1-39.

Winter, Sidney G. 1986. The research programme of the behavioral theory of the firm: Orthodox critique and evolutionary perspective, in Benjamin Gilad and Stanley Kaish (eds.), *Handbook of Behavioral Economics*. Volume A. Greenwich, Connecticut: JAI Press.

Xenophon [ca. 360 B.C.] *Oeconomicus*. Trans. O. J. Todd, Loeb Classical Library 168. Cambridge, MA: Harvard University Press, 1923.

3

Rationality in Economics and Econometrics: Theoretical Devices, Issues and Puzzles

Robin Rowley

"An economist by training thinks of himself as the guardian of rationality, the ascriber of rationality to others, and the prescriber of rationality to the social world." (Arrow, 1974: 16)

"Economics is the science of rational choice in a world—our world—in which resources are limited in relation to human wants. The task of economics, so defined, is to explore the implications of assuming that man is a rational maximizer of his ends in life, his satisfactions— ... his 'self-interest.'" (Posner, 1986: 3)

Introduction

The theoretical commitments of microeconomists to a presumed rationality of individual economic agents (narrowly associated with optimization over alternative actions or decisions and governed by the existence of relationships between means and ends, both fixed for the individual agent) were stimulated by the neoclassical or marginalist revolution that began in the 1870s. These commitments were gradually affected by reliance on basic ingredients of neoclassical theory including equilibrium, competition, and complete markets, as made explicit by Knight (1921). They were subsequently reinvigorated and transformed following the introduction of game theory (with its axiomatic foundations for subjective preferences and probabilities, and with its focus on strategic interactions with "rivals") by von Neumann and Morgenstern about fifty years ago, and later modified when proponents of game-theoretic approaches tried to deal with problems of indeterminacy for solutions of games. Modest encouragement also came from statisticians when they developed the use of personal probabilities rather than frequentist alternatives.

The game-theoretic stimulus added to a revival of "Cournotism" in the late1920s and early 1930s (Hicks, 1935) by bringing uncertainties, subjective probabilities, expected utility, issues of measurement, and some normative or prescriptive concerns (Keeney, 1992) to the forefront of many theoretical discussions among both mathematical economists and their counterparts in other social sciences. Earlier deterministic frameworks were partially displaced by stochastic ones, which dealt with an apparent need to specify how the choices and actions available to "significant others" (and anticipated of them) can impinge on decision-making, and a further mathematization of techniques of analysis was fostered among economic theorists. Some consequences of this historical commitment to *models* of individual rationality by microeconomists include:

(a) The identification by many observers of microeconomic theory with rationality alone (as reflected in the two quotations from Arrow and Posner reproduced above), which weakens interest in the dynamic emergence of individual ends and means as connected with innovative activity and the social embedding of values,

(b) Confusions attributed to an excessive involvement with methodological individualism, which leads to heroic assertions about potential extrapolation of theoretical views to collective choices made by large firms, for example, and which encourages (since models must be tractable) a strong reliance on ubiquitous myopic assumptions that require separation of individual economic agents from the (endogenous) values of others or avoid most aspects of feedback, with familiar "black-box" treatments ignoring the internal structures of firms (clearly significant for determining feasible choices or capabilities, operational controls, the internal and external gathering of information, productive efficiency in various forms, quality assurance, and modes of product development) and the flexibility of their boundaries,

(c) Little recognition for the awkwardness of connecting generic predictions from a fictional microeconomic agent, who is rational in a peculiar (unrealistic, static) context, with the primary characteristics of actual (dynamic), perhaps *average*, economic phenomena and processes as expressed both within markets and outside of them —not least because the diversity and potential irrationality of actual economic agents are removed by a technical device of ignoring aggregation effects in relying on a *representative* individual or by assuming all rivals are rational too (Binmore, 1997: 24)—and also little appreciation of what neoclassical microeconomic theory yields to us in regard to the situation facing individuals or markets in practice,

(d) An exaggeration of the "practicality" of common frameworks involving rational economic choices in the provision of suitable guides to decision-making (whether revealing what decision-makers ought to do or as approximations to what they actually do),

(e) Some hesitation in the appreciation of findings on rule-based behavior, spillover effects and contextual influences from psychological research ("cognitive science") and from developments in political science, geography, and sociology including economic sociology.

This paper has two primary objectives. In the next section, it seeks to identify, outline and clarify *recent* attempts to transform the conventional models of rational decision-making found in microeconomic theory, while noting challenging aspects of choice and some important issues that should be addressed by economists and by those who extend applications of the rational-choice approach to other social sciences. For convenience, comments and observations are expressed in a series of terse paragraphs, all of which merit further elaboration or rebuttal. The second section takes up a development that is connected to *new classical* perspectives rather than neoclassical ones. Emergence of "rational expectations" has affected macroeconomic theory and econometrics. Numerical representations provided by large economy-wide models had been used to illuminate the dynamic characteristics of a changing economic environment and thus permit appraisals of potential fiscal policies, monetary instability, sensitivity to external trading or financial shocks, and the like. This activity was fostered by the Keynesian revolution and the subsequent pursuit of policy interventions focused on stabilization, growth or the dampening of severe dislocations. The new classical perspective rejects the normal bases for these interventions and their support. Technically, the use of rational expectations challenges the stability of structural equations that form Keynesian macroeconometric models (the so-called "Lucas critique"). The new classical framework involves acceptance of three basic ingredients, namely, (a) the view that behavior of economic agents is driven by what they anticipate will happen, (b) the view that such anticipations are quantifiable and can be identified with optimal predictors of the Wiener-Hopf type (Whittle, 1963; Whiteman, 1983), and (c) the view that relevant economic variables (perhaps when written as deviations from their "normal" or equilibrium values) may be treated as generated by linear stochastic processes of the type introduced to economists by Slutsky and Yule in the 1920s (that is, values of the variables are generated by linear difference equations with constant coefficients and subjected to simple random disturbances). Optimal predictors or antici-pations are then merely conditional expectations with linear specifi-cations dependent on both inherent coefficients of underlying pro-cesses and the horizons over which the anticipations are formed.

As stressed by Sargent (1982), new classical theory involving the novel concept of rational expectations "began as an effort to use optimizing economic theory to understand, interpret, and restrict the distributed lags that abounded in the decision rules of dynamic macroeconometric models of the 1950s and 1960s" and the theory addresses "the econometric ideal of discovering objects that are struc-tural, in the sense that they are invariant with respect to the class of policy interventions to be analyzed." This ideal was expressed in terms of *autonomous* relationships by Frisch in the 1930s (Aldrich, 1989) and was an important part of the advocacy that entrenched the "probability approach to econometrics" (Hamouda and Rowley, 1997a) a half century ago. Lucas, Sargent, Prescott and other sup-porters of the rational-expectations (RE) perspective revealed that, in terms of their own theoretical framework, this econometric ideal of structural stability is not met by the models often used to appraise the impacts of policy interventions of national governments and thus econometric models ("Keynesian models") provide inadequate bases to support interventions and display their probable impacts.

Unfortunately, as indicated below, unqualified acceptance of this novel perspective also undermines much econometric estimation, beyond that solely connected with policy interventions—to the ex-tent that special RE-ingredients are retained. In a wider sense, its assimilation within economic research: (a) encouraged the substitu-tion of calibration for estimation of dynamic responses, (b) weak-ened an earlier reliance on asymptotic properties (consistency and asymptotic unbiasedness) for choosing among alternative methods of estimating coefficients, (c) stimulated a widening gap between the focus of econometric theory, as illustrated by our professional journals, and conventional practices of applied model-builders, (d) provided qualitative criteria from NBER records for judging perfor-mance of empirical models of cyclical behavior, (e) provided sup-port for use of equilibrium models of business cycles—"in which prices and qualities are taken to be always in equilibrium" and "the concepts of excess demands and supplies play no observational role and are identified with no observed magnitudes" (Lucas, 1980: 709), reflecting "a discipline imposed by its insistence on adherence to the two postulates ... that markets clear and ... that agents act in their own self-interest" (Lucas and Sargent, 1979: 304)—and (f) dismissed normal statistical testing in favour of exploratory display that emphasizes the primacy of (essentially deductive) economic theory over other considerations.

The strong adversarial feature of this assault on past practices is clear from unqualified assertions of Lucas and Sargent that "modern macroeconomic models are of *no* value in guiding policy" and "this condition will not be remedied by modifications along *any* line which is currently being pursued" (ibid. 296. Emphasis added). The schism between econometricians and RE-proponents remains as wide as ever despite two decades of empirical research since various factions have fundamental differences in regard to referential standards and sources, the attachment to equilibrium versus disequilibrium, diversity and efficiencies within markets, the simulation of artificial economies, desirability of policy interventions, the appropriateness of optimal predictors as representing anticipations, and a host of other factors.

Theoretical Challenges: Issues, Puzzles and Paradoxes

Whether we consider rational choices, decisions or actions, we face a major problem in determining the appropriate *domain* of useful applications for an abstract theory involving rationality, such as that developed around the concept of subjective expected utility (SEU), with its Bayesian or personal approach to probabilities. This domain reflects the nature of means and ends in particular situations, and its determination requires clear identification of basic situational features. Such features include (1) who or what is choosing; (2) what is being chosen; (3) how complete and unambiguous is the framework for choice; (4) how confident or "bothered" is the chooser in the various aspects of that framework (subjective probabilities, options for choice, and potential consequences); (5) what are the perceived consequences of flaws in that framework; (6) does the chooser worry about having "second thoughts" after the initial choice is made; (7) are there differences among choices in regard to revocability or reversibility; (8) is the environment for choice repetitive or unique; (9) how stable is the composition of the choosing unit if the choice is a collective one; (10) must choice be made now or can it be delayed, at least in part; (11) in the event of delay, would preferences, options and consequences be affected or clarified (in the light of new information, changing circumstances and affiliations), or delegated to a different chooser; (12) is a dynamic sequence of choices involved; (13) if choice is collective, do the social dynamics or authority relations within the choosing group (or the nature of their deliberations) affect the presumptions for preferences, options and probabilities; (14) what are group preferences and group (subjective?) probabilities, and will these aggregates satisfy the same "reasonable" axioms as their individual counterparts; (15) are options to be imagined or determined; (16) if the number of effective rivals is relatively small, must the chooser confirm the rationality of his counterparts to determine potential consequences of his envisaged options, and if rivals are not necessarily rational (Binmore, 1997), are these consequences determinate; (17) over what time-horizon are options contemplated and consequences evaluated; (18) are consequences sufficiently quantifiable to support comparisons across options in numerical terms, and so on.

For some advocates of game theory, social situations always involve strategic interactions among participants so the usual domain of application for game-theoretical notions of rationality is wide. Harsanyi (1978: 223-5), for example, argues that "the Bayesian rationality postulates are absolutely inescapable criteria of rationality for policy decisions," "it is *natural* to expect that, in making important policy decisions, *responsible* decision makers *will* take a result-oriented attitude toward risk taking" (emphases added), and the SEU framework "is probably a reasonably realistic prediction; and it is certainly an obvious normative rationality requirement as well as a moral one." Recently, challenged by the problems of indeterminacy and the need for some arbitrary criteria to resolve solution ambiguities, he insisted "one might argue that *proper* understanding of *any* social situation would require game-theoretic analysis" (Harsanyi, 1995: 293, emphasis added)! In sharp contrast, Simon (1983: 16-17) suggests that, in typical real-world situations, no matter how badly they want to do so, decision makers cannot apply the SEU model as "human beings have neither the facts nor the consistent structure of values nor the reasoning power at their disposal that would be required ... to apply SEU principles." In the light of the situational features listed above, the identification of a domain for applicability seems a complex issue. Considerable diversity of views on this issue is revealed by the contributions to Hamouda and Rowley (1997b).

What Predictions? Approximations and Average Behaviour

Microeconomic theory, interpreted as "the science of administration of scarce resources in human society" (Lange, 1945-46: 19), seeks to "discern general patterns of uniformity," or *laws*, within coherent systems of thought (ibid. 20ff)—laws that merely offer conditional statements or predictions, perhaps limited historically in their relevance to particular situations by a dependence on given forms of social institutions and organization. The primary objectives of the theory are not concerned with predictions affecting individuals as individuals, and the conventional norms of rational behavior assumed within our theoretical models are necessarily unrealistic portrayals of some individual actions—as often recognized in transparent assertions to the effect that "the basic economic assumption that human behavior is rational seems contradicted by the experiences and observations of everyday life" and "the assumptions of economic theory are one-dimensional and pallid when viewed as *descriptions* of human behavior" (Posner, 1986: 15. Emphasis added) or that "the theory of rational behavior is a set of propositions that can be regarded either as idealized approximations to the actual behavior of men or a recommendations to be followed" for "living men and women ... do not behave rationally" while the theory's propositions have a two-fold use, namely "to describe approximately the behavior of men who, it is believed, cannot be "all fools all of the time," and to give advice on how to reach "correct" conclusions" (Marschak, 1950: 111-2).

There is a statistical, average or aggregate aspect of microeconomic models involving individual rationality that needs to be emphasized. Note, for example, the following clarifications:

> We shall be able to allow that the individual may diverge from the norm without being deterred from the recognition of a statistical regularity. This is what we do, almost all of the time, in economics. We do not claim, in our demand theory for instance, to be able to say anything useful about the behaviour of a particular consumer, which may be dominated by motives quite peculiar to himself; but we do claim to say something about the behaviour of the whole market — of the whole group, that is, of the consumers of a particular product. ... Economics is rather specially concerned with such "statistical" behaviour. ... It is only a *normal* development for which we are looking, so it does not have to cover all the facts; we must be ready to admit exceptions, exceptions which nevertheless we should try to explain. (Hicks, 1969: 3-6)

Realistic about means as well as ends, economics does not depend on the idea that human beings are effortless and infallible calculators. A market may behave rationally, and hence the economic model of human behaviour apply to it, even if most of the individual buyers (or buys) are irrational. Irrational purchase decisions are likely to be random and hence cancel each other out, leaving the *average* behavior of the market to be determined by the minority of rational buyers (or purchases). ... Although the assumption that human beings ... are rational is important to the construction of mathematically tractable models of economic behavior, the models hold as useful approximations even when the assumption is false. (Posner, 1995: 16-17).

The commitment to generic predictions rather than specific ones (and the implicit reliance on supplemental assumptions of different character in applied economics, such as Posner's claim that random irrationalities cancel out across individual behavior) leaves unsettled the relevance of the considerable diversity of situational factors with which this section began.

Clearly the descriptive usefulness of rationality as a theoretical device is more complicated than many realize, and its role as a normative standard seems obscure—for the advice on how to act must refer to individual events rather than to aggregates or averages with offsetting disparities (and thus situational features remain significant for choices unless we can show otherwise) and we may wonder why economic theorists settle for so little contact with the primary details of actual economic phenomena. Just as the economic theory of the firm may reveal little about the role of management and the internal operations of our primary economic agents, so the economic theory of choice involving individual rationality may shed no light on individual choice or the implications of rational responses to situations facing economic agents. Nor should economists take comfort from optimistic extrapolations to collective choice revealed by Savage (1972: 8, emphasis added):

It is brought out in economic theory that organizations sometimes behave like individual people, so the theory originally intended for people may also apply to (or may even apply *better* to) such units as families, corporations, or nations.

Imagine the process of determining (subjective) probabilities for the SEU model as applied to the large corporations that have dominated the U.S. economy for more than a century, according to the chronicles of Chandler and other business historians, or to nations! Imagine the consultative role of academic economists attempting to advise cabinets, government bureaucracies or corporate boards how to modify their practices and elucidate probabilities, preferences and options so that their collective decision-making is "improved" by an endorsement of the static SEU framework or its non-stochastic counterpart—while ignoring social dynamics, power relations, "horse trading" and transitory concerns that affect their deliberations!

Paradoxes, Violations of Axioms, and Slanting of Probabilities

In view of this discussion of generic predictions, it is difficult to decide if responses to questionnaires or the results from experimental studies illuminate the validity (or refutation) of rationality as a suitable model ingredient or establish the presence/absence of paradoxes, biases and ambiguities as noted in treatments of framing, heuristics, overconfidence and the complex environment of choosing; and clarified by various contributions to Hamouda and Rowley (1997d), Kahneman, Slovic, and Tversky (1982), and the advisory comments for managers of Russo and Schoemaker (1989). Despite this difficulty, some implications from the burgeoning literature on obstacles to individual rationality have stimulated a radical reappraisal of rationality and promoted attempts to generalize the SEU framework as illustrated by Machina (1989), Anand (1993) and Edwards (1992).

Initially, paradoxes (defined by empirical violations of SEU axioms such as intransitivity of preferences) arose from the observation that many individuals and group decisions often give little attention to events with small probabilities of occurrence and are influenced by the unavailability of reliable information. Choice might be based on slanted or distorted estimates of probabilities that reflect a lack of confidence, credibility, consensus and communicability:

> A good many reasonable decision makers ... seem to act differently depending on whether they act under the influence of shaky degrees of belief, i.e., of probabilities the numerical values of which are highly unstable in their minds, or act under the guidance of firm and stable degrees of belief. Degrees of belief that are highly unstable are appreciably influenced by ... "elusive hypotheses." These beliefs usually also have the property of being interpersonally controversial even among the well informed and even among individuals who exchange their information. Such degrees of belief are apt to become unconvincing in retrospect, a fact of which individuals are well aware in advance. (Fellner, 1965: 4).

More generally, economic models of rationality in the presence of uncertain consequences must acknowledge the need to estimate probabilities, the imprecision, incompleteness and instability of these estimates, and the relative degree of support that they deserve if models are to act as useful normative guides or as descriptive summaries. The attitudes of decision-makers to the perceived quality of estimated probabilities are as important as the strength of preferences in any practical context. Theoretical treatments that ignore the problem of estimating probabilities, including the reconciliation of diverse estimates in collective choice (Genest and Zidek, 1986), perhaps through a form of Bayesian dialogue and exchange of information of different quality and coverage, omit a striking feature of systematic choice. Further recognition of this practical obstacle may justify the common reliance on heuristics and "rule-driven" choice that some observers have noted.

The Situational Embedding of Choices and Actions

For managerial decisions, Hamel and Prahalad (1996: 237-238) argue the locational context for significant choices used to be "within the boundaries of industry convention, company tradition, vested authority, national context, functional specialization, the demonstrably feasible, and the here and now." None of these elements seem to receive much attention in the economic literature of rational choice, where means and ends are "given" for economic agents but unrelated to situations facing actual decision-makers, contextual determinants of preferences and options, or inherent (social) bases for optimism and confidence. Hamel and Prahalad also point to the recent emergence of a new looser environment for choice ("managing out of bounds") that involves shifting boundaries of authority, blurring boundaries of control, shifting boundaries of loyalty and affiliation, crumbling boundaries of experience, irrelevance of national boundaries, and changing boundaries between the present and the future—all of which are incompatible with a determinate theoretical framework invoking rationality in the sense of neoclassical optimization for a closed context or in the sense of games with unambiguous solutions.

Locational and historical constraints are also stressed in recent clarifications of various forms of capitalism that have been fostered by rapid growth of the Japanese economic system with its distinctive attitudes to control, information processing, subcontracting, persistent commitments to suppliers and customers, labor practices, collusion, forward planning, and strategic features that provide a special context for sequential decision-making. Economists in North America and Europe have long recognized different informational requirements that will affect efficient choice across the spectrum of alternative industrial structures, but this recognition has begun to receive a cultural texture through the activities of applied economists such Dore and Casson, as revealed in socioeconomic themes explored in Best (1990) and contributions to Okimoto and Rohlen (1988).

At last, the old separation of "pure" economic theory from "applied" topics and other social sciences is crumbling as values, modes of behavior and information gathering, areas of activity, and transactional costs of diverse types are coming to be viewed as endogenous to a transformed multidisciplinary theory of economic phenomena. One visible sign of this change is the emergence of a new economic sociology (Swedberg, 1993; Baron and Hannan, 1994), which may heal the injuries caused during the *methodenstreit* that accompanied the birth of neoclassical economics and of the priority for rationality that is our focus. Another sign is the assimilation of the technical notions of trust, reputation, credibility, custom, transparency and transaction costs in economic theories as applied to decision-making; and of the social construction of economic institutions, networks, property rights and positional goods—see the language adopted by Dixit (1996), Frank (1992) and Sen (1983), and the critical treatment of agents' beliefs by Bacharach (1986).

The intrusion of these interdisciplinary notions becomes especially relevant once we move outside perfect competition to situations for economic choice where strategic activities are based on the presence and exercise of power in determining the consequences of adopting particular options. Then, as Arrow (1990: 31) indicates, the interaction among economic agents acquires a social dimension, threatens an infinite regress in anticipations, and calls for ubiquitous rationality:

> There is a qualitatively new aspect to the nature of knowledge, since each agent is assuming the rationality of other agents. Indeed, to construct a rationality-based theory of economic behaviour, even more must be assumed, namely, that the rationality of all agents must be common knowledge ... Each agent must not only know that the other agents (at least those with significant power) are rational but know that every other agent knows that every other agent is rational, and so forth. It is in this sense that rationality and the knowledge of rationality is a social and not only an individual phenomenon.

Rather than getting involved in this strange environment, it is sensible to admit relevant social influences and other factors associated with power and knowledge into analysis in a direct (and more realistic) fashion.

Diversity and Asymmetric Information

The plausibility of neoclassical theory requires a fulfillment of ideal "structural" conditions in relation to a competitive market structure where prevalent conditions are governed by a "take it or leave it" price mechanism, or to a definite set of supply and demand curves in the presence of imperfect competition so a complete decision tree can exist for all possible actions of significant rivals. With the further restriction to generic predictions, theory also needs a basis for dismissing the impact of disparities among participants in a market situation. Ideal conditions presume an availability of information and special devices (the contingent contracts of Debreu, for example) in some form, and willingness to ignore potential consequences of diversity. Once we admit the absence of common information and permit asymmetries in information and beliefs for individuals, contemplation of rational choices becomes less tractable and the derivation of generic predictions is seriously hampered. Indeed it is unclear what remains for general predictions (as compared with "stories" that deal with "special cases" generated by specifications with differential availability of information). It is worth noting too that information is contextual and non-passive for managerial information systems, which are "marked by the interests and ideologies that make them feasible" and "are also produced in and productive of their host culture, and they often change irrevocably the arrangements and understandings of those involved" (Despres, 1996: 16). The endogenous gathering of information is a fundamental part of an evolving environment. It is susceptible to special circumstances, cultural influences and transactional costs.

Prospects, Regret and Disappointment

When a particular choice is made, accepted consequences and foregone ones are relevant. Neoclassical theory recognizes this with the concept of opportunity costs, which are appraised in terms of what might have been. Such costs may be augmented with "counterfactual" information in regard to *later feelings* that could occur after an "unfortunate" outcome has been determined:

> [I]f it is the case that one would willy-nilly regret the past decision if it turns out to be unfortunate, then it is not in any sense irrational to recognize that fact and take that inescapable feeling into account. (Sen, 1990: 208)

Theories of regret, prospects and disappointment try to amend the conventional SEU framework so as to permit a more complex evaluation of "second thoughts" associated with the hazards of making a "wrong" choice. Some accounts of these theories due to Bell, Loomes, and Sugden, and Kahneman and Tversky are reproduced as contributions to Hamouda and Rowley (1997d). They explain how violations of the axioms might occur, and they offer scope for clarifying apparent paradoxes and their removal by generalizing the SEU framework to deal with a wide range of secondary considerations (in determining the appreciation of outcomes after the fact, as well as before a choice is finalized). An optimistic survey of recent attempts to find a wider framework compatible with many violations is provided by Sugden (1986), who includes violations that stem from a retrospective contamination linked to concerns with "what might have been."

Imagination, Illusions, Mental States and Belief Revision

Economic history reveals an erratic pattern of surprising developments that were not fully anticipated and could not have been fully anticipated. If we accept the account by Schumpeter of creative destruction in the evolution of innovative capitalism, we see that new products, new methods of production and distribution, new locations, new fashions, new structural alignments, and new attitudes constantly disturb the contemporary visions of future change. Many individual choices have consequences in later periods that were inaccurately forecast because subsequent changes were not envisaged when choices were initially made. This characteristic of uncertainty with a stream of qualitative novelties is often incompatible with probability calculations since a range of possible options might expand or contract in unpredictable ways, while the probability calculus requires that range to be determined before weights are attached to the relative likelihood of each alternative. Indeed the future has to be imagined and our limited ability for imagination (coupled with ignorance) is subject to illusions and revisions in beliefs, rational and otherwise.

One difficulty with expected utility is that it requires a comprehensive listing of all possible outcomes, even those that will occur at some future date after actions undertaken by significant rivals, whether choice is part of a repetitive exercise or a novel one. Clearly, any unqualified use of the concept exaggerates the determinacy of future events when the path of economic evolution is unclear. Moreover, economic agents are generally aware of the limitations of their abilities to make accurate forecasts so they often restrict their vision to a consideration of few alternative scenarios. They adopt a short horizon and retain a degree of flexibility which allows them to adjust to unanticipated opportunities that arise. We do not need to go as far as Shackle's notion of a kaleidic society governed by "unknowledge" to realize that such modest safeguards are sensible provisions for dealing with unreliable economic progress.

It is difficult to see how major innovations and unanticipated changes can be meaningfully integrated within the usual SEU framework, and it is clear that other concepts of rational conduct (involving sequentially-improved expertise and prolonged commitments to monitor and amend earlier choices, for example) should be sought. There is a growing body of research on mental states, belief revision and information summarization when knowledge is in flux, as illustrated by Gardenfors (1988) and fuller treatments of information processing and its design in corporations (initiated by Simon and other proponents of a computer-driven cognitive revolution). However it is still unclear where this research leads us, other than to a deeper understanding of corporate structures and informational linkages that affect decisions within firms and among alliances.

Hesitation, Flexibility and the Timing of Choice

Treatments of rational choice presume a restricted time-frame for the dynamic processes of choice among available options (not surprising in view of the static nature of their deductive structures) and they give little indication of any role for entrepreneurial skills in these processes. Many years ago, Knight (1921) pointed to various ways in which the exercise of such skills can affect choice. In particular, he stressed certain matters of time and flexibility. For example, delays may stem from the duration of productive systems and availability of inventories (as well as from strategic commitments to product lives, on-going supplier arrangements, and other contractual or legal obligations) or from the need to generate a sufficient amount of free resources. The means and consequences of choice are necessarily spread through time and must be anticipated. Delays may also partially resolve uncertainty as to means, consequences and ends through the acquisition of further information, and delays permit a spreading or spacing of actions, conditional on prior or revised choices. Most models of individual rationality give inadequate attention to duration, flexibility and spacing but these are important areas in which managerial and entrepreneurial skills may be crucial for economic prosperity.

Entrepreneurs may need to generate confidence and use persuasion to facilitate effective responses that address anticipated opportunities. Their means may not be fixed, but rather could depend on the acquisition of support from other partners—to share or clarify risks, provide expertise, restrain competition, guarantee financial provisions, and create or discover markets for new or modified products. Both individualism and mathematical models are awkward bases for dealing with such ingredients, common features of modern capitalism. Collaborative ventures, partial or fully integrated, cannot be placed in the SEU framework since their constituents are subject to adjustments or differential rates of involvement and since the obligatory bonds of collaboration require a greater interest in flexible structures and time-frames.

It is apparent too that even strong advocates of optimizing models involving rationality and equilibrium move away from new classical perspectives when they contemplate recent history in Eastern Europe and the Far East. See, for example, the retreat of Sargent (1993) to a novel form of transition dynamics with "a wilderness of irrational expectations and bounded rationality" in unstable environments that preclude confidence in the ingredients required for calculations of costs, benefits and possibilities.

Bounded Rationality

Most social scientists are familiar with the advocacy of a bounded form of procedural rationality that stems from a behavioral approach to economics and "takes into account the cognitive limitations of the decision-maker—limitations of both knowledge and computational capacity" (Simon, 1990: 15)—with constant attention to aspects of actual decision-making by corporations and other public bodies. Unlike the static rationality of the neoclassical framework, bounded rationality arises within processes that have (1) new options emerging when discovered by adaptive search procedures that are governed by very limited goals; (2) transitory estimates of probabilities being found; (3) structural alignments of human activities and information flows being coordinated and designed; and (4) "good enough" strategies being sought and monitored in the absence of full optimization. Bounded rationality is not an alternative to the administrative rationality of optimization over fixed resources in neoclassical economics. The two forms of rationality are used for different purposes. One form (with its deductive *a priori* basis) merely seeks generic predictions and does not deal with individual actions, whereas the other form (with its exploratory basis) is functional in orientation, with strong ties to practical demands of actual managerial choices and pragmatic efficiency but with little connection to the auxiliary assumptions of equilibrium and stylized competition that facilitate neoclassical theory.

Rational Expectations: Anticipations and the Demise of Econometrics

A surprising feature of economic analysis since the end of World War II is the emergence of large econometric models (representing the evolution of national economies) that are used to appraise and display the possible consequences of actions by national governments and the results of severe "external" shocks. Interpretation of these models and their technical appraisal require assimilation of a formal framework with a probabilistic basis, introduced by Haavelmo (1944) and promoted by the reports of research findings by the Cowles Commission (Koopmans, 1950; Hood and Koopmans, 1954). This framework assumes that an economic situation can be represented by alternative collections of equations (structural form, reduced form, and final form) with unknown parameters, measurable variables, and errors to which probability properties can be attributed. Since the early 1950s, the conditions under which knowledge of the structural form is required for effective policy decisions have received special attention. Interest in these conditions revived and was redirected when economic theorists explored a concept of rational or consistent expectations during the early1970s, an exploration driven by the view that econometric models failed to deal successfully with the causes of stagflation.

The strength of the theoretical assault on the structural form was unanticipated, especially as the concept of rational expectations (RE) was introduced by Muth (1961) with curious assertions that (a) "expectations, since they are informed predictions of future events, are essentially the same as the predictions of the relevant economic theory," (b) "expectations of firms (or more generally, the subjective probability distributions of outcomes) tend to be distributed, for the same information set, about the prediction of the theory (or the "objective" probability distribution of outcomes)," and (c) "expectations of a single firm may still be subject to greater error than the theory." All variables here are, in an isolated market, deviations from equilibrium values. The variables are presumed to have certainty equivalents, and all errors are normally distributed!

Structural Autonomy

Use of the framework of the Cowles Commission (or SEM for Simultaneous Equation Models) approach to econometrics in order to generate conditional predictions requires a clear understanding of relevant "structures" and the ways in which such structures alter with changing conditions. Marschak (1953: 26) noted:

> In economics, the conditions that constitute a structure are (1) a set of relations describing human behavior and institutions as well as technological laws and involving, in general, nonobservable random disturbances and nonobservable random errors of measurement; (2) the joint probability distribution of these random quantities.

He argued that "every economic theory susceptible to factual tests must describe a structure or a class of structures" (ibid. 26) and he focused special attention both on a perceived stability in relation to any passive environment, noting that a "knowledge of structure is not necessary if the structure is not expected to have changed by the time the decision takes its effect" (ibid. 4), and on a *qualified* replacement in non-passive environments affected by policy interventions:

> Whenever a given change in structure is expected or intended, the attempt to predict the outcome of alternative decisions under the new structure without taking into account experience collected under the old structure is either so lacking in precision or so wasteful of time as to be useless. It is more promising, though not always practicable, to base the choice of best policy upon an estimate of the old structure and on the knowledge of its expected or intended change. (Ibid. 16-17)
>
> The economist is often required to estimate the effects of a given (intended or expected) change in the "economic structure," i.e., in the very mechanism that produces his data. ... The economist can do this if his past observations suffice to estimate the relevant structural constants prevailing before the change. Having estimated the past structure the economist can estimate the effects of varying it. He can thus help to choose those variations of structure that would produce—from a given point of view—the most desirable results. ... Thus, practical considerations bring about the economist's concern with economic structure. (Marschak, 1950a: 2)

This fashionable view led econometricians to find representations, estimate their parameters with data from some past period, and then simulate the potential impacts of changes in government expenditures and tax provisions for example. "Tender loving care" or tuning adjustments (Howrey, Klein, and McCarthy, 1974) dealt, somewhat tentatively, with any anticipated changes in estimated structures. These ad hoc adjustments, which are widely adopted throughout the commercial industry of econometric forecasters, indicate that structures are generally expected to change to some limited extent, while alternative reduced forms and final forms might be subjected to more comprehensive changes. Among academic economists, unfortunately, the practical recognition of such structure change over time did not deter a strong commitment to research on the estimation techniques that enjoy asymptotically desirable properties only for stationary environments.

Interest in rational expectations promoted a less favorable impression of any structural stability or autonomy, with the time paths of anticipations (as dependent on the "laws of motion" for policy variables, and constraints on responses to major amendments to these laws) serving as the intermediary agency through which radical changes might occur. Sargent (1981: 213, 214) illustrates the scope of this perspective:

> The practice of dynamic econometrics should be changed so that it is consistent with the principle that people's rules of choice are influenced by their constraints. This is a substantial undertaking and involves major adjustments in the ways that we formulate, estimate, and simulate econometric models.

In dynamic contexts, a proper definition of people's constraints includes among them laws of motion that describe the evolution of the taxes they must pay and the prices of the goods that they buy and sell. Changes in agents' perceptions of these laws of motion (or constraints) will in general produce changes in the schedules that describe the choices they make as a function of the information that they possess.

The RE perspective rejects the value previously attached to estimates based on earlier data and it embraces the need to cast aside the process envisaged by Marschak and his successors, perhaps to abandon policy activism and conventional econometrics altogether!

A Simple Model Involving Anticipations

Obviously, the advice stemming from the RE perspective needs clarification. A simple model illustrates the principal (technical) arguments behind this perspective and supports the associated condemnation of substantial policy appraisals by econometricians. The model has an inherent structure, a linear equation which links a variable of interest or "endogenous" variable $y(t)$ in some time period with the actual value of another variable $z(t)$, the anticipated value $x^*(t)$ of a third variable $x(t)$, and a random error. Unknown structural parameters of this equation cannot be estimated directly since the anticipations $x^*(t)$ are unknown. The common response is to introduce an auxiliary (often arbitrary, but crucial) assumption that seems to permit estimation.

One approach specifies anticipations $x^*(t)$ as linearly dependent on a few previous values of $x(t)$ and perhaps other variables. This auxiliary specification introduces further parameters that are unknown but presumed constant. Combination of the two linear ingredients produces a "derived" structural equation that acts as the framework for subsequent predictions when confronted with available data. The derived structure expresses the variable of interest in terms of only measured variables and a random error. In particular, the variable of interest now appears to depend on both current and past values of $x(t)$, the current value of $z(t)$ and any additional variables from the auxiliary equation, and an error term, after elimination of the unknown anticipations by substitution. The estimated equation then resembles those used in structural forms for the SEM framework over a half century with the familiar feature of a "distributed lag" involving several values of $x(t)$.

Some hazards of relying on this framework were clearly indicated by Sargent (1971) who was critical both of so-called "identifying constraints" and the neglected horizons for anticipations in specification of the auxiliary equation. Since the SEM framework usually involves a number of structural equations, the simple model is extended to include another equation that links $z(t)$ with actual values of $y(t)$, anticipated values $x^*(t)$ for $x(t)$—again accepting the specification of the auxiliary equation—and another random error. Anticipations are again generally eliminated by substitution to provide a *derived structure* involving only measured variables and random errors, and thus amenable to estimation. The principal complication introduced by this extension is clear although often understated—namely, parameters of the inherent structure can be autonomous in the sense of each being free to change without necessarily affecting values of other parameters but the parameters of the distributed lags in the derived structure are not autonomous. They are affected by the cross-equation constraints which destroy that property. The RE proponents cite this lack of autonomy as a major obstacle to Marschak's conventional view of policy appraisal. The constraints widen the possibility of structural instabilities between the data period and the later period to which policy predictions apply.

This practical problem is enlarged once pertinent questions are asked about the origins of the auxiliary equation. If this equation is meant to represent a process that generates anticipations, the nature of this process needs attention. Following Muth and Lucas, it seemed reasonable to ask whether a generating process can be optimal in the sense that corresponding anticipations can be described as "rational." Clearly, there must be considerable scope for determining what may be considered optimal. The RE perspective offers just one approach; namely, assume a time-series model for $x(t)$ and define an optimal linear process for the generation of anticipations $x^*(t)$ by reference to the statistical theory that focuses on a minimization of mean squared prediction errors, achieved by using conditional expectations—provided a set of well-known conditions hold (Wiener, 1941). Unfortunately, we have little reason to believe that the technical conditions producing a linear process for optimal predictors (rational expectations) are satisfied in economic environments—the random errors of the process must be normally distributed, for example, as dutifully noted by Muth (1961) but the vast majority of economic phenomena are not! We should be skeptical too about presumptions that economic agents, either individually or on average, somehow know the length and parameters of the process generating $x(t)$ and that they are therefore are able to utilize optimal weights for the auxiliary equation that yields $x^*(t)$.

Theoretical Implications and Practical Consequences

Economic predictions are inevitably flawed, irrespective of their particular origins. Some proponents of rational expectations merely stress additional complications that are understated or inadequately understood in the earlier econometric and macroeconomic literature with regard to the fallibilities of applied model-builders, the awkward problems they face, and the devices they employ to handle them. Other proponents display a considerable degree of dismissive hostility and draw exaggerated implications from the inevitable occurrence of structural instability, as the following comments by Willes (1981: 85, 93) illustrate:

> The rational expectations school has demonstrated that all existing macroeconomic models are useless for policy evaluation, because the method used to construct them dooms them to produce forecasts that are incorrect when policy changes.

The rational expectations school has shown that no one knows much about what happens to the economy when economic policy is changed. The methods of evaluating policy that we thought would work don't—and they cannot be patched up. This means that our policies must be much different than they have been in recent years. Specifically, it means that activist macroeconomic policies—those designed to stimulate economic growth by cutting taxes, increasing government spending, increasing money supply, or increasing the federal deficit—must be curbed.

Thus it seems wise to identify what the RE perspective yields when viewed in its most favorable light. First, the perspective extends the static concept of rationality that was used in the second section of this paper and gives a sensible dynamic dimension to decision-making that embodies stochastic processes rather than simple probabilities and that accepts a significant role for complex anticipations as dynamic constraints affect decisions. Second, it clarifies how a change in $x(t)$, seen as the substitution of one time-series model for another process (possibly stimulated by the announcement of a new government policy), may lead to changes in structural parameters —indeed *must* lead to such changes if linkage of optimal predictors with anticipations is a good approximation—and thus fosters imprecision in the appreciation of what a given change in policy might entail. Such imprecision does not mean that policy changes are unnecessary but rather that consequences are more difficult to predict with a sufficient degree of accuracy. There is no real basis for the extraordinary extrapolation to anti-activism by Willes. Third, it implies the need for a substantial re-evaluation of statistical properties associated with estimating procedures, encouraging doubts about the appropriateness of asymptotic properties (consistency, efficiency, and convergence) when structural changes often occur. Preoccupations with statistical tests of the Neyman-Pearson type are weakened and interest in robustness rises.

These are major achievements if we do not take them too far. It should also be noted that anticipations are not limited to the fiscal and monetary policy changes that are initiated by federal governments. The technical argument can be stated in identical terms provided $x(t)$ refers to any innovation—Schumpeterian, say, rather than new classical innovations alone! Thus the current assault on econometric models is not limited to Keynesian models. Rather it affects empirical treatments of all economic phenomena that require substantial structural stability. Indeed the core of Keynesian theory, as found for example in Phillips' models for control and stabilization of economic fluctuations, has always been an active promotion of structural change through induced feedback. Thus it is difficult to separate out Keynesians for special criticism as if they alone are ignorant of a frequent occurrence of instability from various sources, including active governmental interventions.

Rational expectations theories fail when they muddle through with strange connections between objective and subjective probabilities, rely on a representative agent and thus ignore the problems of aggregation and diversity (Geweke, 1985), and opt for "a stochastic form of perfect foresight" (Arrow, 1990: 32ff) that avoids the need to give adequate attention to the acquisition and cost of information. These three elements are similar to those that reveal the weaknesses of a static concept of rationality, including ambiguities due to the incompleteness of markets or the non-uniqueness of equilibria.

The Lucas critique and the associated suggestion that models' performances be evaluated by reference to qualitative patterns linking economic variables (such as general impressions that are derived from NBER chronologies) encouraged the substitution of calibration for estimation of parameters in small models of (real and monetary) business cycles—models represented by simple difference equations subjected to external shocks. These equations have parameters that are to be chosen rather than estimated, perhaps in accordance with those qualitative features that particular values produce, rather than on other grounds. The attraction of calibrated values is a further challenge to conventional econometric practices but the choice of these values is at least as *ad hoc* as the earlier choices of auxiliary specifications for distributed lags that are so often criticized by RE proponents. Advocacy of rational expectations brought a partial substitution of model display for parametric estimation and it attracted simulations of small models, perhaps single equations, in place of the earlier simulations of much larger Keynesian macroeconometric models. Generally, this advocacy stressed the primacy of deductive theory over all empirical concerns and thus it has separated efforts of many econometricians from those of new classical theorists, as noted without much regret by Lucas (1981: 11):

> The prestige of theoretical work is so secure in our profession that its proponents too rarely find themselves on the defensive, and casting meaningless epithets like ad hoc becomes a devastating criticism of empirical work. The cost of this attitude is not that econometric work fails to get done—someone has to do it—but that contact between theorists and working econometricians becomes unpleasant, with the result that the two groups tend to stick to themselves and the necessary interaction between theory and fact tends not to take place.

Consequently, we do not see the demise of conventional econometrics but rather a loss of civility and compromise affecting relationships between the new classical theorists and their econometric counterparts (especially those who apply models to specific policy issues), and to a lesser extent between new classical economists and other theoretical economists who are less enchanted with the eccentric assumptions involving continuous states of equilibrium, stochastic microeconomic foundations, covariance stationarity, and a ubiquitous ineffectiveness of all policy actions.

Concluding Remarks

Where does this discussion lead us in regard to microeconomic theory, macroeconomics and econometrics? Given the assertions of Arrow and Posner with which I began (especially the narrow *identification* of microeconomic theory with rationality and the corresponding focus on static optimization over limited resources), economists have placed themselves in a difficult position. This situation stems, at least in part, from sustained promotion by neoclassical theorists of a "positive" science or "pure theory," which excludes elements usually associated with sociology, history and psychology, and other realistic, relevant aspects of choice, actions and decisions. The situation also stems from persistent denials of the need to deal with aggregation, social embedding of individual and collective choice, those uncertainties and instabilities that are not adequately represented by numerical probabilities, and the complicated nature of decision-making in the world around us.

Rational microeconomic theory is interesting when viewed with the backdrop of immanent standards of theorists, but a wider audience may agree with judgments expressed by Anand (1991: 213) that "for the standard problems and kinds of analysis in which economists trade, rationality is both insufficient and unnecessary" and "the term rational is grossly abused when it is applied to certain economic theories of expectation formation and decision making." Further reliance on such theories may also support the charge of self-deception put forward by Farmer and Matthews (1991), the evolutionary-institutional economist Hodgson (1988), some observers who prefer to place theory closer to time considerations, institutional features, mental attributes, and human frailty and indecisiveness, and those economists such as Casson (1997) who dislike the neglect of cultural intermediation and value rationality that affect the formation of ends.

With respect to econometrics, the situation is dismal. In its most extreme expressions, rational expectations theory implies that most of econometric modeling is invalid as a basis for predictions of actual or hypothetical changes in government policies because of failures to deal with structural instability. This criticism extends to any form of dislocation in the time-series characteristics of relevant variables for which anticipations must be formed and the new specter of chaos arises from an irrelevance of estimates based on earlier evidence. For some, this negative evaluation has revived a radical assault on empirical models of any size, and it has encouraged a reliance on the simulative display of small models based on very simple difference equations with calibrated parameters. Not surprisingly, many applied econometricians have ignored the thrust of the RE theory and continued to practice "business as usual" in regard to policy simulations and parametric estimation. The hazards of structural instability are noted but most predictions are still prepared in the way they have been produced for over four decades with hardly a sideways glance at new classical objections involving rational expectations.

References

Aldrich, John. 1989. Autonomy, *Oxford Economic Papers*, 41: 5-34.

Anand, Paul. 1991. The nature of rational choice and *The Foundations of Statistics*, *Oxford Economic Papers*, 43(2): 199-216.

Anand, Paul. 1993. *Foundations of Rational Choice Under Risk*. Oxford: Clarendon Press.

Arrow, Kenneth J. 1974. Rationality: individual and social, in Kenneth J. Arrow, *The Limits of Organization*. New York: W. W. Norton.

Arrow, Kenneth J. 1990. Economic theory and the hypothesis of rationality, in John Eatwell, Murray Milgate and Peter Newman, (eds.) *Utility and Probability*.

Bacharach, M.O.L. 1986. The problem of agents' beliefs in economic theory, in Mauro Baranzini and Roberto Scazzieri (eds.), *Foundations of Economics*. Oxford: Basil Blackwell.

Baron, James N., and Michael T. Hannan. 1994. The impact of economics on contemporary sociology, *Journal of Economic Literature*, 32: 1111-1146.

Best, Michael. 1990. *The New Competition*. Cambridge, MA: Harvard University Press.

Binmore, Kenneth. 1997. Rationality and backward induction, *Journal of Economic Methodology*, 4: 23-41.

Casson, Mark. 1997. Moral leadership in ethical economics, in Peter Koslowski (ed.), *Methodology of the Social Sciences, Ethics, and Economics in the Newer Historical School*. Heidelberg and Berlin: Springer-Verlag.

Despres, C.J.-N. 1996. Information, technology and culture, *Technovation*, 16: 1-20.

Dixit, Avinash K. 1996. *The Making of Economic Policy*. Cambridge, MA: The MIT Press.

Edwards, Ward. (ed.)1992. *Utility: Theories, Measurements and Applications*. Boston: Kluwer Academic.

Farmer, M.K. and M.L. Matthrew 1991. Cultural difference and subjective rationality: Where sociology connects with the economics of technological choice, in Geoffrey

M. Hodgson and Ernesto Screpanti (eds.), *Rethinking Economics*. Aldershot, UK: Edward Elgar.

Fellner, William. 1945. Note on the law of large numbers and 'fair' games, *Annals of Mathematical Statistics*, 16: 301-304.

Fellner, William. 1965. *Probability and Profit*. Homewood, IL: Irwin.

Frank, Robert H. 1992. Molding sociology and economics: James Coleman's *Foundations of Social Theory*, *Journal of Economic Literature*, 30: 147-170.

Gardenfors, Peter. 1988. *Knowledge in Flux*. Cambridge, MA: The MIT Press.

Genest, C., and J.V. Zidek 1986. Combining probability distributions: a critique and an annotated bibliography, *Statistical Science*, 1: 114-148.

Geweke, John 1985. Macroeconometric modeling and the theory of the representative agent, *American Economic Review*, 75: 206-210.

Hamel. G. and C.K. Prahalad 1996. Competing in the new economy: managing out of bounds, *Strategic Management Journal*, 17: 237-242.

Hamouda, O.F. and J.C.R. Rowley 1996. *Probability in Economics*. London: Routledge.

Hamouda, O.F. and J. C. R. Rowley (eds.) 1997a. *The Probability Approach to Simultaneous Equations*. Cheltenham, UK: Edward Elgar.

— (eds.). 1997b. *Economic Games, Bargaining and Solutions*. Cheltenham, UK: Edward Elgar.

— (eds.). 1997c. *Expected Utility, Fair Gambles and Rational Choice*. Cheltenham, UK: Edward Elgar.

— (eds.). 1997d. *Paradoxes, Ambiguity and Rationality*. Cheltenham, UK: Edward Elgar.

Harsanyi, John. C. 1978. Bayesian decision theory and utilitarian ethics, *American Economic Review*, 68: 223-228.

Harsanyi, John. C. 1995. Games with incomplete information, *American Economic Review*, 85(3): 291-303.

Hicks, John R. 1935. Annual survey of economic theory: the theory of monopoly, *Econometrica*, 3: 12-16.

Hicks, John R. 1969. *A Theory of Economic History*. Oxford: Oxford University Press.

Hodgson, Geoffrey M. 1988. *Economics and Institutions: A Manifesto for a Modern Institutional Economics*. Cambridge: Polity Press.

Hood, William C. and Tjelling C. Koopmans (eds.) 1954. *Studies in Econometric Method*. New York: Wiley.

Howrey, E. Philip, Lawrence R. Klein and Michael D. McCarthy 1974. Notes on testing the predictive performance of econometric models. *International Economic Review*, 15: 366-383.

Kahneman, Daniel, Paul Slovic, and Amos Tversky (eds.). 1982. *Judgment Under Uncertainty: Heuristics and Biases*. Cambridge: Cambridge University Press.

Keeney, R.A. 1992. On the foundations of prescriptive decision, in Ward Edwards (ed.), *Utility Theories: Measurements and Applications*. Boston: Kluwer Academic.

Knight, Frank H. 1971 (1921). *Risk, Uncertainty and Profit*. Chicago and London: University of Chicago Press.

Koopmans, Tjelling C. (ed.). 1950. *Statistical Inference in Dynamic Economic Models*. New York: Wiley.

Lange, Oscar. 1945-46, The scope and method of economics. *Review of Economic Studies*, 13: 19-32.

Lucas, Richard E. 1972. Econometric testing of the natural rate hypothesis, in Otto Eckstein (ed.), *The Econometrics of Price Determination*. Washington, DC: Board of Governors of the Federal Reserve System.

Lucas, Richard E. 1980. Methods and problems in business cycle theory, *Journal of Money, Credit, and Banking*, 12: 696-714.

Lucas, Richard E. 1981. *Studies in Business-Cycle Theory*. Cambridge, MA: The MIT Press.

Machina, Mark J. 1989. Dynamic consistency and non-expected utility models of choice under uncertainty, *Journal of Economic Literature*, 26: 1622-1668.

Marschak, Jacob. 1950. Rational behavior, uncertain prospects, and measurable utility, *Econometrica*, 18(2): 111-141.

Marschak, Jacob. 1950a. Statistical inference in economics: an introduction, in Tjelling C. Koopmans (ed.), *Statistical Inference in Dynamic Economic Models*. New York: Wiley.

Marschak, Jacob. 1953. Economic measurements for policy and production, in William C. Hood and Tjelling C. Koopmans (eds.), *Studies in Econometric Method*. New York: Wiley.

Muth, John F. 1961. Rational expectations and the theory of price movements, *Econometrica*, 29: 315-335.

Okimoto, Daniel I. and Thomas P. Rohlen. 1988. *Inside the Japanese System*. Stanford, CA: Stanford University Press.

Posner, Richard A. 1986. *Economic Analysis of Law*. 3rd edition. Boston: Little, Brown.

Posner, Richard A. 1995. *Overcoming Law*. Cambridge, MA: Harvard University Press.

Russo, J.E. and P.J.H. Schoemaker. 1989. *Decision Traps*. New York: Doubleday.

Sargent, Thomas J. 1971. A note on the 'accelerationist' controversy, *Journal of Money, Credit, and Banking*, 8: 721-725.

Sargent, Thomas J. 1981. Interpreting economic time series, *Journal of Political Economy*, 89: 213-148.

Sargent, Thomas J. 1982. Beyond supply and demand curves in macroeconomics, *American Economic Review*, 72: 382-389.

Sargent, Thomas J. 1991. *Beyond Rationality in Macroeconomics*. Oxford: Clarendon Press.

Savage, Leonard J. 1972. *The Foundations of Statistics*. 2nd edition. New York: Dover.

Sen, Amaryta. 1983. The profit motive, *Lloyds Bank Review*, 147: 1-20.

Sen Amaryta. 1990. Rational behaviour, in John Eatwell, Murray Milgate and Peter Newman (eds.), *Utility and Probability*. London: Macmillan.

Simon, Herbert A. 1983. *Reason in Human Affairs*. Stanford CA: Stanford University Press.

Simon, Herbert A. 1990. Bounded rationality, in John Eatwell, Murray Milgate and Peter Newman (ed.), *Utility and Probability*. London: Macmillan.

Sugden, Richard.1986. New developments in the theory of choice under uncertainty, *Bulletin of Economic Research*, 38: 1-24.

Sugden, Richard.1991, Rational choice: a survey of contributions from economics and philosophy, *Economic Journal*, 101: 751-785.

Swedberg, Richard. (ed.). 1993. *Explorations in Economic Sociology*. New York: Russell Sage Foundation.

Whiteman, Charles H. 1983. *Linear Rational Expectations Models*. Minneapolis: University of Minnesota Press.

Whittle, Peter. 1984 (1963), *Prediction and Regulation* 2nd edition. Oxford: Basil Blackwell.

Wiener, Norbert. 1941. *Extrapolation, Interpolation, and the Smoothing of Stationary Time Series*. Cambridge, MA: MIT Press.

Willes, M.H. 1981. 'Rational expectations' as a counterrevolution, in Daniel Bell and Irving Kristol (eds.), *The Crisis in Economic Theory*. New York: Basic Books.

Part 2

How Rational Are We Really?
Views from Philosophy,
Sociology and Political Science

4

Systemism: The Alternative to Individualism and Holism

Mario Bunge

Introduction

It is usually taken for granted that there are only two possible views of society: that it is just a collection of individuals (individualism), or that it is a whole to which individuals are subjected (holism). Whereas individualism stresses agency and ignores social ties, holism underrates agency and overrates ties. It is seldom recognized that society might be a system, that is, a complex thing constituted by interacting individuals. In fact, when rigorous contemporary social scientists hear the word 'system', they are likely to draw their intellectual guns. They seem to feel threatened by a return to the holism of Hegel, Comte, Marx, Durkheim, or Parsons. They are rightly diffident of such imaginary wholes as collective memory, national spirit, and the will of the international community. So, they take refuge in the equally obsolete individualism of Hobbes, Locke, Smith, Weber, or the neoclassical microeconomists.

To be sure, the social individualists—pardon the oxymoron—do not deny that individual action is now constrained, now stimulated by the social context or situation. But they do not and cannot analyze it in individualist terms: for all their talk of "situational logic," they leave the situation as an unanalyzed whole. And they resist the very idea that individuals flock together—or are thrown together—into social systems such as families, gangs, tribes, villages, business firms, armies, schools, religious congregations, informal networks, or political parties, all of which are just as real and concrete as their individual constituents. Individualists insist that all these are just collections of individuals: they underrate structure or even overlook it.

Individualists also miss one of the most important and intriguing of all kinds of events in society as well as in nature, namely the emergence of novelty. More precisely, they miss the emergence of things with systemic properties, that is, properties that their components or their precursors lack—such as cohesiveness, stability, income distribution, division of labor, social stratification, and social order. By the same token, individualists fail to realize the existence of systemic social issues, such as those of poverty and underdevelopment, that cannot be solved by doing one thing at a time, because they affect several systems at once—the biological, economic, cultural, and political ones.

Systems Everywhere

This situation has no parallel in mathematics, natural science, or technology. Indeed, mathematicians know that every valid reasoning (deductive argument) is a system of statements, and they value hypothetico-deductive systems (theories) well above unstructured sets of formulas. Systemicity is indeed peculiar to modern mathematics. Just think of the concepts of real number system, vector space, system (or family) of functions, system of equations, coordinate system, topological space, algebra, and axiomatic system. As Hardy (1967) stated, the importance of a mathematical idea is somehow proportional to its relatedness to other mathematical ideas. One might even say that, in mathematics, to be is to be a component of at least one mathematical system. Strays do not qualify.

Physicists use the concept of a system just as frequently as mathematicians, for they study such systems as atoms, molecules, liquid bodies, crystals, stars, laser beams, and weather systems. Only particle physicists study non-systems, such as quarks, electrons, and photons—which they often, mistakenly, call "systems." But they know that all such simple things are parts of systems or will eventually be absorbed by some system. Likewise, chemists study systems of interacting chemical reactions. And of course biologists study systems at all levels: subcellular (such as chromosomes), cells, organs, multicellular organisms, populations, and ecosystems. In particular, neuroscientists and biological psychologists have left behind the rival hypotheses that individual neurons can have mental experiences, and that only the brain as a whole can have them. In fact, they have adopted the systemic view that the brain is a super-system of systems of cells, and that different mental functions are the specific functions (activities) of different cell assemblies.

Much the same holds for technology. Indeed, technologists design, redesign, test or repair artifacts. And all of these are artificial systems. Indeed, even the simplest of machines and the simplest of formal organizations is a system, that is, a complex thing whose components are bound together, as a consequence of which the whole has peculiar properties and behaves as a unit in some respects. Think of pulleys, batteries, engines, computers, or broadcasting systems; or of schools, clubs, business firms, or government departments. All artifacts, whether physical like television networks, biological like cows, or social like corporations, are systems. Hence, they should be designed, maintained and repaired in a systemic way rather than bit by bit. That is, they should be examined and handled as wholes, though not as blocs but as systems with a more or less variable composition, environment, structure, and mechanism. Alter any of these four features, and the state of the system will change accordingly.

In sum, systems cannot be evaded in any field of study or action. Hence, the word "system"—or its near-synonym "network"—should not be shunned just because it has occasionally been employed by holists. It is not equivalent to "structure," because this word is usually treated as an adjective or attribute. Hence, whereas it makes sense to talk about the structure of a system, the expression "structure of a structure" is meaningless. I submit that the so-called "structural" and "relational" accounts in sociology are models of systems that highlight their structural features, whereas their rational choice counterparts emphasize their composition. The advantage of a systemic model of a system over its rivals is that it encompasses not only its structure (organization) and composition (constitutive persons in the case of social systems), but also its environment and its mechanism (or dynamics).

Systemism

The ubiquity of the concept of a system is such that it suggests adopting an entire systemic worldview. This is centered in the following postulates:

(i) Everything, whether concrete or abstract, is a system or an actual or potential component of a system;

(ii)   systems have systemic (emergent) features that their components lack, whence

(iii)   all problems should be approached in a systemic rather than in a sectoral fashion;

(iv)   all ideas should be put together into systems (theories); and

(v)   the testing of anything, whether idea or artifact, assumes the validity of other items, which are taken as benchmarks, at least for the time being.

Yet, social individualists resist the systemic approach. They insist on studying only the components of social systems, that is, individuals, while overlooking their structure or set of connections (internal and external). I guess theirs is a defensive strategy: they do not wish to be taken for holists, and they are diffident of the writers who call themselves system theorists although actually they are holists. (Talcott Parsons, Niklas Luhmann, and Erwin Laszlo come to mind.) Their opaque and long-winded utterances have given systemism a bad name. I guess this is why most social scientists shun the word "system" even while studying social systems.

Fortunately, few authentic social scientists practice the philosophy they preach. For example, Karl Marx was a holist in epistemology: in fact, he was the grandfather of the now fashionable social constructivism. But when it came to economic and political matters, Marx insisted that individual action is the source of all social change. Likewise, Max Weber popularized Dilthey's individualism, subjectivism and anti-scientism. But he did not practice these philosophical views: indeed, he proceeded scientifically when tackling sociological and socioeconomic problems. Moreover, Weber studied such systems as the slave society, the caste system, the feudal structure, organized religion, bureaucracy, industrial capitalism, and legal codes.

Closer to us, James S. Coleman (1990: 5) stated that, in his own variant of methodological individualism, "[t]he interaction among individuals is seen to result in emergent phenomena at the system level." Moreover, he criticized the "fiction that society consists of a set of independent individuals, each of whom acts to achieve goals that are independently arrived at, and that the functioning of society consists of the combination of these actions of independent individuals" (300). And he stated that "the correct path for social theory is [. . .] to maintain a single conception of what individuals are like and to generate the varying systemic functioning not from different kinds of creatures, but from different structures of relations within which these creatures find themselves" (197). In other words, once a social system is in place, individuals become replaceable to some extent: their roles can be enacted by different persons. When I told Coleman that his views were not individualist but systemist, he admitted that maybe he was a closet systemist.

A Batch of Examples

Social scientists have performed plenty of micro-macro analyses. These can be condensed in what may be called Boudon-Coleman diagrams (Bunge 1996, 1998). Here is a self-explanatory example:

Figure 4.1
Boudon-Coleman Diagram 1

Macrolevel	*Economic growth* ⟶	*Population stagnation*
	↓	↓
Microlevel	*Old-age security* ⟶	*Decline in fertility*

A holist is likely to be baffled by the information that, in our time, economic growth is bound to be accompanied by population stagnation or even decline; and the individualist must take old-age security as a given—even if it depends partly upon a macrosystem, namely government. The systemist dissolves the paradox by linking the system and individual levels. In so doing he unveils the mechanism that mediates two macrovariables.

Second example: There are two main currents in the study of ideas, the individualist or internalist, and the holist or externalist. Internalists focus on conceptual problems and solutions, whereas holists focus on networks and formal organizations. The internalists tend to deal in disembodied ideas, whereas the externalists tend to study groups while minimizing the importance of ideas: they see the net but miss the fish. The two parties do not talk to each other. And yet it should be obvious that each of them sheds light on only one of the sides of the coin, and that neither captures the complexity of the micro-macro links. For example, internalists cannot explain why science was born only once, in ancient Greece, why it withered a couple of centuries later, and was reborn at the beginning of the Modern Era. Externalists are equally at a loss to explain these processes, because they cannot even distinguish science from magic, religion, or philosophy, all of which are allegedly "social constructions" contrived by groups or networks (see, e.g., Collins 1998).

By contrast, the systemist is likely to look at the problem this way. Every thinker is born into a pre-existing system loaded with a tradition which he either enriches or rebels against. He inherits some findings and problems and, if original, invents or discovers new ones. The solutions he proposes to the problems he tackles are born in his brain, not in society: social groups are brainless, hence they cannot think. Of course, social groups and circumstances stimulate or inhibit thought. But their influence is not such that every idea has a social content, let alone a political purpose.

Obviously, the ideas in social studies have a social content. Hence, they must be judged by their adequacy to social facts or their efficiency in promoting social change. By contrast, the validity of mathematical proofs, and the truth of physical or biological theories, have nothing to do with social class, political power, or economic growth. These social factors are relevant only to the ability of individual researchers to conduct their work without distorting political or ideological pressures. For example, the cultural policy of classical liberalism, which is based on individualism, is one of benign neglect. By contrast, the totalitarian cultural policy, which is based on holism, is one of censorship. (For the holism-Nazism connection see Harrington 1996.)

My third example is Tocqueville's ([1856] 1998) explanation of the backwardness of French agriculture compared with the English in the eighteenth century. The mechanism was landlord absenteeism, far more common at the time in France than in England. Whereas the typical French aristocrat left the administration of his land in the hands of a steward, and took up a position as a civil servant or a courtier, his English counterpart was typically a gentleman-farmer who lived on his estate and saw personally to it that his land was well cultivated, his tenants paid punctually their rent, and his neighbors observed law and custom. In sum, whereas the typical squire remained at the center of his rural network, his French counterpart was marginalized.

In turn, the root of this difference is macrosocial, namely the political organization, which was centralist in France and decentralized in England. A French aristocrat gained more political power and prestige from shuffling papers, socializing and scheming in Paris, than from pottering in his grounds, learning new cultivation methods, and acting as the local magistrate. In this case, individual choice, and its consequence for rural life, were ultimately determined by the political system. As Tocqueville himself wrote (p. 181), "the chief and permanent cause of this fact was [. . .] the slow and constant actions of institutions."

Boudon (1998) regards this case as confirming what he calls contextual individualism and cognitive rationality. I prefer to think of Tocqueville as a systemist *avant la lettre,* particularly since he noted the social aspect of the process in addition to its economic and political ones. Indeed, Tocqueville's main point is that landlord absenteeism destroyed the rural network centered in the landlord, in addition to impoverishing landlord and peasant alike. He was thus a socio-econo-politologist. Indeed, his explanation fits the following Boudon-Coleman diagram:

Figure 4.2
Boudon-Coleman Diagram 2

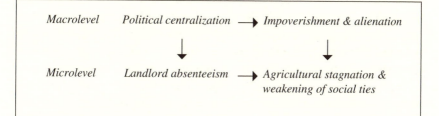

In this case, like in all other social processes, there are uncounted individual choices, decisions and actions. But all of them occur within or between social systems, and they reinforce or weaken the bonds that keep these systems together. Action, bond and context go together. Eliminate either, and no social fact remains.

A Second Batch of Examples

Fourth example: The science-technology-market system. There are two main socioeconomic views on the relation of technological innovation and the market. Individualists claim that inventor proposes and market disposes. Holists hold, by contrast, that invention is market-driven: that market demands and inventor supplies. (Yet, ironically, all market worshippers espouse individualism.) Each party parades a large collection of examples, without bothering about counterexamples. I submit that only a systemic view of the matter attains the whole truth.

The first thing to note is that there are big inventions and small ones: radical novelties and improvements. Whereas the former are motivated mainly by sheer curiosity and the love of tinkering, improvements may also be motivated by profit: these are often commissioned by the technologist's employer with a view to marketing the corresponding products. By contrast, some radically new inventions have created whole new markets. For example, the electrical industry was made possible by electrical engineering, which in turn was the child of experiments and theories on electricity and magnetism. In particular, Michael Faraday discovered the principle of electromagnetic induction, which was used by Joseph Henry to design the electric motor, and by Nikola Tesla to design the dynamo. Industry transmuted these and many other bits of scientific and technological knowledge into welfare and wealth. This is only one of many science-technology-industry systems. The market does not create: it only demands and selects—that is, rewards or punishes. Moreover, it usually rewards the follower rather than the pioneer. (As a wit put it, the early bird gets the worm, but the second mouse gets the cheese.) It would be just as silly to underrate the power of the market as to regard it as the fountain of technological ingenuity.

Fifth example: The combination of competition with cooperation. Whereas individualists stress competition or conflict, holists emphasize cooperation or solidarity. (Marxism is a special case: it stresses interclass warfare but intraclass solidarity.) Actually, competition and cooperation coexist in all social systems, though not in the same respects. Indeed, social systems cannot emerge and persist without a modicum of (spontaneous or coordinated) cooperation in some regard. And, once a system is in place, competition in some respect is bound to arise in its midst precisely because of a common interest in some scarce resource—attention, love, time, space, food, money, job, or what have you.

Think for instance of a scientific community. Some post-Mertonian sociologists of science, notably Latour and Woolgar (1979), claim that there is no such community: that individual scientists are engaged in a selfish and unscrupulous struggle for power. But these writers are poorly informed in this regard as in others. Indeed, every scientist knows that, while researchers compete for peer recognition, they also learn from one another: scientific research is a so-cial endeavor even when it has no social content and no practical value (see Merton 1973). As Wolpert (1992:88) states, "[i]n order to promote the success of their ideas, scientists must thus adopt a strat-egy of competition and cooperation, of altruism and selfishness." In any event, Latour's claim that "science is politics by other means" has recently been falsified by an empirical study of citations (Baldi 1998).

Sixth and last example: Boudon (1974), who calls himself a con-textual individualist, has shown that the proliferation of universities after World War II has had a perverse effect. This effect is the emer-gence of a sizable intellectual proletariat, and the concomitant in-crease in social inequality. The mechanism is this: As the number of university graduates increases, the queues of candidates waiting for qualified jobs lengthen. The practical moral is obvious: to check the massive unemployment of university graduates, either (a) impose quotas in the professional faculties, or (b) raise the level of job speci-fication in industry and government. That is, influence choice from above to minimize failure at the bottom.

Implications for Social Policy Design

The preceding examples suggest two important points, one theo-retical and the other practical. The first is that any deep explanation of social change calls for the unveiling of social mechanisms, which in turn involves micro-macro analyses. This is so because every indi-vidual action is partially constrained by macrosocial circumstances, which may in turn be affected to some extent by individual actions.

The second point is that the design of effective social policies should be based on correct hypotheses concerning the social mechanisms of interest. The reason is that a social policy is expected to set up, repair or dismantle some social mechanism—e.g., of health care, wealth redis-tribution, or conflict resolution. By contrast, the intuitive and the empirical approaches to social policy-making are wasteful and often counterproductive. For example, contrary to popular wisdom, a raise in minimum wage does not increase unemployment, but benefits the economy as a whole because it increases demand (Card 1995).

There is an additional reason for favoring systemic social poli-cies, namely that social problems are typically systemic. That is, they involve many interrelated features and even several social sys-tems at a time. For example, an effective policy of national development must involve factors of various kinds: environmental (e.g., protection of forests and fisheries), biological (e.g., health care and planned parenthood), economic (e.g., industrialization and improved infrastructure), political (in particular political participation), and cultural (in particular education).

The reason for such a multifactorial approach is that all those factors are interrelated. For example, there is no modern industry without educated manpower, and no education on an empty stomach, let alone on a gut full of parasites. For this reason, the sectoral and one-problem-at-a-time approach is bound to fail. Even such a staunch individualist as the financial wizard George Soros (1998: 226) has concluded that, contrary to the opinion of his erstwhile teacher Karl R. Popper, piecemeal social engineering cannot work to solve systemic problems. He suggests that these should be tackled radically and in all their complexity.

Contrast the systemic approach to social issues with its rivals. The radical individualists oppose all social planning in the name of individual liberties (a.k.a. privileges). Hence, they leave individuals to their own resources—which, in an inegalitarian society, are meager for most people. On the other hand, holists swear by top-down planning. Consequently, even when they address the basic needs of the common people, they are likely to ignore their aspirations and rights. In either case, the powerless individual, whether forsaken or corralled, has nothing to gain. The systemic approach to social policy-design is quite different from both libertarianism and totalitarianism: it attempts to involve the interested parties in the planning process, and designs social systems and processes likely to improve individual well-being, revising the plans as often as required by the changing circumstances.

Social Science is about Social Systems

Consider briefly the French Revolution of 1789. Despite its tremendous worldwide consequences, it was a cakewalk: the central government fell in the course of an evening. Tocqueville ([1856] 1998) explains this process clearly and in systemic terms, namely as a result of the replacement of the feudal social networks with four closed and mutually hostile castes: those constituted by the peasants, bourgeois, aristocrats, and the Crown. Those traditional networks were ripped when, in the previous century, the landowners abandoned their land and left their tenants to their own devices as a consequence of the concentration of both government and nobility in Paris. This is how it happened that "the ties of patronage and dependence which formerly bound the great rural landowners to the peasants had been relaxed or broken" (p. 188). The king was thus a victim of his own art "of dividing people in order to govern them more absolutely" (p. 191).

There was more: the centralization of political power left a political vacuum that was filled by the intellectuals, most of whom criticized the unjust social order. This explains the disproportionate influence of the *philosophes*, in particular the Encyclopedists: they occupied the place that the aristocrats occupied in England and elsewhere at the time. "An aristocracy in its vigor not only runs affairs, it still directs opinion, sets the tone for writers, and lends authority to ideas. In the eighteenth century, the French nobility had entirely lost this part of its empire; its moral authority had followed the fortunes of its power: the place that it had occupied in the government was empty, and writers could occupy it at their leisure and fill it completely" (p. 198). A century and a half later, the author of a huge treatise on the sociology of philosophy (Collins 1998) devotes a single page to the Encyclopedists, fails to explain their remarkable influence, and devotes many laudatory pages to the Counter-Enlightenment, from Hegel and Nietzsche to Scheler and Heidegger.

The point of these stories about the French Revolution is to remind ourselves that, contrary to the radical individualist tenet, society is not an unstructured collection of independent individuals. It is, instead, a system of interacting individuals organized into systems or networks of various kinds. In fact, every one of us belongs at once to several systems: kinship, friendship, and colleagueship networks, business firms, schools, clubs, religious congregations, etc. This explains our many "identities" (Tilly 1998: 34).

To be sure, the emergence, maintenance, repair or dismantling of any social system can ultimately be explained only in terms of individual preferences, decisions and actions. But in turn these individual events are largely determined by social interaction and social context. I cultivate the relations and support the systems that benefit me, and neglect or sabotage those that hurt me. In sum, agency and structure are only two sides of the same coin. We see agency through Weber's microscope, and structure through Marx's telescope.

Now, individuals are studied by natural science and psychology, which—along with anthropology, linguistics, demography, and epidemiology—is one of the biosocial sciences. The social sciences proper, such as sociology and economics, do not study individuals except as components of social systems. Thus, anthropology studies entire communities such as villages and tribes. Sociology studies social systems, all the way from the childless couple to the world system. Economics specializes in the study of the social systems engaged in production, services, or trade. Politology studies power relations in all systems, particularly the political ones. And history studies social (structural) changes on all scales.

It is not enough for a social scientist to point out the social context or circumstance of a fact. He is expected to study *social* facts, and a social fact happens to be one that occurs in a social system—such as a strike in a factory—or between social systems—such as an international conflict. Hence, he must study social *bonds* in addition to social contexts, for bonds are what hold systems together.

In short, the social sciences study social systems. True, some of those who dislike the word "system" prefer the term "structure." But structures are properties of things, not things, whereas social systems are concrete things. For example, a corporation is a system with a definite (though perhaps changing) structure, or set of bonds among its components and its environment. The socioeconomists who study the social structure of a corporation do not investigate the structure of a structure—a meaningless expression—but the structure of a thing.

The Competitive Advantage of Systemism

To appreciate the advantages of systemism over its two rivals, it may help to consider briefly three examples, one in sociology, the other in management, and the third in political science. A family sociologist interested in understanding why so many families are breaking up these days is unlikely to be satisfied by lamentations over the decline of family values. Nor will he be convinced by the rational-choice theorist who regards the family as a production unit that ceases to be profitable in producing a certain number of goods, from meals to children, or because, after cold calculation, one of the spouses realizes that his or her marriage had been a mistake (Becker 1976: 244). Neither of these views focuses on the weakening of the interpersonal bonds that gave rise to the family to begin with. In modern society, most people marry or divorce neither because of social pressures nor because of economic calculations.

People marry primarily because they fall in love and share interests to such an extent that they wish to live together; and they divorce when they fall out of love, their interests diverge, suffer from work-related stress, or some other cause. In these matters, interaction or its weakening is all-important, whereas rational calculation and the institutional context are secondary.

Our second example is that of a management consultant, operations research expert, or industrial sociologist intent on understanding how a given business firm works, or else stops to work efficiently. Presumably, he will not be satisfied with holistic considerations about the firm's goal or the business environment. Nor will he try to guess the subjective utilities and probabilities of the firm's members, to see whether the managers succeed or fail in maximizing their expected utilities. He knows that the latter are inaccessible and, like everything subjective, are at most an object of study, never a tool of scientific analysis. He will focus instead on the social structure of the firm, and on various mechanisms that keep the firm going, or that have been allowed to deteriorate or become obsolete. Indeed, he will study the three main mechanisms: work, management, and firm-environment interactions. Unless corrected, a dysfunction in any three will jeopardize the firm's survival, for it will result in a decrease in efficiency, as measured by the output-input ratio—not the inaccessible expected utility. (For the centrality of mechanisms in social studies, see Hedström and Swedberg, eds. 1998, and Bunge 1999.)

Finally, a political example: Why did the Soviet empire collapse? Recall that nobody predicted this momentous event. In particular, it took by surprise the holistic futurologists, the game-theory modelers, and the data-gatherers and hunters of the various American "intelligence" agencies. I submit that the political analysts and spies failed because they did not study seriously the various subsystems of the Soviet society and their inter-relations. In particular, they failed to realize that the so-called dictatorship of the proletariat had cut the non-coercive bonds that hold a civil society together; that the top-down planned economy did not deliver enough consumer goods and functioned at a low technological level in everything but space exploration and arms manufacture; and that the ruling Marxist-Leninist ideology had stunted cultural development and ceased to command popular allegiance because it was finally perceived as having become an irrelevant dogma. The result of the malfunction of all three subsystems—the economy, the polity and the culture—was a rather backward and rigid society made up of low-motivated, mutually suspicious and grumbling individuals. Gorbachev's reforms came too late, were not radical enough, and had the perverse effects of disappointment, relaxing discipline all around, and eroding the authority of the state (see details in Bunge 1998:205-211).

In sum, the systemic approach is superior to both individualism and holism because, instead of studying either empty wholes or individuals that only share a context, it focuses on social systems and the mechanisms that make them tick, namely the interpersonal ties. Interaction, especially participation, is the mortar of society. The context or institutional framework is nothing but the social system (or supersystem) within which individuals and groups act. And the situation that methodological individualists invoke is nothing but the momentary state of such system. (For a general theory of social systems see Bunge 1979.)

Conclusion

Neither of the two most influential approaches to the study and management of social affairs is completely adequate, let alone practically efficient. Individualism is deficient because it underrates or even overlooks the bonds among people, and holism because it plays down individual action. By contrast, systemism makes room for both agency and structure. Moreover, it emphasizes the role of the environment, and suggests studying or altering the mechanisms of both social stasis and social change. The consequence for political philosophy and social-policy design is that systemism takes into account social values (ignored by individualists) as well as individual values (held in contempt by holists). Hence, it is more likely than its rivals to inspire and defend policies that combine competition with cooperation, and enhance individual welfare and liberty while strengthening or reforming the requisite institutions.

References

Baldi, Stephane. 1998. Normative versus social constructivist processes in the allocation of citations: a network-analytic model, *American Sociological Review* 63: 829-846.

Becker, Gary S. 1976. *The Economic Approach to Human Behavior.* Chicago: University of Chicago Press.

Boudon, Raymond. 1974. *Education, Opportunity and Social Inequality.* New York: Wiley.

——.1998. The necessary evolution of rational choice theory, *American Journal of Sociology* 104:817-28.

Bunge, Mario. 1974. *Treatise on Basic Philosophy*, vol. 1: *Sense and Reference.* Dordrecht-Boston: Reidel [Kluwer].

——.1979. *Treatise on Basic Philosophy*, vol. 4: *A World of Systems.* Dordrecht-Boston:
Reidel (Kluwer).

——.1996. *Finding Philosophy in Social Science.* New Haven, CT: Yale University Press.

——.1998. *Social Science under Debate.* Toronto: University of Toronto Press.

——.1999. *The Sociology-Philosophy Connection.* New Brunswick, NJ: Transaction Publishers.

Card, David E. 1995. *Myth and Measurement: The New Economics of the Minimum Wage.* Princeton, NJ: Princeton University Press.

Coleman, James S. 1990. *Foundations of Social Theory.* Cambridge, MA: Harvard University Press.

Collins, Randall. 1998. *The Sociology of Philosophies: A Global Theory of Intellectual Change.* Cambridge, MA: Harvard University Press.

Fogel, Robert W. 1994. Economic growth, population theory, and physiology: The bearing of long-term processes on the making of economic policy, *American Economic Review* 84: 369-95.

Hardy, Godfrey H. 1967. *A Mathematician's Apology.* Foreword by C. P. Snow. Cambridge: Cambridge University Press.

Harrington, Anne. 1996. *Reenchanted Science: Holism in German Culture from Wilhelm II to Hitler.* Princeton, NJ: Princeton University Press.

Hedström, Peter and Richard Swedberg (eds.). 1998. *Social Mechanisms: An Analytical Approach to Social Theory.* Cambridge: Cambridge University Press.

Hirschman, Albert O. 1981. *Essays in Trespassing: Economics to Politics and Beyond.* Cambridge: Cambridge University Press.

Latour, Bruno and Steve Woolgar. 1979. *Laboratory Life: The Social Construction of Scientific Facts.* London and Beverly Hills, CA: Sage.

Merton, Robert K. 1973. *The Sociology of Science: Theoretical and Empirical Investigations.* Chicago: University of Chicago Press.

Smelser, Neil and Richard Swedberg (eds). 1994. *The Handbook of Economic Sociology.* Princeton, NJ: Princeton University Press; New York: Russell Sage Foundation.

Soros, George. 1998. *The Crisis of Global Capitalism (Open Society Endangered).* New York: Public Affairs.

Tilly, Charles 1998. *Durable Inequality.* Berkeley: University of California Press.

Tocqueville, Alexis de 1998[1856]. *The Old Regime and the French Revolution.* Vol. 1. Trans. A. S. Kahan. Chicago: University of Chicago Press.

Wolpert, Lewis. 1992. *The Unnatural Nature of Science.* London and Boston: Faber and Faber.

5

Rational? Agents

Storrs McCall[1]

Introduction

Practical deliberation—*bouleusis*—is discussed by Aristotle in books 3 and 6 of the *Nicomachean Ethics*. Although Aristotle doesn't mention this, it is necessary to distinguish practical deliberation from what may be called "cognitive deliberation." Cognitive deliberation is deliberation over whether something is true or false, while practical deliberation is over what to do. In jury trials for example the jury is asked to decide the cognitive question, is the accused guilty as charged? Its deliberations concern this matter exclusively. If the judgment is "guilty," the judge must deliberate about something quite different, viz. what sentence to impose. The jury's deliberations are cognitive, the judge's practical.[2] In this chapter, I shall be concerned with practical deliberation.

Aristotle makes two remarks about deliberation that are familiar to every philosopher: first that we deliberate about means not ends, and secondly that we deliberate about things that are in our power and can be done (EN 1112a30, 1112b11-16, 1139b6, 1140a32). I need a table; to make a table requires a hammer and saw; I have a hammer but no saw; so let me go out and buy a saw. Again a doctor, *qua* doctor, does not deliberate about whether a patient should be healed, but *how to heal him. No* one will disagree with this. To be sure, one can imagine circumstances in which a doctor might deliberate over whether a patient should be healed, say if there were 1,000 patients and drugs for only 500. But in this case the doctor isn't really deliberating about ends, but about the practical problem of how to treat as many people as possible with the means available. If a doctor were truly to deliberate about ends and ask for

125

example, "Is healing worthwhile?" then that would fall under cognitive rather than practical deliberation.

What exactly is deliberation? In what follows I try to give a philosophically adequate account of it, and to answer some difficult questions. I finish up by speculating about what sorts of structures and neurophysiological functioning in the brain would make possible in real life the philosophical description of the deliberative process that I have given.

Deliberation

Let's start off with a concrete example. Marsha has to decide whether to accept an offer of graduate study in philosophy at UBC, Western Ontario or McGill. Call these alternatives A, B and C. Each one has its advantages and its disadvantages, and it is important to make the right decision. Marsha deliberates.

The first step in the deliberative process is to be clear about the alternatives, to represent them accurately and keep them in focus. Is the list exhaustive? Should she make a last-minute application to McMaster, where her sister is studying? Should she simply do nothing, and not accept any of the offers? Call this last option *D,* the do-nothing alternative. Let's suppose that A, *B,* C and *D* exhaust the alternatives facing her, and that each one is a "live" alternative in the sense that (i) she can choose it, and (ii) if she chooses it her choice determines what happens subsequently. Thus if she chooses UBC, she goes to UBC. We may imagine that Marsha has lined up three envelopes on her desk, addressed to UBC, Western and McGill. All she has to do is to put a stamp on one of them and mail it, or alternatively forget about graduate study. The first requirement for deliberation, then, is the existence of a "choice set," a set of two or more alternative courses of action (A, *B, C, D,*...) each of which it is physically possible for the deliberator to perform or implement, and which together exhaust the available options.

Once the choice set has been established, the process of deliberation begins in earnest. Each option has its advantages, which constitute the reasons for choosing it, and its disadvantages, which constitute the reasons for not choosing it. I shall call these *deliberation reasons.* For example UBC has made a generous scholarship offer, but on the other hand has no member of staff who works directly in Marsha's area of interest. These facts constitute positive and negative deliberation reasons for A, and there will be other positive and negative deliberation reasons for B, C, and *D*. In deliberation, we weigh deliberation reasons. We compare their relative strength with the aim of arriving at an overall comparative evaluation. The process of evaluation is normally but not invariably the most time-consuming part of deliberation, and ideally should result in a list of the options ordered by preference.

Once evaluation is completed, it might seem that the deliberative process is at an end. But this is not so. There is one more step, frequently ignored in studies of rational choice and decision but still essential: the element of choice or decision itself It may seem difficult to imagine, once an ordered evaluation of the options has been made, what more a deliberator could need. But suppose the first two alternatives are very close in the ordering? Suppose they come out equal? What if the deliberator is faced with a difficult decision? Even in the case where an evaluation is unambiguous, with a clear-cut winner, something else besides evaluation is needed for action. The missing element is what Aristotle call *prohairesis,* deliberative choice.

More needs to be said about *prohairesis,* but we should first sum up what has been established so far. Our philosophical account of deliberation has distinguished three separate components of the deliberative process, ordered in strict temporal sequence:

    (i)   Representation of the alternatives,

    (ii)   Evaluation,

    (iii)   Choice.

With decision, which is choice of one of the alternatives, the deliberative process ends. We turn now to decisions and the reasons for them, the latter being distinct from the deliberation reasons for the different options.

In deliberation we weigh and assess deliberation reasons, each being a reason for or against one of the alternatives. When eventually we decide, and choose one of the options, there is normally also a reason why that option was selected over the others. I shall call the latter an *explanation reason, or,* occasionally, a decision *reason.* In the deliberative process there are deliberation reasons, i.e. the reasons for or against the different options, but there are also explanation reasons, which are the reasons why, after examination of the deliberation reasons, one of the options is chosen.

A principal objective of this paper is to be clear about the exact difference between deliberation reasons and explanation reasons. Without a good understanding of the difference, I don't think we can know what deliberation is. Therefore I shall spend some time discussing the relationship between them.

Deliberation and Explanation Reasons

First, is it certain that a sharp line can be drawn between deliberation reasons and explanation reasons? On the face of it, yes. Deliberation reasons, in the deliberative process, have a relatively long life. Some may be present from the start, as when a diner at a restaurant perceives an excellent reason for choosing a chocolate mousse dessert at the very moment he becomes aware that it is on the menu. Others may emerge later, when the calorie count of the mousse is compared with that of the fruit salad. The explanation reason, on the other hand, comes into existence only at the end of the deliberation, when the choice has been made. As long as there is not yet a choice or decision, there cannot as a matter of logic be any explanation of it. Deliberation reasons are reasons for deciding this way or that; explanation reasons are reasons *that* or why a certain decision was made. A typical explanation reason might be of the form "X chose A rather than *B* because in the end X attached more weight to the deliberation reasons for A than to the deliberation reasons for *B.*" If it exists at all, the explanation reason comes into existence only when the decision comes into existence. This isn't the case with deliberation reasons. Hence the two are quite different.

That being said, we still want to know more about explanation reasons. Could they perhaps be associated, or identified, with comparisons among deliberation reasons, or more strictly perhaps with *comparative rankings* of alternatives based on deliberation reasons? If Marsha for example were to conclude that the program and the second language opportunities at McGill were more important than the funding and the friends she has in Vancouver, would this not be a perfectly good explanation reason for the decision to go to McGill? We must proceed carefully here. A reason for going to McGill, even though it results from a comparative weighing of all the deliberation reasons, is still a deliberation reason. One can, if Aristotle is right in maintaining there is such a thing as *akrasia,* conclude that overall the reasons for doing X outweigh the reasons for doing Y, and still do Y. In Davidson's memorable example someone may conclude that there is nothing to gain and everything to lose from drinking a can of paint, and still one day drink it.[3] No matter how strong it is, and how much it dominates all other deliberation reasons, a deliberation reason is not an explanation reason. Not until the decision has been taken, and the choice made, does the explanation reason come into existence.

Secondly, must every decision have an explanation reason? Or are there some totally irrational decisions, for which there is no explanation at all? Is the difference between a decision that is made lightly, casually or thoughtlessly, and a decision that is made carefully and deliberately, the difference between a decision which lacks, and a decision which has, an explanation reason? These questions are not easy to answer. Let us start with Buridan-type situations, in which a choice must or should be made, but in which there is absolutely no reason for choosing one thing rather than another.

Buridan's ass starved to death half-way between two piles of hay because there was nothing to incline his choice towards A rather than B.[4] Here the deliberation reasons for A and B are equally balanced, and as a result no decision is taken. A similar problem, based on fear rather than desire, is the "railroad dilemma."[5] What fascinates us in these examples is not just the spectre of decisional paralysis, but the feeling that the outcome—death by indecision—is in a genuine sense an affront to reason. If the ass had been rational, or more rational than he was, he would not have starved. He would have drawn straws and said "Long left, short right." Failing this, if he had been clever enough, he could simply have made an arbitrary or criterionless choice (Olfstad, 1961; McAdam, 1965). If you believe this is impossible, reflect on how you manage to choose one of a hundred identical tins of tomato soup in a supermarket. The example of the soup tins was a favorite of Macnamara's, who used it with great effect in discussion. If you made the mistake of saying that an arbitrary choice in these circumstances was difficult or impossible, that would indicate that you, like Buridan's ass, were not very intelligent.

Moving from Buridan-type examples to cases where there is a significant difference between the alternatives, but where the deliberation reasons are still equally balanced, the same question arises: can a choice be made for which there is no explanation or decision reason? If Marsha finds it difficult or impossible to decide between UBC and McGill because between them there is "nothing to choose," can she use some tie-breaking mechanism like a coin and in so doing make a choice which lacks an explanation reason? Not really. Although in this case the explanation is different from what it would have been if the evaluation process had produced a winner, an explanation reason still exists. If Marsha is asked why she chose UBC rather than McGill, she may answer that she flipped a coin. The reason why she chose UBC is that the coin fell heads. There need be nothing irrational about this. Compared to the paralysis of the Buridan example, and bearing in mind the approaching deadline for mailing the letter of acceptance, it is a supremely rational procedure. Sometimes we just have to stop deliberating and decide. It's a sign of rationality that we're able to do this.

Although the conclusion towards which we're moving seems to be that decisions always have explanation reasons, even if the reason in question may be something like "Because the coin fell heads," there still remain other cases to be examined. All our examples have been decisions that were made carefully, thoughtfully, deliberately. Even if a coin had to be used to break ties, its use was deliberate and rational. But what of decisions that are taken carelessly, without adequate thought? What if we are inebriated, and our deliberative powers impaired? Such cases may provide examples of decisions without explanation reasons.

The making of a decision, like the activity of evaluation, is a rational process. In fact deliberation as a whole is a rational process, and each of the components which make it up is subject to norms by which it can be judged.

(1) In the formation of the choice set the alternatives should be realizable, and each option should be such that the decision of the deliberator alone is sufficient to implement it, or to initiate its implementation. The alternatives should also be exhaustive: no important or significant alternative should be excluded from the choice set.

(2) For the process of evaluation, different norms apply. Have all the deliberation reasons for all the alternatives been recognized and collected? Has each deliberation reason been appropriately weighted? If there are several deliberation reasons for the same alternative, has the total weighting of all of them, including possible negative reasons, been reasonably assessed? Finally, given appropriate total weighting for each alternative, has the comparison between them been carried out honestly and without bias? Or if there is bias, is the deliberator conscious of it, rather than having it work behind the scenes and affect the evaluation without the deliberator being aware of it? These are the questions to be considered if an evaluation is to be judged rational. It is true that frequently we lack sufficient insight and self-knowledge to be sure whether in a par-

ticular case we are giving due and appropriate weight to a set of deliberation reasons, particularly if the decision is one that touches us emotionally. In many cases the degree of objectivity and detachment required may be beyond us. Nevertheless, if the deliberative process is to be a rational one, a certain level of objectivity and self-knowledge are needed.

Finally (3) there are, in addition to the above requirements, norms for rational choice. The first requirement is that to be considered rational, a choice or decision must have an explanation reason. If for example a choice is made for no reason at all, not even with the aid of a randomizing device like a coin as part of the decision making process, then the decision cannot be considered rational. Furthermore, even in cases where an explanation reason is provided by the deliberator norms of rationality still apply to it, and the rational assessment of a decision must take them into account. For example, if Marsha were to explain her decision to go to UBC by saying "Because I'm a Libra," the relevance and consequently the rationality of this supposed explanation could be questioned. Decision therefore, like choice-set formation and evaluation, is a procedure which it is appropriate to subject to rational norms, and to judge rational only if it satisfies these norms. The same applies, mutatis mutandis, to the whole deliberative process.

An important question which should be addressed is whether an explanation reason for a decision is a cause of that decision. The immediate answer would seem to be no. An explanation reason for a decision comes into existence only once the decision is made, while a cause should antedate the thing it causes. The whole question of causality and its role in the deliberative process is nevertheless of great interest, and must be looked at carefully.

First, our discussion from the start has taken us outside the framework of causal determinism, since the very existence of a choice set with two or more physically realizable alternatives is not consistent with determinism. One might attempt to remove the inconsistency by requiring that in any choice set one and only one alternative was causally possible, the deliberator necessarily being ignorant of which one that was. As long as the deliberator believed (falsely) that each alternative in the choice set was realizable, deliberation could proceed as usual, the eventual decision being taken in favor of the one option that was in fact open. This is deliberation according to the script that would be written for it by a determinist. The re-writing does indeed remove the inconsistency, but at the price of (i) abandoning choice sets with two or more real alternatives, and (ii) drawing a veil of ignorance over the eyes of deliberators as to which is the sole choosable option. Behind the veil, "deliberation" can proceed. But re-writing the script in this way is unnecessary, if it can be shown that it is simpler and more elegant to abandon determinism.

Since the 1920s, quantum mechanics has provided the example of a science which is probabilistic rather than deterministic. As a result, replacing deterministic models of deliberation by indeterministic ones is not such a daunting or unthinkable project today as it would have been for Hume, or Mill or Brentano, or any philosopher working within the paradigm of Newtonian science. This is not the place to speculate exactly how or in what respect the overall neuronal functioning of the brain could be regarded as probabilistic rather than strictly deterministic, but at least the hypothesis that the brain is a complex indeterministic mechanism makes sense, is testable, and may one day be confirmed or falsified.

What is important for present purposes is the fact that if the central nervous system functions probabilistically rather than deterministically, then this functioning permits the formation of choice sets in deliberation. At the neurophysiological level, a choice set requires different physically possible neural states $n(A)$, $n(B)$, $n(C)$,... corresponding to the different actions A, B, C, ..., the states being such that if n(A) obtains then A is performed, if $n(B)$ obtains B is performed, etc. Just as each of A, B, C..excludes the others, so each of $n(A)$, $n(B)$, $n(C)$,...excludes the others. These states are "missing" states of the brain which neuroscientists should one day be able to specify and describe, but which during deliberation are not actual existents. What is essential however for the existence of a choice set is that throughout the deliberative process each one of the neural states $n(A)$, $n(B)$, $n(C)$,...should be physically possible, i.e. capable of becoming actual at the end of the process. Since each state is incompatible with the others, the only way this could be the case would be if the brain functioned indeterministically. Indeterministic neural functioning consequently underpins choice set formation in the sense that it makes it possible, that it is a necessary condition for its existence. If we believe in choice sets, with each option separately realizable, I don't see how we can avoid regarding the operations of the brain as in some yet-to-be-discovered way indeterministic.

The next step is to consider probabilities. If each of the outcome neural states $n(A)$, $n(B)$, is physically possible, it will have a probability value, and the probability values of all the members of a given choice set will sum to one. Needless to say, in keeping with the idea of the brain as a complex indeterministic mechanism, we are talking of objective probability values, not epistemic ones. With the introduction of probability comes the possibility of saying something about causality and perhaps ultimately being able to conclude whether deliberation can be considered a causal process.

At the beginning of the deliberative process, once the choice set is formed, the existence of the underpinning neurological mechanism, with the different target neural states, gives each alternative of the choice set a precise probability value. An interesting and important question is whether these probabilities change during deliberation.

If the probabilities change during the deliberative process, considerations of probabilistic causality may apply. For example if J is some factor that enters consciousness during deliberation (a thought, a desire, a fact, a memory, a goal)—and if A is one of the options of the deliberator's choice set, then if

$$p(A|J) > p(A|\text{not-}J)$$

we may say that *J* is a (prima facie) *probabilistic cause* of A.[6] This is not equivalent to saying that J causes the alternative A to be chosen, since together with the above inequality we may also have

$$p(B|J) > p(B|\text{not}|J),$$

and could not be the cause of A being chosen and also *B* being chosen. Hence probabilistic causality is of limited interest in connection with deliberation.

Again, the factor J may increase the probability of option A's being realized, but can it increase it to unity? Can any deliberation reason, or deliberative factor, be of such strength that it makes it physically or causally impossible for any alternative other than A to be selected? Might it, before the choice is made, reduce the choice set to a single choosable option? This takes us back once more to determinism. One cannot rule out the possibility that during deliberation something should occur, e.g., paralysis or a violent fit, which restricts the alternatives to one option only. But such cases are so far removed from the norm as not to qualify as instances of deliberation at all. At the end of a deliberation we are left either with the choice set with which we began, or with a reduced choice set, or an enlarged one, but in any case a set consisting of at least two members. The probabilities of these options can change, but if any of them reaches the value one deliberation ceases.

A final question concerning probabilities, which reintroduces the subject of explanation or decision reasons, is this. At the end of the deliberative process, before a decision is made, the deliberator is faced with a choice set of different alternatives A, *B*, C,..., each with a corresponding neural state *n(A), n(B), n*(C),... The objective probabilities of realizing these different options, and hence of the different target neural states becoming actualized, will not in normal circumstances be known to the deliberator. Each probability will in fact be non-zero and some may be exceedingly small. Is it possible for a deliberator to choose, deliberately and intentionally, an alternative of very low objective probability?

From the point of view of probabilistic science, the occurrence of an event of low probability is not impossible, but would not be expected. If it happened, the only explanation that could be given would be something like "By the laws of chance, improbable events do occasionally occur. By pure chance, a bridge player may be dealt a hand of 13 spades." There exists no better causal/probabilistic explanation than this of why an improbable event occurs. But this isn't true of a choice made by a deliberator. No matter how objectively improbable the chosen option may be, a perfectly good explanation reason for the choice may be forthcoming. The deliberator who has for years drunk nothing but whiskey may say that this time he chose a Tia Maria, no matter how objectively unlikely his choice may have been, because he felt like it.

The lesson here, I think, is that in the realm of deliberation and choice there may occur events for which there is no causal/probabalistic explanation, but for which there is an intentional explanation. Some intentional explanations may be of the form "Ivan chose the Tia Maria because he felt like it;" others may be of the form "Unbelievably, Sally isn't here today because she deliberately and intentionally chose to go to jail." Perhaps the clearest examples of intentional explanations are those given in circumstances where non-intentional explanations, i.e. causal/probabilistic ones, don't exist. But detailed examination of the difference between intentional and causal/probabilistic explanation is a lengthy matter, and must await another occasion.

Conclusion

Summing up, I began by listing the three essential components of a deliberation. These are, in strict temporal order, (i) choice set formation, (ii) evaluation, (iii) decision. In evaluation the reasons for and against the different options (deliberation reasons) are both appropriately weighted and weighed by the deliberator. Eventually one option is chosen. Each element of the deliberative process is subject to rational norms by which it may be judged, a common but non-mandatory norm of element (iii), choice or decision, being the existence of an explanation reason for the choice once it is made. If choice set formation is underpinned by an indeterministic neural mechanism, with a specific neural state $n(Ai)$ and a specific probability corresponding to each alternative Ai of the set, then the explanation of why the deliberator chooses one of the alternatives will not in general be a causal/probabilistic explanation based on those probabilities. Instead it will be an intentional explanation. The precise relationship between intentional and causal/probabilistic explanations in deliberation remains to be investigated.

Notes

1. John Macnamara and I talked about many things, over many years, in the area of practical deliberation and intention. As I write this paper I imagine his voice, objecting, sometimes chiding, but always encouraging, and I dedicate these pages to the memory of a true friend.
2. The distinction between practical and cognitive deliberation is discussed in McCall (1994), p. 254, and McCall (1987).
3. Davidson (1980[1963]), p. 4.
4. The dilemma antedates Buridan. See Rescher (1959) for why the problem of "Buridan's ass" should more justly be known as "al-Farabi's dates." Buridan's problem is discussed in Bratman (1987).
5. You are hiking with your partner in a mountainous wooded country and come to a horseshoe shaped valley with a railway track at the bottom. While crossing the track a heavy branch falls on your partner's leg, pinning him/her to the rails, and while trying vainly to move the branch you hear the whistle of an approaching train. Unfortunately, the echoes in the valley make it impossible to tell which direction the train is coming from. Game theory tells us you have a 50% chance of saving your partner's life if you pick a direction arbitrarily and run as fast as possible down the track to stop the train, but how many of us would have the strength of mind to do this as the whistle grows louder and the uncertainty becomes more agonising?
6. Suppes (1970), p. 12; Fetzer (1988), p. 118; Cartwright (1989), p. 55; Eells (1991), p. 56; Devito (1997). This definition of probabilistic cause is normally supplemented by requiring that $p(A|J) > p(A|\text{not}J)$ in all partitions of A's causal factor-space, meaning in all circumstances in which combinations of other causal factors of A are held fixed and only J is allowed to vary. In the case of deliberation,

however, we are concerned with a single unique process, not in general repeatable, and so this supplemental requirement cannot be met. Nor would it be appropriate to require, in addition to $A|J)>p(A|\text{not}|J)$, that the anticipated probabilistic effect A actually occurs, since if A occurs then in the probability calculus $p(A)=1$, and hence $p(A|C)=1$ for an C, provided $p(C)\neq0$.

References

Bratman, Michael. 1987. *Intention, Plans, and Practical Reason*. Cambridge, MA: Harvard University Press.

Cartwright, Nancy. 1989. *Nature's Capacities and their Measurement*. Oxford: Clarendon Press.

Davidson, Donald. 1980 (1963). Actions, reasons and causes, in Donald Davidson, *Essays on Actions and Events*. Oxford: Clarendon Press.

DeVito, Scott. 1997. *Probabilistic Causality Without Propensities*, typescript, University of Pittsburgh.

Eells, Ellery. 1991. *Probabilistic Causality*. Cambridge: Cambridge University Press.

Fetzer, James H. 1988. Probabilistic metaphysics, in James Fetzer (ed.), *Probability and Causality*. Dordrecht: D. Reidel Publishing Company.

McAdam, James. 1965. Choosing flippantly or non-rational choice, *Analysis* 25:132-6.

McCall, Storrs. 1987. Decision, *Canadian Journal of Philosophy* 17:261-87.

McCall Storrs. 1994. *A Model of the Universe*. Oxford: Oxford University Press.

Ofstad, Harald. 1961. *An Inquiry into the Freedom of Decision*. Oslo: Norwegian University Press.

Rescher, Nicholas. 1959. Choice without preference, *Kant-Studien* 51:142-75.

Suppes, Patrick. 1970. *A Probabilistic Theory of Causality*. Amsterdam: North-Holland Publishing Company.

6

Penser la guerre, Clausewitz

John A. Hall

Introduction

The conference from which this volume derives sought to maximize interest and to improve cognition by bringing together proponents and opponents of rational choice theory. Accordingly, I felt a slightly unwelcome guest for the most basic of reasons. Either-or oppositions, so beloved of Levi-Strauss, are very often the bane of human inquiry. To place rational choice theorists against their critics seems to me to reify an entirely false opposition. Differently put, both sides on their own advance positions of little merit. What matters is finding a middle way. All of this is contentious, and it deserves at least minimal justification.

There is everything to be said for the view that human beings calculate. The view of the world that says that people are so constrained conceptually by some system of norms or ideas, that they cannot think in any other way at all, seems to me profoundly unconvincing. Meaning does not make the world go round. Belief systems tend to be loose and baggy monsters so filled with escape clauses as to lack the capacity for constraining thought. That this is so brings us back to questions of interest and calculation: we need to know why a particular clause in a belief system makes sense to, or is advanced by, a particular group in particular circumstances.

Yet preferences are not the same at all historical moments-as many wedded to rational choice style theory imagine. One thinks in this context of Jeremy Bentham's reply to a critic who wondered how much a principle of rational material self-interest helped us understand the behavior of someone who lashed himself until he bled—to the effect that this was the form that self-interest took for that particular person. If you define self-interest like that everything becomes completely tautological and does not actually get us anywhere. So we need to think about the way in which preferences are formed and structured.

It is within this middle range, it seems to me, where people calculate as best they can but within a certain set of ideas, that the most interesting work is currently being done within the social sciences as a whole. People who produce sophisticated work on rational choice theory know these things extremely well, and we can learn a great deal from them.

Normally I do not write on a topic when I know I have to say things which are rather banal and boring. But on this occasion I will do so because of a comment made by Michael Smith in a characteristically brilliant recent public lecture. He made a contrast, in talking about different types of theories, between a rigorous, clear, more or less rational choice view of the world, and "something fuzzier." There was an echo here of William James's distinction between tough and the tender minded. Smith certainly exemplifies toughness himself. But is rational choice theory really so very rigorous? Certainly the attraction of rational choice theory is its hidden promise, the notion that perhaps it can really deliver the goods in some hard and powerful way for social sciences as a whole. I have already hinted at doubts as to this claim. But let me try to prove my case, to insist that rational choice matters but that its salience and intellectual power should not be exaggerated, by turning to Clausewitz. More particularly, my title is that of Raymond Aron's (1976) great book; this is no accident as my purpose here is to highlight the contribution that Aron's interpretation of Clausewitz makes to the understanding of rationality.

Soldier and Theorist

Clausewitz is not well known by social theorists, for all that *On War* is one of the greatest treatises of social theory ever written. Hence it may be useful to recall some biographical facts of the Prussian soldier and theorist. Particular attention must be paid to the arguments in Book 11 of *On War* for it is here that the soldier most clearly confronts the theorist.

Clausewitz joined the Prussian army at the age of twelve in 1792 and he had, therefore, by the end of his life, accumulated an enormous amount of historical experience. He was trained in the old-fashioned eighteenth-century "war of the minuets." This was a formal style of warfare, designed to minimize deaths within a very controlled setting. Frederick the Great, for example, was desperate not to have his troops killed if he could at all possibly avoid it. But the young Clausewitz was at Auerstadt and experienced defeat at the hands of Napoleon. This Napoleonic took things to the extremes, insitituting a no holds barred concentration of force in every possible way. One point to be underlined here is that Clausewitz was as tough-minded as one could possibly be. He knew what battle and killing was lik—that describes the experience of warfare in some detail.

He was also tough as a theorist. He had no time whatsoever for those practical men who did not want to theorize at all. Clausewitz believed that such a position was useless, he maintained that we must try to be as rigorous as we can be. We need theory, he said. People need tools with which to think. But he was also tough as a theorist in another way. He says that there are a lot of military theorists who are absolutely useless. While they may look tough on the outside, all they really do is to produce "truth-machines." Inside they are soft, weak and misleading. Moreover, they appear to be more rigorous than reality allows us to be. Instead what we need is some theory which allows us to think in open situations, and that is precisely the way that Clausewitz himself theorized.

One further comment about Clausewitz's rather dramatic life. Although he started working on his book in 1815 (he eventually died in 1831), it is only in 1827 that he finally fully worked out what he wanted to say. It is only in the very first chapter of this 700-page book that he reaches a mature theory of war. He never had a chance to revise the rest of the book to be in line with these last observations of the first chapter. Initially he was so enamored of Napoleon's revolutionizing of war that his initial definition of war was something to the effect that the logic of the situation always leads one to go to the extremes. One must never stop, if one stops one will lose, one must escalate and escalate until victory is achieved. However, from 1827 onwards Clausewitz started to change his mind. This was mainly due to the fact that not only was he trained in eighteenth-century warfare, and a witness to Napoleon's many victories, he also saw Napoleon defeated. Near the end of his life, Clausewitz started to calculate, to think what it meant that Napoleon had lost. He also started, ever so slightly, to change his mind about his original position.

For example, in the first chapter of *On War* there is a crucial passage where he says that war logically—that is to say in a Platonic sense—should escalate to the extremes, yet in real life it seldom does. He then goes on, in a combination of descriptive and prescriptive statements, to say that war is actually a trinity made up of the politician, the military commander, and the people. For Clausewitz, the most important element in this trinity is the politician. That is to say that the political purpose of war must be kept in mind at all times, otherwise the consequences could be disastrous. Napoleon really did not pay enough attention to this aspect of war, observed Clausewitz, in comparison to someone like Frederick the Great who calculated much more carefully. Perhaps it was for that reason that Frederick the Great had, in the long run, gained more with his various campaigns. Clausewitz, then, has a very clear definition of war, however, he does not really explain why it is that war is in some instances limited and unlimited in other instances. I will offer an explanation designed to complement Clausewitz in a moment.

The Nature of Theory in International Relations

First however, I want to say some general things about Clausewitz's view of theory. He says, very definitely, that no theory of war can be a science. Such a thing, in his view, is an impossibility. He also argued that anyone who claims that a theory of war can be a science is simply producing another misleading truth machine. Eventually this will cause more problems than it is worth. He develops, at a basic level, three reasons why he thinks this is so; all of which have to do with the nature of rationality.

The first reason that war is not a science is that it always has some friction attached to it. It is like being in a swimming pool: everything that happens within it moves rather slowly. It is also like Tolstoy's description of Borodino in *War and Peace:* a fog comes in, you lose touch with your troops, it rains (and there is much discussion of weather in Clausewitz) and you can not really keep control of things. Everything looks simple but really everything, in fact, becomes extremely complicated. Therefore, clear, simple plans become much more difficult to execute than one originally imagined, and any simple, naive, rational plan will often get one into trouble.

The second reason, and I believe that Clausewitz is the first theorist to point this out, is that morale matters enormously in war. This is so because of the importance of friction. Morale matters in a number of ways, but especially in terms of the military commander. The military commander needs to have certain, very particular, qualities. It is very much like the poor woman on the railroad track whose experience is theorised by Storrs McCall in this volume: the first quality one needs is determination. In the middle of battle, Clausewitz says, there is always a moment when it seems as though something is going to go wrong. In this instance what one needs is determination to make a plan and the courage to stick with it. However, neither obstinacy nor a mindless digging oneself into a grave will do, rather one needs the capacity to carry on acting even when things are going against you. The commander also must have the special capacity, very much like a chess player, of being able to see the whole board. He needs to gain perspective over the whole situation. In a sense the commander should have certain moral qualities and so, in a way, should his troops. I will also point out that these moral qualities that I am speaking about are the ones most necessary for battle.

Yet, it is the third reason that is most important in Clausewitz's view when arguing that war can not be a science. In a way it is again close to what Storrs McCall said in his chapter: War—like life—is a dialectic. One is constantly in a duel with someone who is often like oneself. They have different levels of behaviors. For instance, I know that you might fight in a particular way. If you know that I know you will fight in this way you might fight in yet another way. But if I am really clever I might be able to guess that actually you have figured out that I know that you know that I know. This is, in a very real sense, an endless game of mirrors, an endless regress. It cannot be closed, it is an open world and we cannot have a formal theory of these things.

However, Clausewitz insists that theory is still necessary. He says that theory can help us to think more and more clearly. Yet, while war is not a science, it definitely is not an art either. On the contrary, it is very different from art because of this process of interaction that I just mentioned. It is not like you with a pen and paper trying to write a poem: something or someone is talking back to you. Clausewitz says that war is not a science and not an art, it is similar to commerce and politics. By commerce he does not mean capitalism, instead he means mercantilism (an economic duel between people). In fact Marx and Engels and even Lenin all adore Clausewitz because they think he is speaking about capitalism when in fact he is speaking about mercantilism.

The major thing that a theory can do is to train judgment. Theory must train people, through means that are carefully analyzed, to be flexible. The crucial thing however, is that these people must then leave the theory behind in the classroom because it will be of no use to them once they get into battle. That is so because everything there depends upon the capacity to think freshly and not with stale formulas.

But is Clausewitz really saying anything against rational choice theory? Is it not the case that this concern with interaction between two separate worlds is one of the things that actually created game theory in its strongest form? The RAND Corporation, for example, developed the ideas of game theory because of the nuclear revolution. Cannot these ideas be modeled in exactly the same rational choice game theoretic game terms that this conference is about? The answer is: yes they can. Nonetheless, I still want to stick with Clausewitz, in a sense unfairly and in an ad hoc manner, because of the experience of Vietnam. Aron, in a tremendously moving lecture in 1968 at the height of Vietnam—remember that he was a sort of conservative, anticommunist French intellectual who had no trouble with the Americans fighting in Vietnam—said that Americans had forgotten how to think. Their military strategists had been so obsessed by this RAND Corporation style thinking, that they had forgotten what Clausewitz was saying. They had forgotten that one has to think and think most carefully about what the stake of the competition is for the other side. The Americans had slipped into a situation where they thought that they were speaking the same language when, in fact they had stopped thinking and they had stopped seeing the flexibility of the other side. They were totally outside of historical context and they had become a truth machine rather than thinking in an open system, as Clausewitz had suggested. I think that, therefore, there can be a tendency for this kind of game theory to mislead, because it can become "scientificity"—or overdoing it. We need to be as rational and as scientific as the material will allow. However in the case of the Vietnam war I think that the Americans got it slightly wrong.

Conditions of Rationality in International Affairs

Let me now turn to Clausewitz's move, at the end of his life, towards the more complicated definition of war already noted. In particular I want to point to his discovery that wars do not always go to the extreme. He did not actually explain this. Marvelous work in this area has been done by people writing within a rational choice perspective. As an example we could look to Keohane's *After Hegemony* (1984). This book seeks to explain the 'long peace' that had settled in amongst the advanced nations after 1945. Keohane's argument was that this peace had become an iterated game, the same set of players sitting down time and time again (think of the G7 meetings) and talking. If you, for example, sit down once with a group of people it might make sense to try to take advantage of them. However, if you know that you are going to meet them again then you know that they might try to do the same thing to you. As a result, a certain moderation is built into things simply because the game is played over again and again.

However, I still think that there is something missing here. What I think is missing is that Keohane never really explains why it is that this community ever gets born in the first place. This is the question of norm creation. The point that I want to make here is that if you just look at the absolute pure logic of realism, it would tell you that if you try to grab too much there will be a coalition of people against you. This is a point that Clausewitz makes against Napoleon, the fact that he was too greedy. Yet is that what really explains throughout history the periods of escalation and diminution of conflict?

One factor that explains the rise and fall of conflict over the ages are things that are very sociological, like trust and knowing other people. The periods where conflict has been diminished have been periods in which there have been norms amongst state leaders. These norms are not created rationally, in the sense that it was a rational decision to create those norms, but they are norms like Christian norms, eighteenth-century upper-class solidarity, and anti-revolutionary sentiment after 1815 designed to counter everthing that Napoleon had done. We can study these social processes in our own time--for example, in those CIA funded conferences after 1945, all of which created some kind of transitional sense or feeling. Such norms matter greatly. While Keohane may be very good at explaining how things work once the situation is established, he does not have a strong explanation for how the situation comes about in the first place.

A second condition helps quite as much to explain periods of diminished violence: it is the very ability of states themselves to calculate. The important point here is that states do not always calculate very well. States occasionally make disastrous mistakes. The

German state in the twentieth century, for example, decided on two occasions to fight a war on two fronts. On both occasions it was bound to lose. Why did it do so? Well, as sociologists we can say that the state did not know how to think because it did not have a proper state structure which could prioritize things.

Conclusion

Clausewitz often slips between description and prescription. What the latter consideration brings to mind is a change in tense. States should try to think. They need to establish state structures that can prioritize. This point is also evident in rational choice theory. Sometimes it appears as descriptive at an individual or even a group level, but actually and very often it is really prescriptive. There is a very great deal to be said at a normative level-as in this case-in favor of developing and spreading rationality. But that is a task to be achieved, precisely because the world is often not like that.

References

Aron, Raymond. 1976. *Penser la guerre, Clausewitz.* Paris: Gallimard.

Clausewitz, Carl von. 1976 (1831). *On War.* Michael Howard (ed. and trans.). Princeton, NJ: Princeton University Press.

Keohane, Robert. 1984. *After Hegemony: Cooperation and Discord in the World Political Economy.* Princeton, NJ: Princeton University Press.

7

On the Use of the Prisoners' Dilemma to Analyze the Relations Between Employment Security, Trust, and Effort

Michael R. Smith

Introduction

Programmatic treatments of the idea of economic sociology tend to emphasise two aspects of behavior: limits on calculative capacity and the diffuseness of motives. *Neoclassical* economics is inadequate, it is argued, because it fails to recognize the extent to which preferences—and therefore motivations—are diverse, unstable, and dependent on social milieus and situations (e.g., Zelizer, 1989; Zukin and DiMaggio, 1990: 23; Hirsch, Michaels and Friedman, 1990: 43; Swedberg, Himmelstrand and Brulin, 1990: 61; Elster, 1990a: 98; DiMaggio, 1990). This complexity in the environment of motives is itself a challenge to calculative capacities. There are multiple optima, poor and/or costly information, strategic interactions through which individuals have to adjust their choices of action on the basis of their expectations of the behavior of others, and some forms of behavior that can be considered irrational (Elster, 1990b).

Despite widespread and frequent assertions of the positions described above, political scientists and sociologists writing on economic phenomena display ambivalence. Accounts that assume clear and limited preferences and very highly developed calculative capacities remain common. In what follows I examine in some detail a rational choice approach, in terms of the so-called "prisoners' dilemma", to one particular economic problem—the relationship between employment security and work effort, although the argument can be applied to the entire employment contract.

Effort and Employment Security

Effort is problematic (e.g., Offe, 1985: 20-25). Employees vary in the extent to which they exert themselves, agree to move between tasks, or take initiative when initiative is called for. There is good reason to believe that average levels of effort—in the forms listed above—vary between work sites. It is also thought that there is variation across countries, with consequences for relative levels of competitiveness and aggregate economic performance.

A major component of the history of management is successive attempts to secure consistent effort from employees (e.g., Pollard, 1968). There are two standard approaches to doing so—supervision, and incentive systems. There are difficulties with each. Close supervision is costly and sometimes not technically feasible—for example, where work is remotely located or where it involves the exercise of skills that complicate supervisory judgments of effort. Piecework most directly ties pay to effort. It is the most reliable incentive system. But, among other difficulties, much work has team-like characteristics that make it impossible to attribute output to any particular individual. Other incentive systems that allocate rewards to groups encounter problems of free riding within those groups. Miller (1992) concludes that, for most jobs, suitable levels of effort cannot be achieved through supervision and incentive systems alone.

So what else is available to secure effort levels that ensure that firms and industries are competitive? One answer is that effort is most effectively secured if managers can earn the *trust* of their employees. A variety of measures can be used to accomplish this.[1] But in all versions of the argument *employment security* is a requisite.[2] The provision of employment security helps employees to trust their employer; in response, employees deploy amounts of effort that produce internationally competitive firm performance (e.g., Rosow and Zager, 1984: 16-38; Streeck, 1992: 21; 1997: 201; Miller, 1992: 116-118; Buttler and Walwei, 1993: 258-261; Osterman, 1988: 44-46, 61-67; Kochan and Osterman, 1994: 52-55). Note that the employment security that is thought to increase trust can take one of two forms. It can be *institutional*—that is, based on either law (as in Sweden or Germany) or custom and social pressure (as in "lifetime employment" in Japan). In each case, the right of employers to dismiss is limited. Or it can be de facto in the sense that, even in the absence of legal or social pressure, individual employers choose to refrain from dismissing (cf. Buechtemann, 1993: 7-8).[3]

In the rest of this chapter I examine an approach to constructing a theory linking the employment contract, through trust, to performance—that is to say, to *effort*. I examine rational choice analyses couched in terms of the logic of the prisoners' dilemma game.

De Facto Employment Security and the Prisoners' Dilemma

Assume, to start with, that the sort of matrix of payoffs that establishes the prisoners' dilemma describes reasonably well possible outcomes in labor relations. Employers offer a package of terms and conditions of employment. That package will include a variety of components: a wage level, a policy on the provision of information to employees, internal disciplinary procedures, and an approach to employment security. Some of these may be contractually specified; others, including employment security, may be part of an implicit contract. Employees offer in return some level of effort, including a degree of willingness or unwillingness to expend effort when the growth of wages slows or stops.

For the purposes of this chapter, I am particularly concerned with employment security. Employers may or may not provide employment security.[4] Employees may or may not exert more than the minimal amount of effort required by the existing supervisory arrangements and incentive schemes. The provision of effort and employment security coincides with the "cooperate" options in the game. The failure to provide employment security and effort coincide with the "defect" options. A schematic payoff matrix is diagrammed in figure 7.1.

Figure 7.1
Employment Security and the Prisoners' Dilemma

	EMPLOYEE	
	Effort, wage restraint	**Shirking, short-run wage maximization**
Employment security, etc.	Employer=High Employee=High	Employer=Very Low Employee=Very High
EMPLOYER		
Employment *in*security, etc.	Employer=Very High Employee=Very Low	Employer=Low Employee=Low

The point about this matrix is that, in the one-shot game, the best outcome for each party is to act self-interestedly while the other acts with generosity. Employers do best if their workforce expends significant amounts of effort, but the employer still responds to a temporary decline in demand by laying people off. Workers do best if they shirk but their employer guarantees them employment security. But to avoid the risk of doing very badly, employers lay off at will and employees shirk. Each ends up with small rewards whereas, had each followed the cooperative route (employment security, effort), each would have done better than they do *at the point at which they end up* (no employment security, shirk). That point is the Nash equilibrium where "no individual can gain by playing differently, given that opponents stick to their prescribed strategies" (Rizvi, 1994: 7). It diverges from the Pareto optimum (employment security, effort), from which no change would be possible without a loss in rewards to at least one of the parties (Miller 1992: 22-25).

A response to this is to argue that the relationship can better be described as an *iterated prisoners' dilemma game*—rather than as the one-shot version. That is to say, the choice of cooperating (employment security, effort) or not is (or may be) infinitely repeated. Endless repetition makes possible the use of a *tit-for-tat* strategy. The principle underlying it is the following: cooperate on the first round of the game then copy the other party's choice on all subsequent rounds. It would imply that in a first time period employers offer employment security and employees do not shirk. Then, mimicking the other's choice in all subsequent time periods, each continues to cooperate into the indefinite future. In Axelrod's tournaments this strategy produced better scores than any other (Axelrod, 1984).[5] It makes sense that it would. The payoff matrix for the game means that the aggregate scores produced by the continuous choice of the cooperative strategy by each party will produce the best overall result. The possibility of retaliation induces the other party not to defect. This, however, raises two questions. First, what does the tit-for-tat strategy have to do with *trust*—which features prominently in interpretations of the effects of employment security? Second, to what degree is it plausible to model labor relations as an iterated prisoners' dilemma game?[6]

Miller settles the first issue as follows: "Stable cooperation in a team shirking game requires that members of the group have high subjective probabilities that others are playing tit-for-tat—playing cooperatively as long as the others do. We will denote this latter belief state by the term 'trust'" (Miller, 1992: 186). In this approach trust is purely calculative. Employees trust their employer to follow a tit-for-tat strategy. They do not vest any emotional content in their relationship. They have no illusion that the employer has any concern with their welfare. Trust means that, like them, the employer has determined that tit-for-tat will yield the largest cumulative return. That it also yields the largest cumulative return for employees is only relevant to the employer because that fact shapes employees' choice of strategy. The employer takes no pleasure in the fact that the employees are better off.

There are, however, some difficulties in treating labor relations as an iterated prisoners' dilemma game and inferring cooperation from it.

1. The tit-for-tat strategy only works in a game that has some probability of being infinitely repeated. Strictly speaking, a game repeated many times but with a finite ending point reduces to the one shot version. This is because of *backward induction*.[7] On the last of a repeated series of plays neither party risks punishment for subsequent defection. Each then calculates that the other will defect on the last play, as they would in the one shot game. But if they calculate that the other will defect on the last round there is no reward to cooperation in the penultimate round. So they defect on that round too. And so on, all the way back to the first round choice (Heap and Varoufakis, 1995: 168-170). This makes strong assumptions about the calculating capacity of the two parties. But doing so is very much within the rational choice spirit that informs Miller's approach to the problem.

Can it not be argued that labor-management relations do have an indefinite character? Most work sites have no scheduled termination date. A new automobile factory or retail store will remain in business as long as it remains profitable.[8] However, while the capital/labor relationship within a particular work site may be indefinite that will not be the case for individual employees. Some will plan to quit. Those that do not quit will sooner or later retire. Each individual employee has a finite time with a firm, limited at the extreme by the retirement age. Consequently, within the prisoners' dilemma logic each would choose to shirk. In fact, the course and outcome of the GM strike in the summer of 1998 *was* influenced by the relatively short time horizons of a group of employees with an average

age approaching fifty (Dionne, 1998). Of course, the problem disappears if some common employee culture is established that persuades employees to think of themselves as a group rather than as individuals. This leads to the next problem.

2. The tit-for-tat strategy was successful in tournaments involving two opposing players. Labor relations normally involve multiple participants on the side of labor, and sometimes on the employer side too. The fact of multiple participants poses the problem of free riders. Even if it is in the interests of employees as a group to play a tit-for-tat game, individual members of that group (again, assuming the narrowly self-interested motivations that underpin the rational choice approach) are best off shirking while other employees refrain from doing so. But if this is in the interests of one employee, it is in the interests of all, and the basis for the tit-for-tat strategy, with its welfare-maximizing outcomes, collapses. Employees are engaged in a multi-party prisoners' dilemma game, with the same likelihood of a perverse outcome as in the two-party game. Wherever a group of employees is involved the difficulty of generating a cooperative outcome, even when the prisoners' dilemma is iterated, is compounded.

Axelrod (1986) and Heckathorn (1989) have addressed the problem of cooperation within a multi-party prisoners' dilemma. They argue as follows: work groups may enforce second order norms on their members. Within the work group there is not only a first order norm that says, *don't shirk!*; in addition, there is a second order norm that says, *punish a co-worker who shirks!* The commitment to a second order norm need not imply that employees abandon self-interest. On the contrary, *if* they recognize the benefits of cooperation in an iterated prisoners' dilemma game they might sanction shirking by their colleagues while seeking to shirk themselves. Heckathorn calls this "hypocritical cooperation." The point is that second order norms can be effectively implemented if a sufficient number of members of a group cooperate hypocritically.

Is it reasonable to see second order norm enforcement as a solution to the problem that the risk of free riding poses to the development of a tit-for-tat strategy in an iterated prisoners' dilemma game? Consider, first, the situation of employees.

Miller (1992: 188-195) uses the classic Bank Wiring Room study to illustrate the possibility of work group norm enforcement in pursuit of productivity. Assume for present purposes that the study actually lends itself to that interpretation.[9] While the research was taking place the Bank Wiring Room had fourteen employees. Olson (1965) has argued plausibly that the effective enforcement of normative sanctions is inversely related to the size of the work group. Two mechanisms produce this result. As the size of the workgroup increases the proportionate effect on output of any single employee decreases and the difficulties in enforcing discipline increase. While there are many workplaces with, say, less than twenty employees, a very large proportion of employees is concentrated in workplaces with much larger numbers. What is not clear is the extent to which secondary norm enforcement is practicable as the size of a relevant work group increases. Certainly, simulations by Coleman (1990) that model the process of norm generation and enforcement through the classification of participants into strangers (for whom there is no shared norm) and acquaintances (for whom the possibility of a tit-for-tat relationship encourages the development of a norm) reveal considerable sensitivity to group size. Moreover the maximum group size in his simulations is ten. Even at that relatively small number there is a high proportion of defections.

Another difficulty is that the abstract versions of multi-party prisoners' dilemmas assume that the groups are comprised of individuals. But in real organizations individuals are usually segmented into different parts. In an organization of any size employees will be divided into occupations and departments. We know from organizational ethnographies that the work process can generate resentments between occupations (e.g., production versus maintenance employees in Crozier, 1964: 93-100) and departments (e.g., Burns and Stalker, 1961: 177-192). Employers might try to segment the bargaining process. But there is reason to think that it is hard to do so and that fairness concerns limit management discretion in larger organizations (e.g., Williamson, 1985: 150).

Many larger workplaces have more than one union or union local. This sometimes produces resentments between unions or union locals that equal or exceed those between locals and management.[10] Many companies have more than one plant with a single union representing the employees at the several plants. Since the technical modernity of plants varies, the interests of union members across them are likely to diverge. Those in older plants might wish to make concessions to protect jobs; those in more modern ones are less likely to want to do so. Insofar as the bargaining process is linked

across establishments it will be difficult to generate the shared preferences that second order norms require. Are employees in a modern plant forced to accept smaller wage increases to protect the jobs
of those in older plants likely to enforce the second order norm that
shirkers should be punished?[11] Surely that is rather unlikely. The
employees in the more modern plant may think that the sacrifice
they have made to protect the employment security of their co-workers should be compensated in some way—perhaps by a reduced
expenditure of effort. But if management concedes a wage increase
that embodies the higher productivity level of the more modern plant
the initial commitment to employment security on which the tit-for-
tat strategy rested is undermined. Finally, union locals within a single
plant are usually part of national trade unions that attempt to implement policies thought to serve some broader industry labor force
interest. The constraints by national or international union policies
may limit the room for the local negotiation of mutually agreeable
outcomes (Lichtenstein, 1985).

What about the employer side? Can employers sensibly be treated
as single bargaining entities? Once again, the likelihood that this
will be so decreases with organization size. Larger organizations
are divided into departments. A departmental structure introduces
divisions of interest within management, as it does among workers.
If skill composition varies across departments and there is variation
in the demand for different skills, managers are likely to seek local
contractual modifications to ensure an adequate labor supply. Since
it is clear that wage relativities *matter* to employees it is also clear
that this sort of process of adaptation will, at the very least, complicate efforts to preserve the broader agreement necessary for the
maintenance of the united front upon which the tit-for-tat strategy
rests.

There is also the problem of the relationship to head office of
managements in firms with multiple work sites. Oddly, Miller (1992:
209) uses Gouldner's (1954) classic study of *the indulgency pattern* in a gypsum mine and factory to illustrate the possibility of a
commitment by employees to high effort and productivity. What *I*
think it illustrates, however, is the vulnerability of any stable exchange of effort for employment security (or any other employer-
provided benefit) at the local level to disruption from the center of
an organization. Gouldner's indulgency pattern was accepted by
the local workforce and management. It was disrupted because head

office viewed as unsatisfactory the factory performance that the local settlement had produced. Whether or not the center's judgment was right is neither here nor there.[12] What matters for present purposes is that it is likely to be difficult to maintain a tit-for-tat strategy that produces consecutive decisions to cooperate where an external power that is not party to the settlement can at any time disrupt it.[13]

Overall, then, while de facto employment security may sometimes elicit suitably productive efforts from employees in some organizations, the likelihood that it will do so diminishes as the size and complexity (the departmental structure, the range of occupations) of the organization increases. In large unionized plants of the sort that Osterman (1988) treats as models of effort-restriction caused by employment insecurity, a tit-for-tat strategy that produces consecutive and persistent cycles of cooperation seems particularly unlikely.

Institutional Employment Security and the Prisoners' Dilemma

In much of the writing employment security is based in law rather than voluntary agreement between employers and employees. Thus Osterman (1988) associates a set of favorable performance outcomes in Germany and Sweden with the legislated basis for employment security in those two countries (see also, Buttler and Walwei, 1993; Streeck, 1997).[14] To what degree can the effects of legislated employment security be understood in terms of the prisoners' dilemma?

Consider, once more, Figure 7.1. Cooperative behavior *may* be forthcoming when a prisoners' dilemma is iterated indefinitely. But this has nothing to do with good will. (Remember Miller's definition of trust!) Each party chooses to cooperate because of the potential loss from retaliation to defection, and *only* because of the potential loss from retaliation. Suppose government legislation effectively prohibits layoffs. This would have the effect of removing the entire bottom row of the pay-off matrix, as illustrated in Figure 7.2. Here, there is no constraint on employees; employers *cannot* play tit-for-tat. Employees can choose either to shirk or exert effort and, within the logic of the prisoners' dilemma game (where it is assumed that their effort involves disutility), they would decide to shirk. So legislated employment security cannot produce the choice of effort at the level of the work site, *within a prisoners' dilemma framework*.

Figure 7.2
Cooperative Behavior, Government Legislation, and Employment Security

	EMPLOYEE	
	Effort, wage restraint	**Shirking, short-run wage maximization**
Employment security, etc.	Employer=High Employee=High	Employer=Very Low Employee=Very High
EMPLOYER		
Employment *in*security, etc.		

There is another option. Employee choices at the work site might be equally constrained. That is to say, a union or union federation might negotiate rules with respect to effort (for example, broad job classifications, unsociable hours of work) and require that their affiliate work sites conform to those roles. This would produce the payoff matrix in Figure 7.3 which reduces the matrix to a single cell!

Figure 7.3
Neocorporatism, Employee Choice, and Effort

	EMPLOYEE	
	Effort, wage restraint	**Shirking, short-run wage maximization**
Employment security, etc.	Employer=High Employee=High	
EMPLOYER		
Employment *in*security, etc.		

This is the way the situation would look at an individual work site where there is neocorporatist centralized bargaining. Centralized bargaining (and the political arrangements that accompany it) provide a relatively high degree of employment security along with central union constraints on employees that induce them to expend the amount of effort required (in the appropriate forms) by a high productivity growth strategy (e.g., Pekkarinen, Pohjola and Rowthorn, 1992; Crouch, 1993). As a result, the prisoners' dilemma is displaced from the individual work site to the level of the economy as a whole. This is embodied in Figure 7.4, which is identical to Figure 7.1, except that the labeling has been changed to reflect the shift of levels.

Figure 7.4
Macro Level Prisoners' Dilemma

	THE WORKING CLASS	
	Effort, wage restraint	**Shirking, short-run wage maximization**
Employment security, etc.	Capital=High Working Class=High	Capital=Very Low Working Class=Very High
EMPLOYER		
Employment *in*security, etc.	Capital=Very High Working Class=Very Low	Capital=Low Working Class=Low

A Macro Level Prisoners' Dilemma?

Arguments are quite common in which, for the purposes of analysis, labor and capital confront each other as homogeneous units. Thus, in a widely cited paper by Przeworski and Wallerstein (1982) "workers consent," "workers choose their strategy," "workers opt for a compromise," while in response to workers' choices capitalists as a whole have a set of best responses. Przeworski and Wallerstein do not treat the construction of aggregates capable of self-conscious strategies as inevitable. On the contrary, they associate this outcome with "corporatist arrangements" (p.232). They do not use the language of the prisoners' dilemma but they do sketch a two party bargaining game, in which the choice of strategy is contingent on the time horizons of each party (see also Schott, 1984a, 1984b). *If* labor and capital can be treated as homogeneous entities facing an infinite time horizon one might imagine a class compromise emerging from tit-for-tat strategies in the same way that, according to Miller, they can emerge in a single plant. Macro level employment security would be a crucial element of the bargained outcome. And, in a number of versions, *trust* (albeit, imprecisely defined) is an intervening variable between the negotiated exchange of employment security and the ultimately resulting connection between negotiated wage increases and productivity growth (e.g., Barber and McCallum, 1982: 2; McCallum, 1983: 785).

In this chapter I am concerned with a prisoners' dilemma game involving an exchange of employment security for effort. Most of the literature that models employee-employer relations at the aggregate level, however, deals with an exchange of wage restraint on the part of employees (wage growth tied to productivity growth) for an employer-provided share in the growth of revenue produced by productivity growth. However, in this sort of modeling employment security is often bundled into the package provided by employers (e.g., Blais and McCallum, 1986: 164-166). At the same time, extra effort is an adequate substitute for wage restraint (as in so-called "productivity bargaining"). More generally, the exchange between the classes of employers and employees can involve any combination of effort, wage restraint, employment security and profit shares. In this section I refer to all these potential elements of an exchange within a prisoners' dilemma framework. Nonetheless, my main concern remains the effects of employment security.

With that in mind, even were it reasonable to assume that the employees and employers in a single firm form homogeneous entities capable of choosing strategies (and that will not usually be the case), the assumption is much more problematic at the level of the economy as a whole. Focus, for the moment, on employees alone.

The analyses of neocorporatism that attempt to infer from centralized bargaining a set of beneficial effects for economic performance must treat labor as a more or less homogeneous entity. Corporatist macroeconomic models normally accomplish this by asserting that relevant union movements have a "representational monopoly."[15] But how is it possible to secure *democratically* a "representational monopoly," given the range of interests among employees? It might be possible to secure such a monopoly through coercion—but that would get us back to the fascist forms of corporatism from which the writers on neocorporatism are quite determined to distinguish the modern form.

Lange (1984) has addressed this issue directly—but in a way that should now be familiar. Neocorporatism, he says, produces a performance bonus because it establishes the conditions for sufficient wage restraint to allow investment.[16] There is the familiar problem of free riding: employees maximize their welfare by not restraining their own wages but drawing the longer term welfare benefits of restraint by everyone else. Following Hardin (1971), Lange says that this situation can be described as a multi-person prisoners' dilemma. The one-shot-game produces the familiar perverse outcome; in this case, maximized wage demands and reduced investment.

But, says Lange, where the future of an economy is involved "the Prisoners' Dilemma game" is *"played repeatedly over time"* (p.100).[17] This implies that the time horizon of employees approximates infinity—as the cooperative solution to the iterated prisoners' dilemma requires. Lange does not explicitly refer to tit-for-tat as the source of wage restraint. But he argues that, in a repeated game, it is possible for players to "play *contingently rational strategies*" (p.103) and to take future benefits into account in their choice of strategies—which is, of course, what tit-for-tat involves. In effect, Lange is arguing that because the relationship between employees can be described as an iterated prisoners' dilemma, as for the relation between employers and employees, the conditions necessary for a cooperative solution are present. At the level of the economy as a whole that cooperative solution would involve employees exchanging wage restraint and other productivity-relevant behaviors (exertion, flexibility, and initiative) for a share in productivity growth along with employment security guaranteed by the government (see also Crouch, 1985).

For the economy as a whole, then, Pareto optimal outcomes rest on at least two iterated prisoners' dilemmas: one between employers and employees and a multi-party one among employees. In fact, there is a third prisoners' dilemma among employers. A more productive employer needing scarce labor might choose to break ranks and increase wages above the agreed norm in order to meet that need, while profiting from the better economic performance procured by the restraint of other employers.

How likely is the iteration of a multi-party prisoners' dilemma involving either employees or employers to produce a cooperative solution? Lange (1984:100) rests his argument on what he sees as evidence of the success of negotiated wage restraint in several rich countries—"Wage regulation *has* occurred in advanced industrial democracies, sometimes for extended periods of time and with at least partial success." Even this qualified judgment with respect to the record of wage regulation ("at least partial success") probably overstates the performance of the countries usually treated as exemplars of a centrally negotiated restraint made possible in part by the provision of employment security—Germany, Sweden, and Austria. The critical issue is the extent to which outcomes match wages to productivity growth. In none of these countries does detailed consideration of the evidence suggest that they do (Smith, 1992: 183-204).

Still, it is clear that institutional conditions *can* make possible coordinated positions among employees, on the one hand, and employers, on the other. In Sweden, control of unemployment insurance seems to have played a crucial role in locking workers into unions that in turn supported the centralized bargaining system—at least until the late 1980s. The employers' federation also had instruments of control at its disposal—although, perhaps, weaker ones.[18] It is also clear that the centralized negotiation had effect—if not in tying wage and productivity growth more closely then certainly in reducing pay differentials (Hibbs, 1991; Edlin and Topel, 1997: 167-175). So I do not think that it would be sensible to rule out the possibility of a constructive outcome of an iterated prisoners' dilemma at the aggregate level.

But the difficulties in preserving the conditions that make it possible appear formidable. Those conditions have to be present for three different iterated prisoners' dilemma games, two of which are multi-party games! To produce the cooperative outcome all three games have to work simultaneously. Is this likely?

While the time horizon for the economy as a whole can reasonably be characterized as infinite, that is not at all the case for the individual employees of that economy who, as they age, are likely to heavily discount future flows of income produced by current restraint. Insofar as those same employees are protected from job loss by the law or by seniority provisions in a collective agreement they are, moreover, much less likely to share the same concern with *generalized* employment protection as their younger employees. A concern with the welfare of their children *may* lead them to extend the time horizon they use to judge between alternative policies. But not everyone has children; not all of those who do maintain good relations with them; and those who do maintain good relations with their children may decide that individual strategies to protect their children's interests—that is, personal income maximization and the transfer of that income to the children in one way or another—will pay off better than will making current sacrifices in the interests of the economy as a whole, which includes the children of others for whom (within the calculative context assumed) they have no sympathy whatsoever!

Moreover, whatever problems are caused by numbers and segmentation at the level of the firm or plant are, surely, magnified at the level of the economy. Consider the problem of second order norm enforcement. It works in Heckathorn's analysis not because employees renounce their self-interest but, rather, because they recognize that cooperation on the part of their co-workers serves their personal interests. So they try to enforce a cooperative norm—effort or wage restraint—while attempting to evade respecting the norm themselves. The success of this as an option must depend on the extent to which it is possible for parts of the relevant aggregate to shelter themselves from scrutiny by others.

Now, where an entire economy is the relevant unit it is easy to imagine conventions and meetings at which delegates hypocritically urge respect of some shared norm on their fellow delegates and implement sanctions when violation of the norm is evident. But without an expensive monitoring apparatus norm violations are surely likely. After all, a delegate who enforces a norm that does not serve the perceived interests of the local membership is likely to lose office. We know that norm violation goes on within centralized union movements. The magnitude and generality of *wage drift* in such contexts provides ample evidence of it (e.g., Flanagan, 1987: 166-169). Further evidence of the difficulty centrally negotiated restraint encounters comes from the apparent gulf between leaders and members in the highly centralized Swedish bargaining system, even during its heyday (see Korpi, 1978: 225-229). And, of course, there are the well-documented splits in Sweden between more and less skilled employees (Edlin and Topel, 1997: 192-193) and (partially overlapping with skill) public and private sector employees (Ahlén, 1988a, 1988b, 1989; Albåge, 1986). While a different interpretation may have been defensible at the end of the 1970s, in retrospect, the segmentary tendencies within centralized bargaining systems appear both powerful and pervasive, and raise serious questions with respect to the feasibility of a tit-for-tat solution to the iterated prisoners' dilemma.

What about employers? Clearly, there is segmentation by age of plant and equipment and by industry. However, employers also have the possibility of stepping out of the game, so to speak. They can decide that the matrix of payoffs provided by the domestic prisoners' dilemma is unsatisfactory and shift the bulk of future investments to a better game, in another country. Once they choose to do so, the game in plants from which they withhold investment becomes effectively finite, with the familiar consequences for the feasibility of tit for tat.

They may be limited in their use of this option. Part of the existing tit-for-tat settlement, so to speak, may involve agreements on how to dispose of profits, including substantial disclosure of investment decisions. Employers may choose to respect this agreement as long as it generates a rate of return that they find satisfactory. But what they define as satisfactory will certainly be a function of what is available in other economies. A large enough gap will almost certainly induce an employer to decide that the domestic game is not worth playing. There is also the possibility of capital controls. Assume that they are effective in preventing unapproved overseas investments. The problem here is that most countries decide for one reason or another (the need for scale economies, the advantages of proximity to a market) to allow overseas investment by domestic firms. Once they do so it becomes hard for the country of origin to control the finances of the firm's overseas branches. Insofar as that is so, firms confronted with an unsatisfactory matrix of payoffs in the domestic market are likely to go to some lengths to avoid repatriating profits.

There is evidence that something like this went on in Sweden during the period leading up to the onset of economic crisis at the beginning of the 1990s. In the 1970s and 1980s rates of return on invested capital were low compared to other comparable countries (Aliber, 1987: 405-406). Not surprisingly, the rate of domestic investment per worker was also low and falling (Leamer and Lundborg, 1997: 412-413). This is consistent with what one would expect to observe where employers decide that the local payoff matrix is much less attractive than overseas alternatives.

So while it is possible to theorize a tit-for-tat strategy that involves an exchange of employment security and other benefits, on the one

hand, for wage restraint and effort, on the other, the practical difficulties in a modern open economy where there are three separate
games involved are enormous.[19] Furthermore, while the process of
negotiation *might* have as its outcome an enhanced capacity to deal
with the adjustments necessary as a result of economic shocks (the
oil crisis, the current economic difficulties in Asia) it is surely just as
likely that the uncertainties and confusions that they introduce into
a bargaining situation—for example, what constitutes an accept-
able rate of return—will overwhelm a centrally negotiated agreement. Lacroix (1987) presents an analysis in which uncertainties in
the bargaining process produce this sort of outcome.

Conclusion

From time to time, relatively stable bargaining arrangements have
been established in different plants, firms, and countries. Those arrangements *may* have produced better economic performance, in
part through an exchange of employment security for flexibility and,
perhaps, wage restraint. But I would argue that it is rather uncom-
mon for the process generating that outcome to be suitably described
in terms of the iterated prisoners' dilemma, accompanied by the
entirely calculative definition of trust used by Miller. What then might
produce satisfactory negotiated outcomes? There are, I think, two
possible routes.

First, the matrix of payoffs may differ from that of the standard
prisoners' dilemma. Heckathorn (1986) has explored the implications of this in some detail. If the benefits of mutual cooperation
become very high, and the benefits of exploiting the other party in
a game become only moderate the incentives are changed. The incentives for cooperation become much stronger so that each party
will choose the cooperative solution simply on the basis of the assurance of cooperation from the other party. This is called an *assurance* game and is illustrated in Figure 7.5.

It is also possible that at the beginning of a game (the opening of
a new plant?) the employees and/or the employer *believe* that the
matrix of payoffs looks like the prisoners' dilemma while, in fact, it
is an assurance game. Playing consecutive rounds allows one or
both parties to revise their estimates of the rewards to cooperation
in the light of experience, and to change their estimate of the likelihood that the other party will cooperate. This sort of mechanism
would be consistent with models of sequential games involving

Figure 7.5
Assurance Game

	EMPLOYEE	
	Effort, wage restraint	**Shirking, short-run wage maximization**
Employment security, etc.	Employer=Very High Employee=Very High	Employer=Very Low Employee=High
EMPLOYER		
Employment *in*security, etc.	Employer=Very High Employee=Very Low	Employer=Low Employee=Low

bounded rationality—that is, uncertainty with respect to the true pay-off matrix (e.g., Kreps and Wilson, 1982a; Kreps, 1990: 65-77). This approach has an interesting implication. If beliefs about the payoff matrix are consecutively revised by one or both parties, backward induction is impossible, since the final payoff matrix is unknown. This makes possible cooperative outcomes over a significant number of rounds of a finite game (Kreps and Wilson, 1982b).

There is not space to discuss here whether or not it is appropriate to model labor relations as an assurance game, or whether uncertainty with respect to the payoff matrix provides an incentive for cooperation. But, in either case, it is likely that segmentation within groups will continue to create obstacles to the choice of cooperative strategies.

Second, while this is perhaps less likely at the level of an economy as a whole, it is possible that the mechanism that produces preferred outcomes at the level of the plant or firm is not purely calculative. It is possible that decent behavior by the employer (employment security and so on) produces loyalty, trust and other psychological states that are conducive to better performance at work. This is the sort of thing implied in Misztal's definition of trust (1996: 24), which is very different from the purely calculative version found in Miller. Thus: "Trust can be said to be based on the belief that the person, who has a degree of freedom to disappoint our expectations, will meet an obligation under all circumstances over which they have control. If unforeseen circumstances arise which could prevent the fulfilment of those obligations, through no fault of the parties concerned, it will not be perceived as a case of betrayal. Thus, although we are willing to forgive mistakes or unintended consequences, the intended betrayal of our trust is a cause for enormous pain and distrust."

This is non-calculative trust. Violating it produces emotional hurt. Such trust, perhaps, yields superior performance in some firms. Misztal (1996: 5) is sympathetic to interpretations of Japanese labor relations along these lines. Obviously, however, confirming this interpretation requires research that is not purely aggregate but, rather, looks at the incidence of trust and loyalty (is it associated with secure employment?) and the extent to which the presence of trust and loyalty is associated with superior performance. Such research exists. As far as I can tell it has been ignored in writings on the positive effects of employment security. It has, in fact, yielded quite mixed results.[20] But I suspect that trust and loyalty in their more diffuse forms provide a more promising route to explanation of any relationship between employment security and effort than the purely calculative one that is most commonly adopted in treatments of the issue.

Notes

1.   Miller (1992: 223-234) lists symbolic gestures (e.g., the elimination of managers' parking spaces), employee representation, less obtrusive supervision, broadened tasks, improved training, profit- and gain-sharing plans, and employee stock ownership plans.

2.   In this paper I mean security of employment with the current employer, rather than security of employment in the sense of a high probability of finding another job, were the current one lost. I do not mean by this job security, which refers to an employee's probability of keeping a particular job. This latter assumes narrowly defined job categories that would normally be associated with reduced effort, in the form of inflexibility. See Buechtemann (1993: 5-6).

3.   Buechtemann puts employment security provisions in collective agreements into the institutional category. Since, in bargaining, employers may or may not choose to concede on this issue I am inclined to put bargained employment security into the de facto category.

4.   Employment security may be treated as a condition guaranteeing that a prisoners' dilemma game will be repeated rather than as a component of the payoff matrix. But it is hard to justify this choice. In most analyses of wage differentials employment security is usually treated as one compensating differential among several. While Miller (1992: 195-196) treats employment security as a condition of repeated play rather than as part of the payoff matrix, in his substantive discussion it looks much more like part of the package offered by employers (e.g., p.118).

5.   But Nachbar (1992: 314-316) argues that Axelrod's tournament games did not constitute truly infinite prisoners' dilemmas. Among other things: i) Axelrod calculated the payoff matrix for a finite number of plays and ii) no participant submitted the always defect option. Nachbar argues, however, that these factors probably would not have made much difference to the success of tit-for-tat.

6.   A third problem is that the iterated prisoners dilemma game contains multiple Nash equilibria (Kreps, 1990:97-99; Rizvi, 1994: 9-12). This is because there is no a priori way of fixing the chosen strategy of the playing partners. If a partner has never cooperated as a preferred strategy, then never cooperate must be the chosen strategy of the other partner. This means that tit-for-tat depends on some previous recognition on the part of each party that this is a sensible choice for the other one. Or it might be an outcome of a learning process, of the sort described in the conclusion.

7.   Bounded rationality in the form of uncertainty about the opponent's pay-off matrix modifies this. I return to this in the conclusion.

8.   Some work sites—like construction—do have finite termination dates. So even if employers offered to their employees something other than employment security in exchange for cooperation, it would not allow them to escape from the one-shot prisoners' dilemma outcome, because the end date of the exchange is (more or less) fixed.

9.   This was not the interpretation of Roethlisberger and Dixon themselves who treated it as an example of an informal organization "which at many points worked against the economic purposes of the company" (1943: 560-561).

10.   This is often the case in North American paper mills, where a single plant may contain both a paper workers union and a series of craft unions for some or all of the maintenance employees. In many mills the paper machine operators, on the one hand, and the pulp and maintenance employees (not in separate craft unions), on the other, are in different locals of the same union. This sometimes produces considerable inter-union or inter-local conflict.

11.   For a relevant case study see Elbaum and Wilkinson (1979). The history of international unions in Canada illustrates these difficulties. Resentments caused by settlements influenced by larger North American concerns, and related issues, have led Canadian locals to break away from the international union. Still useful discussions of this process can be found in Abella (1973), Laxer (1976), and Thompson (1983).

12.   Such judgments provide the rationale for multidivisional structures in organizations. See Williamson (1970).

13.   Axelrod, (1984: 81-82) is aware of this. His favorite example of sustained cooperation within an iterated prisoners' dilemma is the mutual restraint displayed between opposing trenches during the first world war. This restraint was, however, vulnerable to disruption by both the General Staff of the opposing armies and the artillery, neither of which was a party to whatever agreed upon restraint had been settled on by the small groups of soldiers facing each other across no man's land. Head office, I am arguing, is the more-or-less pacific equivalent of the General Staff and the artillery.

14.   In Germany, Works Councils, which have a statutory basis, have a right to consultation on lay-offs and, if they disagree with management, can have layoff plans submitted to binding arbitration (Osterman, 1988: 119-120). In Sweden, since the mid 1970s unions have had the right to substantial layoff notification, to bargain over layoffs, and to solicit the opinion of a so-called 'wage-earners consultant' to provide an independent judgment on whether proposed layoffs are warranted (Smith et al., 1995: 689-718).

15. For a general treatment of this issue see Smith (1992).

16. Lange uses the term "wage regulation" for what I refer to here as "wage restraint."
     The basic principle is that workers do not maximize their benefits in any one year
     but, rather, under specific circumstances accept that their longer term interests are
     served with wages that allow a suitable amount of investment to take place.

17. The emphasis here and in subsequent quotes is in the original.

18. Ingham (1974: 56) listed fines and expulsion from the employers' federation as
     potential sanctions. The fact of substantial wage drift is evidence that the controls
     were quite a bit less than complete.

19. One or more additional games involving the government and the bargaining par-
     ties might also be added. This, I think, would further reduce the likelihood of a
     successful tit-for-tat outcome.

20. Broadly speaking, the relevant research shows that employment insecurity does
     reduce organizational commitment (within which loyalty and related psychologi-
     cal states are subsumed), trust, and job satisfaction. However, while reduced
     organizational commitment increases the likelihood that respondents will plan to
     quit it has no effect on whether or not they actually do so. Moreover, perceived
     employment insecurity has no effect on employment and, "Although higher levels
     of commitment may relate to performance in some situations .... the present find-
     ings suggest that commitment has relatively little direct influence on performance"
     (Mathieu and Zajac, 1990). See also Ashford, Lee, and Bobko, 1989; Arthur,
     1994; Fenton-O'Creavy et al., 1997). A study that attempts to resurrect the com-
     mitment-performance relation is Benkhoff (1997), but it has a number of method-
     ological problems, including the fact that the commitment measure used includes a
     substantial performance component—hard work!

References

Abella, Irving Martin. 1973. *Nationalism, Communism, and Canadian Labour: The
    CIO, the Communist Party, and the Canadian Congress of Labour 1935-1956.*
    Toronto: University of Toronto Press.

Ahlén, Kristina. 1998a. Recent trends in Swedish collective bargaining: Collapse of the
    Swedish model, *Current Sweden.* No.358 .

Ahlén, Kristina. 1998b. Recent trends in Swedish collective bargaining: Heading toward
    negotiated incomes policy? *Current Sweden.* No.359 .

Ahlén, Kristina. 1989. Swedish collective bargaining under pressure: Inter-union rivalry
    and incomes policies, *British Journal of Industrial Relations.* 27: 330-346.

Albåge, Lars-Gunnar. 1986. Recent trends in collective bargaining in Sweden: An
    employer's view, *International Labour Review.* 125: 107-122.

Aliber, Robert Z. 1987. Financial markets and the growth of Europe. in Robert Z.
    Lawrence and Charles L. Schultze (eds.), *Barriers to European Growth: A Transat-
    lantic View.* Washington, DC: Brookings Institution.

Arthur, Jeffrey B. 1994. Effects of human resource systems on manufacturing perfor-
    mance and turnover, *Academy of Management Journal.* 37: 670-687.

Ashford, Susan J., Cynthia Lee, and Philip Bobko. 1989. Content, causes, and conse-
    quences of job insecurity: A theory-based measure and substantive test, *Academy of
    Management Journal.* 32: 803-829.

Axelrod, Robert. 1984. *The Evolution of Cooperation.* New York: Basic Books.

——. 1986. An evolutionary approach to norms, *American Political Science Review.* 80:
    1095-1111.

Barber, Clarence L. and John C.P. McCallum. 1982. *Controlling Inflation: Learning
    from Experience in Canada, Europe, Japan.* Toronto: Lorimer.

Benkhoff, Birgit. 1997. Ignoring commitment is costly: New approaches establish the missing link between commitment and performance, *Human Relations*. 50: 701-726.

Blais, André and John McCallum. 1986. Government, special interest groups and economic growth, in David Laidler (ed.), *Responses to Economic Change*. Toronto: University of Toronto Press in cooperation with the Royal Commission on the Economic Union and Development Prospects for Canada.

Buechtemann, Christoph G. 1993. Introduction: Employment security and labor markets, in Christoph G. Buechtemann (ed.), *Employment Security and Labor Market Behavior: Interdisciplinary Approaches and International Evidence*. Ithaca, NY: ILR Press.

Burns, Tom and G. M. Stalker. 1961. *The Management of Innovation*. London: Tavistock.

Buttler, Friedrich and Ulrich Walwei. 1993. Employment security and efficiency: Assumptions in the current debate and empirical evidence for West Germany, in Christoph G. Buechtemann (ed.), *Employment Security and Labor Market Behavior: Interdisciplinary Approaches and International Evidence*. Ithaca, NY: ILR Press.

Coleman, James S. 1990. Norm-generating structures, in Karen Schweers Cook and Margaret Levi (eds.), *The Limits of Rationality*. Chicago: University of Chicago Press.

Crouch, Colin. 1985. Conditions for trade union wage restraint, in Leon N. Lindberg and Charles S. Maier (eds.), *The Politics of Inflation and Economic Stagnation*. Washington, DC: Brookings Institution.

Crouch, Colin. 1993. *Industrial Relations and European State Traditions*. Oxford: Clarendon Press.

Crozier, Michel. 1994. *The Bureaucratic Phenomenon*. Chicago: University of Chicago Press.

DiMaggio, Paul. 1990. Cultural aspects of economic action and organization, in Roger Friedland and A.F. Robertson (eds.), *Beyond the Marketplace: Rethinking Economy and Society*. New York: Aldine de Gruyter.

Dionne, E.J., Jr. 1998. Fear drove workers to fight GM, *Guardian Weekly*, August 16: 16 (reprinted from the *Washington Post*).

Edlin, Per-Anders and Robert Topel. 1997. Wage policy and restructuring: The Swedish labour market since 1960, in Richard B. Freeman, Robert Topel, and Birgitta Swedenborg (eds.), *The Welfare State in Transition: Reforming the Swedish Model*. Chicago: University of Chicago Press.

Elbaum, Bernard and Frank Wilkinson. 1979. Industrial relations and uneven development: A comparative study of the American and British steel industries, *Cambridge Journal of Economics*. 3: 275-303.

Elster, Jon. 1990a. Marxism, functionalism, and game theory, in Sharon Zukin and Paul DiMaggio (eds.). *Structures of Capital: The Social Organization of the Economy*. Cambridge: Cambridge University Press.

——. 1990b. When rationality fails, in Karen Schweers Cook and Margaret Levi (eds.), *The Limits of Rationality*. Chicago: The University of Chicago Press.

Fenton-O'Creavy, M.P., P.Winfrow, H. Lydka, and T. Morris. 1997. Company prospects and employee commitment: An analysis of the dimensionality of the BOCS and the influence of external events on those dimensions, *British Journal of Industrial Relations*. 35: 593-608.

Flanagan, Robert J. 1987. Efficiency and equality in Swedish labor markets, in Barry P. Bosworth and Alice M. Rivlin (eds.), *The Swedish Economy*. Washington, DC: The Brookings Institution.

Gouldner, Alvin. 1954. *Patterns of Industrial Bureaucracy*. New York: Free Press.

Hardin, Russell. 1971. Collective action as an agreeable N-person prisoners' dilemma, *Behavioral Science*. 16: 472-481.

Heap, Shaun P. and Yanis Varoufakis. 1995. *Game Theory: A Critical Introduction*. London: Routledge.

Heckathorn, Douglas D. 1989. Collective action and the second order free rider problem, *Rationality and Society*. 1: 78-100.

Heckathorn, Douglas D. 1986. The dynamics of collective action, *American Sociological Review*. 61: 250-277.

Hibbs, Douglas A. 1991. Market forces, trade union ideology and trends in Swedish wage dispersion, *Acta Sociologica* 34: 89-102.

Hirsch, Paul, Stuart Michaels, and Ray Friedman. 1990. Clean models vs. dirty hands: Why economics is different from sociology, in Sharon Zukin and Paul DiMaggio (eds.), *Structures of Capital: The Social Organization of the Economy*. Cambridge: Cambridge University Press.

Ingham, Geoffrey K. 1974. *Strikes and Industrial Conflict: Britain and Scandinavia*. London: Macmillan.

Kochan, Thomas A. and Paul Osterman. 1994. *The Mutual Gains Enterprise: Forging a Winning Partnership among Labor, Management, and Government*. Boston: Harvard Business School Press.

Korpi, Walter. 1978. *The Working Class in Welfare Capitalism: Work, Unions and Politics in Sweden*. London: Routledge & Kegan Paul.

Kreps, David M. 1990. *Game Theory and Economic Modelling*. Oxford: Clarendon Press, 1990.

Kreps, David M. and Robert Wilson. 1982a. Reputation and imperfect equilibrium. *Journal of Economic Theory*. 27: 253-279.

———. 1982b. Sequential equilibria. *Econometrica*. 50: 863-894.

Lacroix, Robert. 1987. *Les grèves au Canada: Causes et conséquences*. Montréal: Les presses de l'Université de Montréal.

Lange, Peter. 1984. Unions, workers and wage regulation: The rational bases of consent, in John H. Goldthorpe (ed.). *Order and Conflict in Contemporary Capitalism: Studies in the Political Economy of Western European Nations*. Oxford: Clarendon Press.

Laxer, Robert. 1976. *Canada's Unions*. Toronto: James Lorimer & Company.

Leamer, Edward E. and Per Lundborg. 1997. A Heckscher-Ohlin view of Sweden competing in the global marketplace, in Richard B. Freeman, Robert Topel, and Birgitta Swedenborg (eds.). *The Welfare State in Transition: Reforming the Swedish Model*. Chicago: University of Chicago Press.

Lichtenstein, Nelson. 1985. UAW bargaining strategy and shop-floor conflict: 1946-1970, *Industrial Relations*. 24: 360-380.

Mathieu, John E. and Dennis M. Zajac. 1990. A review and meta-analysis of the antecedents, correlates, and consequences of organizational commitment, *Psychological Bulletin*. 108: 171-194.

McCallum, John. 1983. Inflation and social consensus in the seventies, *Economic Journal* 93: 784-805.

Miller, Gary J. 1992. *Managerial Dilemmas: The Political Economy of Hierarchy*. Cambridge: Cambridge University Press.

Misztal, Barbara A. 1996. *Trust in Modern Societies: The Search for the Bases of Social Order*. Cambridge: Polity Press.

Nachbar, John H. 1992. Evolution in the finitely repeated prisoner's dilemma, *Journal of Economic Behavior and Organization*. 19: 307-326.

Offe, Claus. 1985. *Disorganized Capitalism: Contemporary Transformations of Work and Politics*. Cambridge, MA: MIT Press.

Olson, Mancur. 1965. *The Logic of Collective Action*. New Haven, CT: Yale University Press.

Osterman, Paul. 1988. *Employment Futures: Reorganization, Dislocation, and Public Policy*. New York: Oxford University Press.

Pekkarinen, Jukka, Matti Pohjola, and Bob Rowthorn. 1992. *Social Corporatism: A Superior Economic System?* Oxford: Clarendon Press.

Pollard, Sidney. 1968. *The Genesis of Modern Management: A Study of the Industrial Revolution in Great Britain.* Baltimore, MD: Penguin Books.

Przeworski, Adam and Michael Wallerstein. 1982. The structure of class conflict in democratic capitalist societies, *American Political Science Review.* 76: 215-238.

Rizvi, S. Abu Turab. 1994. Game theory to the rescue? *Contributions to Political Economy.* 13: 1-28.

Roethlisberger, F.J. and William J. Dickson. 1943. *Management and the Worker: An Account of a Research Program Conducted by the Western Electric Company, Hawthorne Works, Chicago.* Cambridge, MA: Harvard University Press.

Rosow, Jerome and Robert Zager. 1984. *Employment Security in a Free Economy.* New York: Pergamon Press.

Schott, Kerry. 1984a. *Policy, Power and Order: The Persistence of Economic Problems in Capitalist States.* New Haven, CT: Yale University Press.

——. 1984b. Investment, order, and conflict in a simple dynamic model of capitalism, in John H. Goldthorpe (ed.), *Order and Conflict in Contemporary Capitalism: Studies in the Political Economy of Western European Nations.* Oxford: Clarendon Press.

Smith, Michael R. 1992. *Power, Norms, and Inflation: A Skeptical Treatment.* New York: Aldine De Gruyter.

Smith, Michael R., Anthony C. Masi, Axel van den Berg, and Joseph Smucker. 1995. External flexibility in Sweden and Canada: A three industry comparison, *Work, Employment & Society.* 9: 689-718.

Streek, Wolfgang. 1997. Beneficial constraints: On the economic limits of rational voluntarism, in J. Rogers Hollingsworth and Robert Boyer (eds.), *Contemporary Capitalism: The Embeddedness of Institutions.* Cambridge: Cambridge University Press.

——. 1992. *Social Institutions and Economic Performance: Studies of Industrial Relations in Advanced Capitalist Economies.* London: Sage.

Swedberg, Richard, Ulf Himmelstrand, and Göran Brulin. 1990. The paradigm of economic sociology, in Sharon Zukin and Paul DiMaggio (eds.), *Structures of Capital: The Social Organization of the Economy.* Cambridge: Cambridge University Press.

Thompson, Mark. 1983. International unionism in Canada: The move to local control, *Industrial Relations.* 22: 71-86.

Williamson, Oliver E. 1970. *Corporate Control and Business Behavior.* Englewood Cliffs, NJ: Prentice-Hall.

Williamson, Oliver E. 1985. *The Economic Institutions of Capitalism: Firms, Markets, Relational Contracting.* New York: Free Press.

Zelizer, Viviana. 1989. Beyond the polemics of the market: Establishing a theoretical and empirical agenda, *Sociological Forum.* 3: 614-634.

Zukin, Sharon and Paul DiMaggio. 1990. Introduction, in Sharon Zukin and Paul DiMaggio (eds.), *Structures of Capital: The Social Organization of the Economy.* Cambridge: Cambridge University Press, 1-36.

8

Judges as Rational Actors: Strategic Behavior and the Emergence of Judicial Supremacy in Canada

Christopher P. Manfredi

Introduction

On April 2, 1998 the Supreme Court of Canada delivered its judgment in *Vriend v. Alberta* ([1998] 1 S.C.R. 493). At issue was the constitutionality of Alberta's Individual Rights Protection Act, which did not include sexual orientation among its prohibited grounds of discrimination. The Court's judgment that the Act's exclusion of sexual orientation rendered it unconstitutional under section 15 of the Charter of Rights and Freedoms, and that the "appropriate and just" remedy consisted of reading sexual orientation into the Act, was a bold exercise of judicial power in at least three ways. First, the Charter's equality rights provision itself does not include sexual orientation among its constitutionally prohibited grounds of discrimination, and the provision's extension to sexual orientation is the product of prior judicial interpretation. Second, "reading in" is among the most intrusive remedies available for Charter violations, and its use in this instance had the effect of extending the jurisdiction of the Alberta Human Rights Commission in a direction expressly rejected by the legislature. Finally, the Court devoted several paragraphs of its judgment to the institutional legitimacy of its interpretive and remedial activism. In its view, the Court's role as "trustee" of the Charter requires that it "scrutinize the work of the legislature and the executive not in the name of the courts, but in the interests of the new social contract that was democratically chosen" (*Vriend*, paragraph 135).

The assertiveness of the Court's approach to the morally controversial issues raised by *Vriend* stands in marked contrast to its cautious foray only a decade earlier into the equally morally charged
arena of abortion politics. To be sure, in 1988 the Court did declare
the abortion provisions of the Criminal Code unconstitutional under section 7 of the Charter (*Morgentaler, Smoling and Scott v. The
Queen* [1988], 44 D.L.R [4th] 385 [SCC]). However, only one justice of seven—Bertha Wilson—was willing to extend the right to
liberty to include a right to reproductive freedom that would render
the criminalization of abortion unconstitutional under almost all circumstances. The four justices in the plurality preferred to base their
judgment on narrow procedural grounds. Indeed, Chief Justice Brian
Dickson declared that it was "neither necessary nor wise" to "explore the broadest implications" of liberty in analyzing the abortion
question (*Morgentaler, Smoling and Scott* 1988: 397). Instead, he
focused on the law's administrative deficiencies, which he found to
produce unjustified delays and unequal access to legal abortions
across Canada. The effect of the judgment was to nullify the existing law while leaving enough legislative maneuvering room to re-
establish criminal regulation of abortion under a different administrative scheme.

Why did the 1998 *Vriend* Court choose to exercise judicial review in more confrontational terms than the 1988 *Morgentaler* Court?
One obvious explanation is an attitudinal shift associated with
changes in judicial personnel. Indeed, only one justice (Lamer) was
a member of the Court for both cases. While this change in the
Court's membership cannot be entirely ignored, there are several
reasons to doubt that it provides a complete explanation. First, it is
unlikely that the pool of potential appointees to the Court would
have changed so drastically during the decade between *Morgentaler*
and *Vriend* as to produce a dramatic shift in judicial attitudes. Second, even if the selection pool had changed, conventional analyses
of judicial attitudes suggest that the conservative prime minister
(Mulroney) responsible for appointing six of the eight justices on
the *Vriend* Court would have selected the most conservative members of that pool. Finally, both individual and aggregate measures
of voting patterns show very similar voting behavior among the
1988 and 1998 justices (Kelly 1999). Individually, support for Charter claims by the *Morgentaler* justices ranged from 22 percent
(MacIntyre) to 55 percent (Wilson), with four justices clustered be-

tween 32 and 37 percent. Support rates for the *Vriend* justices ranged from 26 percent (Gonthier) to 38 percent (McLachlin), with four justices clustered between 32 and 36 percent. On an aggregate level, the support rates were identical (33 percent) for both the 1984-92 and 1993-97 periods. Interestingly, the support rate for challenges to statutes and regulations actually declined from 39 percent during the Courts first 100 Charter decisions to 30 percent during decisions 101-195 and 24 percent during decisions 196-345. The restraint of *Morgentaler* and the activism of *Vriend* were thus *atypical* of their respective time periods.

A second explanation for the shift from restraint to activism concerns the level of government under review in each case. Since final courts of appeal tend to favor central governments (Bzdera 1993; Feeley and Rubin 1998: 171-77), the Court may have been less willing to interfere directly with the federal government's abortion legislation than it was to interfere with a provincial human rights statute. The problem with this explanation is that the evidence for such a tendency in Charter cases is weak. In quantitative terms, the Charter has not affected provincial policies more negatively than federal policies (Morton, Russell, and Riddell 1994; Kelly 1999). Between 1984 and 1997 the Supreme Court nullified thirty-four federal and seventeen provincial statutes. In more general terms, in the forty-six cases where the Court has ruled against government policies without necessarily nullifying a statute, it has ruled against the federal government thirty-three times and against provincial governments thirteen times. Not only has the Supreme Court ruled against federal policies more than twice as often as it has ruled against those enacted by provincial governments, but provincial governments have been more successful (72.3 percent) than the federal government (62.5 percent) in defending their policies against Charter challenges. Central judicial hostility to provincial policy preferences is not, therefore, a satisfactory explanation of the shift from *Morgentaler* to *Vriend*.

In this chapter I explore a third explanation: that the shift in judicial assertiveness from *Morgentaler* to *Vriend* reflects a change in the justices' strategic calculations. Starting from the assumption that judges, like other political actors, must at times act strategically to advance their policy preferences, the paper argues that each judgment reflects a different moment in the institutional struggle over constitutional authority between judges and legislators. To be more precise, the chapter argues that judicial institutions were uncertain in 1988 about the nature and extent of their authority to enforce the Charter against democratic institutions. By 1998, however, this uncertainty had been significantly reduced, and the Court could be more confident in confronting legislators. The chapter develops this argument in three stages. First, it sets out a theory of judicial strategy. Second, it examines the broader institutional context that affected judicial strategy in both cases. Finally, it analyzes the strategic calculations that may have led to restraint in *Morgentaler* and activism in *Vriend*.

A Theory of Judicial Strategy

Since C. Herman Pritchett's classic study of the Roosevelt Court, political scientists have recognized that judicial decision making, particularly in appellate courts, is driven primarily by policy rather than legal considerations (Baum 1997: 57; Pritchett 1948). There are several reasons for this characteristic of judicial decision making, especially among senior appellate courts like the U.S. and Canadian supreme courts (Baum 1997: 64 and 69). First, cases reach these courts precisely because the applicable legal rules are ambiguous, and legal ambiguity enhances the importance of judicial policy goals. Second, institutional characteristics of both courts elevate policy over law: each court exercises discretionary jurisdiction and neither court is subject to higher court review.

In addition to the role that policy plays in supreme court decision-making, political scientists have also recognized that judges, like other political actors, must be strategic in pursuing their policy objectives despite institutional provisions (e.g., security of tenure and formal independence) designed to insulate them from ordinary political pressures.[1] There are at least two reasons for strategic judicial behavior. First, on multi-member appellate courts the successful transformation of individual policy preferences into law requires coalition building. Second, while judges may be insulated from politics, they are not isolated. Judges must be cognizant of the possible reaction to their decisions by other institutions whose actions can either advance or frustrate the achievement of their objectives. In this section I sketch out the theory underlying the use of judicial strategy.

Strategic choice is a function of decision making within institutions, where institutions are defined as "set[s] of rules that structure social interactions in particular ways"(Knight 1992: 2).[2] Institutions affect decision-making by providing information about the nature of sanctions for noncompliance with the rules, and the probable future actions of other actors involved in the interaction (Knight 1992: 17). Judicial decision-making takes place within the context of two overlapping institutions. On the one hand, judges are constrained individually by specific intra-court rules, which govern their interactions with colleagues. On the other hand, courts are constrained collectively by general constitutional rules that govern their interactions with other political institutions. Judges are thus faced with the task of advancing their individual policy preferences while preserving the general institutional power and prestige of their court, without which there would be little possibility of achieving policy objectives (Baum 1997: 123). Judges behave strategically, therefore, when they "take actions intended to advance their policy goals in collective decisions of their own court or in the decisions of other institutions" (Baum 1997: 92).

Perhaps the most important element of judicial strategy (to use Murphy's term) is strategic voting, where judges support case outcomes and/or doctrinal statements that do not necessarily reflect their true preferences (Baum 1997: 91). The principal incentive for such behavior is to avoid provoking a reaction by other institutions that might negate the court's decision, which would harm both the short-term policy goals and long-term institutional authority of the court. For example, where a court is subject to further appellate review, the threat of reversal may prevent judges from setting doctrine at their ideal preference point (Baum 1997: 115). In this sense, an incremental, if imperfect, gain is more valuable than appellate reversal of a judge's most preferred policy position. Even where a court is not subject to appellate review judges may have strategic reasons for adopting positions that diverge from their policy preferences. For example, research suggests that the U.S. Supreme Court votes strategically on statutory issues because of the possibility of reversal by the legislative and executive branches. If the broader political context suggests that reversal is a possibility, the justices "will compromise by adopting the interpretation closest to their preferences that could be predicted to withstand reversal" (Baum 1997: 119). Compromise may also be necessary in constitutional adjudication, where reversal is highly unlikely but where the controversial nature of an issue exposes the Court to political risk. In such cases, collective preservation of the Court's institutional authority may require subordination of individual policy preferences to achieve unanimous support for both outcome and doctrine (O'Brien 1986: 214-15, 221-22, 233).

The theoretical implications of this approach to the study of judicial behavior can be summarized as follows. Supreme Court decision making, in Canada as in the United States, is primarily policy-oriented and takes place within an institutional context of rules that structures the interactions between the Court and other political actors. As a result, where judicial decision-making generates potential conflict between the Court and other institutions the justices adjust their behavior strategically in response to information communicated by those rules. The purpose of these strategic adjustments is to maintain the Court's institutional authority and legitimacy vis-à-vis other political institutions. Strategic shifts in judicial behavior thus indicate a change in the information communicated by the rules of the game under which the Court operates.

The Institutional Context

The theory of judicial strategy laid out in the preceding section suggests that the different doctrinal, if not decisional, outcomes in *Morgentaler* and *Vriend* represent a strategic shift in judicial behavior that can be attributed to a change in the information communicated by the broader institutional environment in which the Court operates. In this section I focus on the changes in that environment that may have affected the information communicated to the Court.

Although table 8.1 summarizes the chronology of key events that affected the strategic environment faced by the Court, the unfolding of these events merits further elaboration.

The story begins on September 8, 1980, when the Liberal government, under Pierre Trudeau's leadership, presented a constitutional reform package to a meeting of provincial premiers. Four days of meetings failed to produce an agreement on constitutional change, and on October 2 Trudeau announced that his government would proceed unilaterally. On October 6, the Liberal government placed a package of amendments to the constitution, which included, among other items, a domestic amending formula and a constitutionally entrenched charter of rights, before the House of Commons for its approval. Eight days later (October 14), five provinces (British Columbia, Alberta, Manitoba, Québec and Newfoundland) announced that they would challenge the legality of unilateral amend-

Table 8.1
Chronology of Key Events

Date	Event
8-12 September 1980	First Ministers' Conference on constitutional reform: fails to produce agreement
2-6 October 1980	Trudeau announces unilateral patriation with Charter, amending formula and other items; places unilateral patriation before House of Commons
14 October 1980	Five provinces—BC, AB, MB, QC, NFLD—decide to challenge legality of unilateral patriation in the courts of three provinces. PEI joins challenge later. NS and SK hold out. ON and NB support federal government.
6 November 1980	Hearings of the Special Joint Committee of Senate and House of Commons begin
3 February 1981	Manitoba Court of Appeal supports federal government by a majority of 3-2
13 February 1981	Special Joint Committee reports to Parliament
February 1981	NS and SK join the six dissentient provinces, creating the "Gang of Eight"
31 March 1981	Newfoundland Court of Appeal unanimously supports provinces
15 April 1981	Quebec Court of Appeal supports federal government by a majority of 4-1
16 April 1981	Vote in Parliament on final amendments to federal constitutional package. Eight dissentient provinces sign a Constitutional Accord opposing the package.
28 September 1981	Supreme Court judgment that federal unilateralism is legal but contrary to constitutional convention
2-5 November 1981	First Ministers' Conference on the constitution; agreement reached on constitutional changes; inclusion of s.33 (legislative override "notwithstanding clause") makes agreement possible; Quebec dissents
17 April 1982	Constitution Act, 1982, including Charter, proclaimed in force
23 June 1982	Quebec passes Bill 62, attaching s.33 to all existing provincial laws; begins practice of attaching s.33 to all legislation
31 January 1986	Saskatchewan attaches s.33 to "back-to-work" legislation for public sector employees
6 March 1986	Quebec (under Liberal government) stops practice of attaching s.33 to all legislation
7-10 October 1986	Supreme Court hearings in *Morgentaler*

(continued on next page)

9 April 1987	*Alberta Labour Reference*: Supreme Court holds that freedom of association does not encompass a constitutional right to strike
2-3 June 1987	First Ministers' agree to a constitutional amendment (Meech Lake Accord) that satisfies Quebec's requirements for approval of the 1982 constitution
28 January 1988	*Morgentaler* decision: Supreme Court nullifies Criminal Code abortion provisions on procedural grounds
28 July 1988	Government seeks non-binding advice from House of Commons on legislative response to *Morgentaler*: pro-life resolution receives most votes (105)
15 December 1988	*Ford* decision: Supreme Court nullifies Quebec sign law, but rejects substantive review of legislative overrides under s.33
18 December 1988	Quebec government announces new sign law will be implemented and contain a legislative override
19 December 1988	Manitoba government withdraws Meech Lake ratification resolution from legislative consideration
2 February 1989	*Andrews* decision: Supreme Court adopts substantive equality and acknowledges that list of protected groups in s.15 is not exhaustive
6 April 1989	Prime Minister Mulroney condemns s.33 as the "fatal flaw" of the 1982 constitution
6 April 1990	Newfoundland rescinds ratification of Meech Lake Accord
29 May 1990	House of Commons passes Bill C-43: maintains distinction between legal and illegal abortions, but further liberalizes the process for obtaining legal abortions
3 June 1990	Ratification period for Meech Lake Accord ends without ratification
31 January 1991	Bill C-43 defeated in Senate by tie vote
9 July 1992	*Schacter* decision: Supreme Court accepts "reading in" as an "appropriate and just" remedy for some Charter violations
25 May 1995	*Egan* decision: Supreme Court incorporates sexual orientation into s.15
4 November 1997	Supreme Court hearings in *Vriend*
10-11 March 1998	Alberta introduces bill to compensate victims of provincial eugenics laws from 1929-72; proposes to use s.33 to prevent victims from suing province for additional compensation; Alberta withdraws eugenics compensation bill under intense public pressure
2 April 1998	*Vriend* decision: Supreme Court orders Alberta to include sexual orientation in human rights statute

ment in the courts of three provinces. Although Prince Edward Island would subsequently join the legal challenge, Nova Scotia and Saskatchewan remained neutral; only Ontario and New Brunswick supported the federal government. The federal government responded by establishing a Joint Committee of the Senate and House of Commons to undertake public hearings on the constitutional reform proposals. The political purpose of these hearings, which ran from November to February was clear: to undermine provincial government opposition by generating popular support for Trudeau's self-styled "People's Package" of entrenched rights and freedoms. Not surprisingly, most of the groups that testified before the Committee supported the charter in principle and lobbied for one "with terms which were as broad and potent as they could be" (Romanow, Whyte, and Leeson 1984, 248).

As the federal government pursued its political strategy of public hearings, the dissentient provinces were mounting their legal challenge in the courts of appeal of Newfoundland, Manitoba and Québec. This legal strategy produced mixed results: In February, the Manitoba Court of Appeal narrowly supported the federal government; in March the Newfoundland Court unanimously supported the provinces; and in April the Québec Court supported the federal government. During these judicial hearings, Nova Scotia and Saskatchewan ended their neutrality and joined the dissentient provinces, creating what came to be known as the "Gang of Eight." These provinces signed a Constitutional Accord opposing the federal government's action on the same day (April 16, 1981) that Parliament voted on final amendments to the constitutional reform package. The mixed outcome of the appellate court decisions and the continued political stalemate over constitutional amendment ensured that the issue would go before the Supreme Court of Canada, which heard arguments on the federal government's right to proceed unilaterally between April 28 and May 4. Almost five months later, on September 28, the Court held that federal unilateralism was legal but contrary to constitutional conventions.

The Court's judgment, which gave each side a partial victory, created the conditions for a return to the federal-provincial bargaining table. Consequently, in a First Ministers' conference held in early November, the Premier of Saskatchewan proposed to break the stalemate by incorporating into the charter of rights a legislative override provision that would apply to everything except language rights, democratic rights and fundamental freedoms (Romanow, Whyte, and Leeson 1984: 193-215). Attracted by this proposal, the other dissenting provinces pushed for its extension to fundamental freedoms. Sensing the opportunity for an agreement, Trudeau accepted the proposal on condition that the premiers' agree to a five-year limitation clause on any specific use of the legislative override. This "classic example of raw bargaining" (Romanow, Whyte, and Leeson 1984: 211) produced section 33 of the Charter, which allows the federal and provincial governments to declare that a law shall operate "notwithstanding" the Charter's fundamental freedoms, legal rights, or equality rights provisions. As a result, every province with the exception of Québec was now willing to support constitutional change.

The inclusion of section 33 in the Charter meant that the *Constitution Act, 1982* was deliberately ambiguous about the institutional source of authoritative constitutional meaning with respect to rights-based challenges to government action. On the one hand, section 52 of the *Act* declares the principle of constitutional supremacy and authorizes courts to nullify unconstitutional statutes. Moreover, section 24(1) of the Charter gives "anyone whose rights or freedoms, as guaranteed by this Charter, have been infringed or denied" the right to "apply to a court of competent jurisdiction to obtain such remedy as the court considers appropriate and just in the circumstances." On the other hand, section 33 gives legislatures the authority to override judicial decisions, or even to immunize legislation from judicial review under the Charter altogether. As the federal justice minister argued during the House of Commons debate on the matter, the "notwithstanding" clause was a "safety valve" to ensure that "legislatures rather than judges would have the final say on important matters of public policy." Section 33, the minister continued, would allow legislatures "to correct absurd situations without going through the difficulty of obtaining constitutional amendments" (*House of Commons Debates*, 20 November 1981, 13042-43). This ambiguity of constitutional authority is a crucial element of the institutional environment in which the Court would render its *Morgentaler* judgment.

Not surprisingly, the one province that withheld its consent to the 1982 constitution was the first to use section 33. On June 23, 1982 Québec passed Bill 62, which attached a "notwithstanding clause" retroactively to all existing provincial laws, and began the practice of attaching such a clause to all legislation. Québec remained the only jurisdiction, however, to use section 33 until 1986, when Saskatchewan attached a "notwithstanding clause" to legislation forcing public sector employees back to work during a labor dispute. Concerned that the courts might find such interference with the collective bargaining process contrary to "freedom of association," the province declared that its *Saskatchewan Government Employees' Union Dispute Settlement Act* would operate notwithstanding section 2(d) of the Charter. Although the use of section 33 by these provinces generated criticism among constitutional scholars (Scott 1982: 287-303; Arbess 1983: 115-41; Greschner and Norman 1987: 155-98), there was little publicly visible opposition that might undermine the legitimacy of a constitutional provision initially proposed by a politically progressive premier and supported by most provincial governments. Thus, although a new Québec government stopped the practice of attaching section 33 to all legislation in March of 1986, the legislative override was a viable component of the constitutional order when the Supreme Court heard oral arguments in *Morgentaler* from October 7-10, 1986. Indeed, perhaps in recognition of the institutional authority granted to legislatures by section 33, the Court transformed the principle underlying Saskatchewan's use of the "notwithstanding clause" into constitutional law in 1987 when it held that freedom of association does not encompass the right to strike.

The political legitimacy of section 33 began to unravel on December 15, 1988, less than eleven months after the *Morgentaler* judgment on January 28, 1988. In *Ford v. A.-G. Québec* ([1988] 2 S.C.R. 712) the Court nullified provisions of Québec's language law that prohibited the use of English on commercial signs. However, in an indication of the Court's own assessment of the legislative override's legitimacy, it rejected the argument that the use of section 33 should be subject to substantive review. Three days after the judgment, the Québec government announced that a new sign law, shielded from judicial review by the "notwithstanding clause," would be passed and implemented. The judgment, and Québec's reaction, occurred in the midst of a second process of constitutional amendment (the Meech Lake Accord) intended to secure Québec's agreement to the 1982 constitution. Québec's decision to override the Court's *Ford* judgment provoked a hostile reaction from the Manitoba government, which withdrew its resolution ratifying the Accord from legislative consideration on 19 December. With the

Accord now in political trouble because of Québec's action, Prime Minister Brian Mulroney attempted to shift the blame toward the earlier compromise that had resulted in the inclusion of section 33 in the Charter. Speaking in the House of Commons, Mulroney called section 33 "that major fatal flaw of 1981, which reduces your individual rights and mine." This provision, he continued, "holds rights hostage" and makes the entire constitution "not worth the paper it is printed on" (*House of Commons Debates*, 6 April 1989, 153). Despite Mulroney's rhetorical effort the damage was done. Public support for the Accord slipped from 56 percent in June of 1987 to 30 percent in June of 1989; and in April of 1990 Newfoundland rescinded its earlier ratification of the Accord. The deadline for ratification (June 3, 1990) arrived without the unanimous consent required to make the Accord part of the constitution.

The decline in support for section 33 caused by its role in the demise of the Meech Lake Accord is evident in the change in attitude towards it by the important constitutional analyst Patrick Monahan. In his 1987 book on the Charter, Monahan disagreed with those who criticized section 33 as a "constitutional anomaly" that trivialized rights. He argued that it was instead a "powerful and blunt expression" of confidence in the political process and the principle that government action is not necessarily a threat to individual liberty. Section 33, Monahan argued in 1987, does not "legitimate tyranny" but merely ensures "that the political process will not be subject to unreasonable or perverse judicial interpretations" (Monahan 1987: 118-19). However, writing four years later about the collapse of the Meech Lake Accord, he concluded that "the inclusion of the notwithstanding clause in the 1982 constitution was clearly a very serious mistake" (Monahan 1991: 169). Indeed, according to one analyst, the Meech Lake episode so undermined the political legitimacy of section 33 that there was emerging a binding constitutional convention against using it (Heard 1991: 147).

As support for section 33 waned, two other sets of events were also contributing to changes in the institutional environment faced by the Supreme Court. First, the Mulroney government was finding it impossible to respond legislatively to the *Morgentaler* judgment.[3] Six months after the decision, the government asked members of the House of Commons to indicate their position toward several possible revisions to the Criminal Code's abortion provisions in a set of non-binding votes. The proposal that garnered the most support (105 votes) was a pro-life resolution that would have restricted access to abortion even more than the law the Court had nullified. No other proposal, including the government's preferred position, received more than 76 votes. Chastened by the outcome, the government waited until after its re-election in November 1988 to raise the issue a second time. On May 29, 1990 the House of Commons finally passed Bill C-43, which redressed the procedural deficiencies of the nullified statute while maintaining the regulation of abortion within the Criminal Code. However, on January 31, 1991 Bill C-43 failed to gain Senate approval as a result of a tie vote (43-43). The government subsequently announced that it would not attempt to enact new abortion legislation, leaving it unregulated at the national level.

The second set of events consisted of a series of Court decisions that would prove highly relevant for the *Vriend* decision. In 1989, the Court decided its first equality rights case, *Andrews v. Law Society of British Columbia* ([1989] 1 S.C.R. 143). In this judgment the Court adopted a theory of substantive equality and declared that the list of groups explicitly protected under section 15 of the Charter is not exhaustive. Three years later, the Court delivered its judgment in *Schacter v. Canada* (1992), in which it acknowledged that reading additional benefits into legislation is an "appropriate and just" remedy for certain Charter violations ([1992] 2 S.C.R. 679). Finally, in *Egan v. Canada* (1995) the Court incorporated sexual orientation into section 15 and came within one vote of extending spousal benefits under the *Old Age Security Act* to same sex couples.

From the preceding narrative, one can discern two critical moments in the evolution of the strategic environment in which the Court decided *Morgentaler* and *Vriend*. The first was the initial decision to include a legislative override provision in the Charter. The presence of section 33 made it more difficult for the Court to assert ultimate authority over the articulation and enforcement of constitutional rights because it provided a clear institutional mechanism for legislatures to resist any commitment to judicial supremacy in this area. The second critical moment was Québec's decision to invoke the legislative override in the midst of a constitutional ratification process designed to secure that province's acceptance of the 1982 constitution. This decision produced two casualties: the proposed constitutional amendment itself and the political legitimacy of the legislative override. With this institutional check on judicial supremacy significantly weakened, the Court could assert its authority more boldly. In the next section I elaborate how these two critical moments may have affected the Court's strategic choices in *Morgentaler* and *Vriend*.

From Restraint to Activism:
Strategic Behavior and Judicial Supremacy

The argument of this section of the paper is that the shift from restraint in *Morgentaler* to activism in *Vriend* resulted from a change in Supreme Court's capacity to assert supremacy over the development of Charter-based rights policy. *Morgentaler* was only the forty-ninth Charter case decided by the Court, and it was arguably the first case to engage the Court in an issue of broad public visibility and controversy. Moreover, unlike the nineteenth century statue overturned by the U.S. Court in *Roe v. Wade* (410 U.S. 113 [1973]), the provision under review in *Morgentaler* was a liberalizing one less than twenty years old. In addition, the government in power was a politically conservative one with a significant number of members who supported stricter regulation of abortion. Finally, the existence of a still politically viable notwithstanding clause meant that the federal government had the institutional capacity to reverse a decision with which it fundamentally disagreed.

The combination of these factors produced a highly fractured outcome: seven justices produced four separate reasons for judgment, ranging from support for the status quo (upholding the constitutionality of the existing law) to nullification based on a novel interpretation of liberty (right to reproductive freedom). Figure 8.1 sets out these judgments.

Justices William McIntyre and Gerard La Forest, who voted to support the existing law, based their judgment on the Charter's si-

Figure 8.1
Ideal Points of Supreme Court Judges

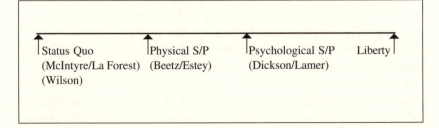

lence on the question of abortion rights. According to McIntyre, "the proposition that women enjoy a constitutional right to have an abortion is devoid of support in the language of s.7 of the Charter or any other section" (*Morgantaler, Smoling, and Scott* 1988: 143). Without such support, McIntyre argued, there was no constitutional reason to nullify the abortion law. Justices Beetz and Estey, like Chief Justice Dickson, focused their attention on the delays women faced in securing permission for a legal abortion as a result of the procedural mechanisms contained in s.251 of the Criminal Code. In their view, these delays created an additional risk to women's health, and thus threatened their section 7 right to security of the person. The Chief Justice and Justice Lamer broadened this procedural approach to include psychological and emotional integrity within the meaning of security of the person. Examining the procedural operation of section 251, he characterized it as "a law which forces women to carry a foetus to term contrary to their own priorities and aspirations and which imposes serious delay causing increased physical and psychological trauma to those women who meet its criteria" ([1988] 44 D.L.R. [4th] 385, 407). Finally, Justice Wilson argued that the right to liberty enumerated in section 7 of the Charter included reproductive freedom, which was essential to "modern women's struggle to assert her dignity and worth as a human being" ([1988] 44 D.L.R. [4th] 385, 491). This meant that all government regulation of abortion during at least the early stages of pregnancy should be prohibited.

How might strategic considerations have affected judicial decision-making in *Morgentaler*? Faced with uncertainty about whether judicial nullification of the federal abortion policy would trigger use of the notwithstanding clause, the justices confronted the possibility that the Court might "lose" its first direct confrontation with Parliament over a highly visible policy issue. In the long-term this outcome could have seriously undermined any future claims to supremacy the Court might make. The solution, particularly evident in the Chief Justice's lead judgment, was to nullify the existing law while maximizing the feasible set of alternatives to legislative override. The overall structure of the judgment was such that Parliament could set a new abortion policy anywhere to the right of the Dickson/Lamer judgment and be reasonably confident that it would survive future constitutional scrutiny under the doctrine articulated in

Morgentaler.[4] Had the overall doctrine been set closer to Justice Wilson's ideal point, Parliament would have had much less room to maneuver. In fact, the plurality judgment in *Morgentaler* excluded only two choices from Parliament's feasibility set: the existing law and re-criminalization of all abortions. With the exception of these two options, however, Parliament retained relatively wide power to regulate abortion even after *Morgentaler*.

The moderate approach to judicial review evident in *Morgentaler* was not at all evident in *Vriend*. The decision generated three judgments. Justices Cory and Iacobucci split the task of articulating the Court's overall judgment. Cory presented the Court's unanimous judgment that provincial human rights acts must prohibit discrimination on the basis of sexual orientation in order to comply with section 15(1) of the Charter, and Iacobucci presented the Court's judgment that this prohibition should be read into the Alberta law and defended the democratic character of this remedy. Justice L'Heureux-Dubé wrote a separate judgment that essentially agreed with the Cory/Iacobucci position. Although he accepted Justice Cory's part of the joint judgment for the majority, Justice Major dissented from Iacobucci's remedial declaration. In essence, the *Vriend* Court minimized Alberta's feasible set of alternatives by presenting the province with a dichotomous choice between accepting the Court's human rights policy preference or invoking the notwithstanding clause.

The Court was able to do this because of the decline in the notwithstanding clause's political legitimacy after December 1988. Moreover, less than a month before the Court issued its *Vriend* judgment, the Alberta government had to withdraw a proposal to invoke the notwithstanding clause. On March 10, 1998 Alberta introduced a bill to compensate victims of provincial eugenics laws in place between 1929 and 1972. One element of the bill was a provision to prohibit victims from suing for additional compensation, and the government proposed to shield that provision from judicial review through the notwithstanding clause. One day later, the provincial attorney general withdrew the bill under intense political pressure. The province's premier explained the decision in the following terms: "It became abundantly clear that to individuals in this country the Charter of Rights and Freedoms is paramount and the use of any tool...to undermine [it] is something that should be used only in very, very rare circumstances."[5] As this statement makes clear, changes in the rules of the political game were communicating a new piece of information to the Court: the notwithstanding clause was a weak, and perhaps even inoperative, obstacle to assertions of judicial supremacy. The Court could thus set its doctrine on this issue at its ideal point.

The strategic explanation of judicial decision-making elaborated in this analysis of *Morgentaler* and *Vriend* rests on two assumptions. The first is that the justices are aware of key elements of the political environment in which they operate, and the second is that they take these elements into account when making decisions. In the context of these two cases, these assumptions require that the justices evaluated the political status of the notwithstanding clause and used that evaluation to determine the extent to which their actual decisions could reflect their ideal policy preferences. Although there is as yet little firm evidence to support this inference, there is at least some foundation on which to construct a circumstantial case. For example, in a speech delivered five months after the *Morgentaler* judgment, Justice Bertha Wilson noted that the notwithstanding clause had "only rarely been invoked, presumably because it might spell political suicide for any government that invoked it!" (Wilson 1988: 375, exclamation in original). This statement suggests that Justice Wilson had reflected on the notwithstanding clause's political status and concluded that there was a low probability of its being invoked. This may explain why she chose a rationale for nullifying the abortion law that left Parliament with the option of either withdrawing from abortion regulation or invoking the notwithstanding clause to override a declaration that the Charter protects a woman's right to reproductive freedom. In her calculation, the probability that the government would select the second option was low enough that she could risk setting her judgment very close to her ideal point. That she may not have been so imprudent as to consider the probability of legislative override to be zero is perhaps indicated by her willingness to allow regulation of late term abortions.

Further evidence that the justices are aware of the notwithstanding clause's political status can be found in recent statements by retired justice Gerard La Forest. In a newspaper interview, La Forest conceded that governments have the power to overrule court judgments, but that "generally speaking it [s.33] is not a clause that the population has wanted any wide us of. I suspect that is why they [governments] have not used it."[6] Like Wilson's 1988 statement, La

Forest's statement indicates that the justices are cognizant of the political capacity of governments to challenge the institutional authority of courts to make rights-based policy. As Justice La Forest appears to recognize in this interview, and as the Alberta government discovered in March of 1998, public opinion acts as a sanction against use of the notwithstanding clause. What occurred in the time between *Morgentaler* and *Vriend* is the development of a rule that legislators will not review in "hard" review of judicial decisions by invoking section 33. Consequently, the Court can be less restrained in exercising rights-based judicial review.

Conclusion

The framing of Canada's 1982 constitution left the institutional authority of courts and legislatures ambiguous with respect to the politics of rights. For a Supreme Court invested with newly expanded powers of judicial review, this ambiguity encouraged the strategic use of these powers in order to avoid a political confrontation that might undermine its long-term institutional status. Consequently, when it entered the moral and political minefield of abortion policy, a majority of the justices chose a rationale for nullification that left Parliament with several options short of legislative override. However, the unfolding of events after December, 1988 gradually shifted the balance of power toward the courts. Justice Iacobucci's assertion in *Vriend* of the Court's broad remedial powers and of the democratic nature of its role under the Charter highlights the magnitude of this shift. In answering the critics of broad judicial review, Justice Iacobucci declared that democratic actors had chosen to give the Court this power, and that the Court would exercise it to its full extent. He further challenged legislatures, almost in the form of a dare, to invoke section 33 if they conclude that the Court has overstepped its authority. From this perspective, *Vriend* may be understood as the final step in a sequence of institutional interactions that completed the transition from legislative to judicial supremacy in Canada.

Like most analyses of its type, the one undertaken in this paper serves primarily to demonstrate the plausibility of judicial strategic behavior and explore how it might operate under certain circumstances. The approach has the advantage of directing our attention to the political nature of judicial decision-making, even in the absence of electoral imperatives. Judges, this approach argues, pursue policy objectives in an environment characterized by uncertainty over outcomes. As a result, they must attempt to predict how other actors might respond to their decisions and adjust their own choices accordingly (Knight and Epstein 1996, 113). Judges must still defend their decisions in legal terms, but their choice among a wide array of alternative legal outcomes may be the product of strategic considerations.

Notes

1. See Murphy (1964); Knight and Epstein (1996). Although subject to much less systematic study than the U.S. Court, there is anecdotal evidence that similar forms of strategic behavior are present on the Canadian Court. See Sossin (1997).
2. See also Tsebelis (1990: 92-118).
3. For an analysis see Flanagan (1997).
4. This assumes, of course, stability in terms of the court's membership and the individual justices' attitudes toward abortion.
5. See www.edmontonjournal.com/archives/031298eugenics2.html (*Edmonton Journal Extra*, March 12, 1998).
6. *National Post*, February 22, 1999, p. A2.

References

(1988) 44 D.L.R. (4th) 385, 407.
[1988] 2 S.C.R. 712.
[1989] 1 S.C.R. 143.
[1992] 2 S.C.R. 679.
[1998] 1 S.C.R. 493.
410 U.S. 113 (1973).

Arbess, Daniel J. 1983. Limitations on legislative override under the Charter of Rights and Freedoms: A matter of balancing values. *Osgoode Hall Law Journal* 21:115-41
Baum, Lawrence. 1997. *The Puzzle of Judicial Behavior.* Ann Arbor: University of Michigan Press.
Bzdera, André. 1993. Comparative analysis of federal high courts: A political theory of judicial review. *Canadian Journal of Political Science* 26:3-29.
Feeley, Malcolm M. and Edward L. Rubin. 1998. *Judicial Policy Making and the Modern State: How the Courts Reformed America's Prisons.* Cambridge: Cambridge University Press.
Flanagan, Thomas. 1997. The staying power of the legislative status quo: Collective choice in Canada's Parliament after *Morgentaler. Canadian Journal of Political Science* 30:31-53.
Greschner, Donna and Ken Norman. 1987. The courts and Section 33. *Queen's Law Journal* 12:155-98.
Heard, Andrew. 1991. *Canadian Constitutional Conventions: The Marriage of Law and Politics.* Toronto: Oxford University Press.
House of Commons Debates, 20 November 1981, 13042-43 (Jean Chrétien).
House of Commons Debates, 6 April 1989, 153 (Brian Mulroney).
Kelly, James B. 1999. The Charter of Rights and Freedoms and the rebalancing of liberal constitutionalism in Canada, 1982-1997. Osgoode Hall Law Journal 37:625-695.

Knight, Jack and Lee Epstein. 1996. On the struggle for judicial supremacy. *Law & Society Review* 30:87-120.

Knight, Jack. 1992. *Institutions and Social Conflict*. Cambridge: Cambridge University Press.

Monahan, Patrick. 1991. *Meech Lake: The Inside Story*. Toronto: University of Toronto Press, 169.

———. 1987. *Politics and the Constitution: The Charter, Federalism and the Supreme Court of Canada*. Toronto: Carswell/Methuen.

Morgentaler, Smoling and Scott v. The Queen (1988), 44 D.L.R (4ᵗʰ) 385 (SCC).

Morton, F.L., Peter H. Russell, and Troy Riddell. 1994. The Canadian Charter of Rights and Freedoms: A descriptive analysis of the first decade, 1982-1992. *National Journal of Constitutional Law* 5:1-60.

Murphy, Walter F. 1964. *Elements of Judicial Strategy*. Chicago: University of Chicago Press.

National Post, February 22, 1999, p.A2.

O'Brien, David M. 1986. *Storm Center: The Supreme Court in American Politics*. New York: W.W. Norton.

Pritchett, Herman. 1948. *The Roosevelt Court: A Study in Judicial Politics and Values 1937-1947*. New York: Macmillan.

Romanow, Roy, John Whyte, and Howard Leeson. 1984. *Canada Notwithstanding: The Making of the Constitution, 1976-1982*. Toronto: Carswell/Methuen.

Scott, Stephen A. 1982. Entrenchment by executive action: A partial solution to 'legislative override'. *Supreme Court Law Review* 4:287-303.

Sossin, Lorne. 1996. The sounds of silence: law clerks, policy making and the Supreme Court of Canada. *U.B.C. Law Review* 30:294-97.

Tsebelis, George. 1990. *Nested Games: Rational Choice in Comparative Politics*. Berkeley: University of California Press.

Vriend vs. Alberta, paragraph 135.

Wilson, Bertha. 1988. The making of a constitution: approaches to judicial interpretation. *Public Law* Vol. 1988, 375.

www.edmontonjournal.com/archives/031298eugenics2.html (*Edmonton Journal Extra*, March 12, 1998).

Part 3

Wrapping Up

9

Concluding Remarks[1]

Ian Shapiro

Introduction

Perhaps the best way to begin would be to start with a summary of my own views on rational choice theory. Second, I will say something about the difficulties with a rational choice approach, again, mostly centred on my own understanding of the theory. Finally, I will make some suggestions in terms of the path forward when thinking about what might make rational choice scholarship in the social sciences more productive, and what rational choice scholars might contribute to those who are engaged in trying to understand the social world.

Problems of Rational Choice

Let me start with some observations about the pathologies of rational choice theory we identified in our original book (Green and Shapiro, 1994). These pathologies have to do with three different issues: the ways in which hypotheses are formulated, the ways in which they are operationalized, and ways in which they are tested. Specifically, in the matter of formulating hypotheses our principal complaint was that the rational choice enterprise tends to be method-driven or theory-driven: it seems to be a method in search of an application. In other words, 'this is my theory, what can it explain?' This way of thinking tends to motivate much of what is done in rational choice theory. I believe that in Professor Hechter's chapter he indeed regards it as a plus of rational choice approaches that they are motivated in this way. On the contrary, we argue for the importance of a problem-driven approach: we say start with a problem, then try to come to grips with efforts that have been made to study it, and then think theoretically about one or another explanations that might contribute to enhancing a fuller understanding of the problem. So in formulating hypotheses we argued against method-driven approaches, of which rational choice theory is only one, perhaps extreme, illustration.

With respect to operationalizing hypotheses, we argued that contrary to the claims about deductive rigor that are often made when talking about rational choice theory's merits, when one turns up the headlamps on the ways in which these hypotheses are operationalized they are often slippery, switching among different definitions of rationality, and moving as well among different definitions of the parameters within which rationality is supposed to operate. As a result, often one cannot get a clear grip on what would be a decisive falsifying instance of a hypothesis, even in principle, in many of the formulations. It is certainly true that writing all one's assumptions down can give a rigorous formulation of an argument and can reveal contradictions that might be missed if they had not been expressed in the first place. I have nothing against writing down the assumptions behind arguments. But in reality, we showed in *Pathologies*, a lot of the apparent rigor in many rational choice formulations conceals muddy thinking about the way in which hypotheses should be operationalized.

Third, in terms of the testing of hypotheses, we discerned a systematic lack of attention to alternative hypotheses and a general tendency to search for confirming illustrations of the theory rather than any systematic attempt to test it. H.J. Hexter was fond of saying of doctrinaire Marxists that the game was "Button, button...where is the bourgeoisie?" while sifting the historical record. We showed that, more often than not, rational choice theorists operate in a like spirit, finding *homo economicus* beneath every rock. Our general finding was that despite the great increase in theoretical sophistication in these literatures, there was not much empirical advance since the seminal formulations by Arrow, Downs and Olson in the 1950s and '60s.

Limits of Rational Choice

Beyond this, we asked: What would make rational choice applications more likely to contribute to advances in social knowledge? I will to say a little more about that later. First let me make a few remarks about why there is so much heat generated by rational choice theory, at least to the extent that the debate has moved outside of economics in the social sciences in the USA and particularly within political science and law. The point that cannot be stressed enough is that with the advent of the rational choice revolution in the social sciences three great claims were made for it. The first was that this was the first seriously deductive and rigorous science to come along in a long time. Second, that because it was concerned with the search for equilibria, it could be a genuine science (it is often thought that the search for equilibrium is a necessary condition of science). And thirdly, that this was a truly interdisciplinary venture.

Each of these three claims contributes, in one way or another I think, to the heat and debate about rational choice theory. On the deductive rigor front many people are alienated and intimidated by rational choice because they do not understand the pyrotechnics. Yet they seem, at the same time, at least dimly aware that a number of the claims for its deductive and rigorous character are overblown. On the question of the search for equilibria, I think people believe that it has turned out to be a bust in the sense that the problem of multiple equilibria is so profound that if in fact that the *sine qua non* of a genuine science were the discovery of predictable equilibria then there could be no science of politics. Rational choice does not seem to be able to deliver even on its own terms. Finally, in terms of interdisciplinary ambitions, to outsiders it looks more like imperialism because from the standpoint of most practitioners of rational choice theory the relevant conception of interdisciplinarity is that others should adopt their methods. In fact, with the first generation of rational choice scholars there has been very little interest in seeing what knowledge had been developed elsewhere in the social sciences and how that might inform what they do.

My own view is that discovering equilibria is not an necessary condition for science. Well-tested middle-level empirical generalizations can indeed contribute to the advancement of knowledge. Perhaps the most profound division between people who are attracted to rational choice theory and those who are repelled by it really comes down to a view of what the purpose of science is: whether its purpose is to generate knowledge or whether its purpose is to generate theory. I think that most people who are strongly attracted to rational choice theory tend to be people who think that the point of the exercise is to generate theory. Those who are resistant to this general *weltanschauung* have an instrumental view of theory. They think that the point of social science is to generate knowledge—conceding that all knowledge claims are corrigible[2].

Let me now briefly move on to say a few things about the difficulties with the rational choice approach. First however, I want to bracket the critique of economics that we had from Professor Rowley. This is a foundationalist critique of the elements of the whole enterprise, which I do not think has much to do with the debate elsewhere in the social sciences. If one looks at what actually fills up the political science journals in the name of rational choice theory, one gets a pretty good sense of some of the complaints we are talking about in our book.

For example, a paper that was sent to me to be refereed by the *American Political Science Review* pretty much contained all the pathologies of rational choice theory that we have talked about. It dealt with the South Africa transition that we have all witnessed since 1990. The authors had clearly found some model in the economics literature and were trying to apply it to explain the transition to democracy in South Africa. A key claim in the model was that as the ratio of the disenfranchised majority to the enfranchised minority went up, revolution would be less likely to occur. Why would this be the case? The assumption was that blacks, when thinking whether to allocate their time between revolutionary activity or productive work (these were the only alternatives posited) would be less likely to devote their energies to revolutionary activities as their relative numbers increased. Why? Assuming that a revolution was successful, all appropriated resources would be equally distributed. Individual blacks thinking about this would realize that they would be getting less in relation to their relative size as the black population grew. They would, therefore, have less of an incentive to be revolutionary militants. Whites, realizing that blacks would reason in this way, would be less likely to negotiate as their relative numbers diminished, because they would realize that blacks would be less likely to be militant. The argument was that as the relative size of whites shrunk, revolution would be less likely.

Now, this analysis was accompanied with the usual fifteen pages of math, and then a conclusion saying that this was a good illustration of the theory. However, you really need to be an academic to take something like that seriously. The reason I mention this particular paper is that, although I sent it back pointing out it obvious inadequacies, three months later there it was again on my desk as a second round resubmission at the *APSR*. So I sent it back pointing out yet again that if this were true, why was the Apartheid government not paying whites to leave the country in the 1970s and 1980s? Here is someone who knew very little, if anything, about South African politics, probably found the model by flipping through an economics journal, and by some sort of contorted associative thinking was led to the idea that this was going to illuminate the transition to democracy in South Africa. There was no discussion of how the case was selected. There was no attempt to address obvious counter-intuitive possibilities. And yet there it was as a second resubmission to the *APSR*.

This example illustrates something of the hegemony that rational choice theory has achieved: that so poor a piece of work would not be screened out by the editor rather than refereed in the first place. Perhaps people who do not understand the math are so intimidated by it that they think that this must be rigorous thinking.

That, however, is the bad work, and there is bad work in every field. In a sense, we really should be more constructive in pointing out what the good work could be or might be. After all, that is what we should all aspire to do. I think that if you look to the better scholars of rational choice theory they do not do work of the kind I just described. However, they are a small minority. If you asked what is characteristic of good rational choice scholarship, I think that it has backed off a great deal on the claims of universalism. It has backed off in three different ways.

One of them we call "limited universalism," capturing the aspiration to give universalistic explanations but only within certain domains. So the question becomes: what are the domains within which rational choice models will explain the outcome? This is one set of questions that I think is worthwhile to debate. A second way in which people have backed away from universalism is what we call "partial universalism" which differs from limited universalism in that it is not about marking off domains in which rational choice theories give you the answer, but rather it is about thinking about strategic variables in combination with other variables when accounting for the variance of any given outcome. In this case the question becomes: how much of the variance in any particular outcome is dealt with by strategic considerations versus other considerations? For example, there is a literature in international relations for why wars begin. There is a rational choice literature that says that they begin as a by-product of nations pursuing their strategic interests. But how much of the variance does that actually explain?

One of my recent colleagues, Alan Stam, did an empirical study of all the different rational choice theories and the most helpful ones seemed to explain a very minor part of the variance of why wars begin. Interestingly enough, what explains vastly more of the variance is whether or not the countries are next to each other. We can, of course, still usefully theorize about the 2 percent or whatever it is, but nonetheless, the use of partial universalism is the following: how much of the variance are we talking about, and in conjunction with which other variables for explaining the outcome?

The third way of backing off on the claims to universalism is to say that rational choice theory is not a theory at all but actually a family of theories or set of approaches. I think that that is often the case. People who actually call themselves rational choice theorists often share very little in common with others who also call themselves rational choice theorists.

Limited and partial universalism are healthy moves within the discipline. I would like to say just one thing before I move onto the recommendations for a partial or limited type of rational choice theory. It is important not to forget that once we abandon the universalism in any of these forms, we are also abandoning the claim that what is being done within rational choice theory is something qualitatively different and superior to what is being done elsewhere in explanatory social science.

Conclusion

My recommendations are basically four: first, to avoid method-driven research. If one's tool is only a hammer, then everything in sight starts to look like a nail. One should always start with a problem, see what the state of the art knowledge is about the study of it is, and then see whether it is possible to do better with a new theory (Shapiro, 2002).

Second, I think it is much more likely to be fruitful if people stick to one definition of rationality and see where it works and where it fails, rather than constantly manipulating and adjusting to look for some account of rationality that fits every possible circumstance (as when voting is said to be the strategic maximization of one's sense of civic duty). Rather than multiply family members in order to have some variant of rationality that accounts for anything and every-thing, it is better to stick to one definition of strategic maximization and see how much work it can actually do.

Third, scholars should indeed think of strategic maximization in combination with other variables when accounting for the variation of outcomes, rather than trying to get rational choice theory to ex-plain all of the variance.

Finally, and perhaps most important, scholars should think about the conditions under which rational choice explanations are likely to do better or worse in the empirical world. This is substantially an empirical endeavour, to which the following six considerations seem relevant[3] : First that the stakes be high and the players be self-con-scious optimisers. Second, that preferences be well ordered and rela-tively fixed, which in turn probably requires individuals to be ho-mogeneous or corporate agents. (Otherwise we have the problem of disagreement within the units expected to do this maximizing, firms, classes, etc.). Third, actors must confront a range of clearly defined options. Fourth, the strategic complexity of the situation must not be overwhelmingly great for the actors. Fifth, there should not be great differences in the strategic capacities of the actors—no great differences in dumbness. Last, rational choice explanations are likely to do well in circumstances where the actors have the capacity to learn from feedback in the environment and adapt. At least as a point of departure, these considerations, and no doubt there are others, seem likely to help demarcate those areas where we would expect rational choice theories to do well. These consid-erations are not derived analytically from a deductive argument. They involve empirical claims which would have to be subjected to empirical tests.

Notes

1.   These remarks draw from and build upon my paper with Donald Green (Green and Shapiro, 1996).
2.   For elaboration of what is at stake here, see Shapiro, (2003: chs.1, 6 and 8).
3.   [Eds. Note]: Compare Taylor (1996,1993); Tsebelis (1990: 32-33), Chong (2000).

References

Chong, Dennis. 2000. *Rational Lives: Norms and values in politics and society*. Chicago and London: University of Chicago Press.
Green, Donald P. and Ian Shapiro. 1996. Pathologies revisited: Reflections on our crit-ics, in Jeffrey Friedman (ed.) *The Rational Choice Controversy: Economic Models of Politics Reconsidered*. New Haven, CT and London: Yale University Press.

Green, Donald P. and Ian Shapiro. 1994. *Pathologies of Rational Choice Theory: A Critique of Applications in Political Science*. New Haven, CT and London: Yale University Press.

Shapiro, Ian. 2003. *The Moral Foundations of Politics*. New Haven, CT and London: Yale Univrersity Press.

Shapiro, Ian. 2002. Problems, methods, and theories in the study of politics, or: What's wrong with political science and what to do about it? *Political Theory*, 30: 588-611.

Taylor, Michael. 1996. When rationality fails, in Jeffery Friedman (ed.) *The Rational Choice Controversy:Economic Models of Politics Reconsidered*. New Haven, CT and London: Yale University Press.

Taylor, Michael 1993[1989]. Structure, culture and action in explanations of social change, in William James Booth, Patrick James and Hudson Meadwell (eds.) *Politics and Rationality*. Cambridge and New York: Cambridge University Press.

Tsebelis, George. 1990. *Nested Games. Rational Choice in Comparative Politics*. Berkeley and Los Angeles: University of California Press.

Conclusion

Hudson Meadwell and Axel van den Berg

Introduction

In this chapter we pick up some of the themes of the previous pieces. In particular, given the mix of contributors, we first discuss the relationship between rational choice theory and economics. In a second section, we then turn to the relationship of rational choice theory and some of its rivals in other social science disciplines, especially in sociology and political science. Finally, we will comment on the "bifurcationist" psychological model (based on the distinction between beliefs and desires) which influences work on rational choice.

George Grantham and Robin Rowley have provided an historical and analytical survey of the concept of rationality within the discipline of economics. At the same time, several other contributors, including Michael Hechter and Ian Shapiro, have noted that the "homeland" (Hechter) of rational choice theory is in fact economics, and that its influence in the social sciences has spread outward from this origin. We might assume, then, that all rationalist work is economic, and that resistance to rational choice is strictly directed at maintaining the integrity of other social science disciplines against economic "imperialism" (Shapiro).[1] The resistance to the intrusion of economics is directed at arguments that are general in scope or that can easily be generalized, more than at specific arguments about limited economic phenomena. Other social scientists have been using economic theory for years. Theories of international trade, for example, theories of growth, including endogenous growth, theories of cartels, or theories of national economic performance are now so central to contemporary political economy that it would be difficult to imagine this field absent these contributions.[2] These types of middle-range theory are not typically the objects of criticism. Rather, resistance seems to be directed against claims that the only theoretical language in the social sciences is economic. So, for example, the economics of information is more likely to be a focal point of dispute than the economics of trade because the former has more general implications.

Disciplinary insecurities aside, however, what if not all rationalist work in the social sciences is economic? We could then limit the extension of economic theory, for example, without giving up a rational theory of action. Put differently, we could construct an alternative to, say, an economic theory of politics or of society by arguing that there are constitutive features of the social and political that are not economic and, further, by arguing that at least some of these features imply rational agents.[3]

Therefore in the first part of this chapter, we set out to disentangle economic theory and method in order to consider the possibility that there is rationalist work in the social sciences that is not economic. We examine a central intellectual problem in neoclassical economics—the existence of competitive equilibrium—in light of (relatively) recent innovations in method (game theory) that reflect the mathematization of rationality discussed by Grantham (see also the contribution by Smith). Game theory, especially in its most ambitious versions, raises some fundamental issues about the prospects and limits of rational choice theory in the social sciences. This is so particularly in light of the kind of claim made by Harsanyi (1995: 293) that in principle every social situation involves strategic interaction, thus making game theory the theoretical language for all social science.

If there is such work as alluded to above—rationalist yet not economic—the charge of economic imperialism cannot be laid at its feet and, more importantly, it implies that rational action is an intrinsic feature of the subject matter of other social science disciplines. Yet such work does not imply that rational action exhausts this subject matter.

Thus, as we observed in our Introduction, issues arise concerning the relationship of rational action to other types of action, and the relationship of theories of rational action to other theories in the social sciences. We argued that the possibility of theory-building across the polemical lines of debate around rational choice theory has been obscured. Several of our contributors, such as John Hall and Ian Shapiro, have argued for a middle way—that is, for ways in which "strategic variables" (Shapiro) combine with other variables to generate outcomes. Both Hechter and Manfredi work with models of rational agents that imply that theories of rational action complement other theories, whether institutional or structural. Hechter opts for "thick" models of rational action at the macro level in historical sociology that include the analysis of motives; Manfredi does the same at a micro level in his contribution on strategic voting in the Canadian Supreme Court. Michael Smith, however, questions whether pure calculation (a purely calculative form of trust) can account for the relationship between employment security and employee effort in modern industry. His argument is that the calculative trust endogenously generated within prisoners' dilemma games is not sufficient to account for effort. We touch on a related issue in the first section, where we discuss endogeneity and game models in the context of economic theory, but in the second section of this chapter we are more concerned with how rational choice theory might complement other theories, particularly in political sociology.

Finally, several of our contributors see rational choice theory as resting on intentional explanations and on a psychological model that includes beliefs and desires which we call, following Vogler (2002), the "bifurcationist" model. These features are fairly explicit in the chapter by Hechter, and are present, if not directly addressed, in the contributions of Manfredi and Hall. On the other hand, some contributors are more critical. Grantham concludes his chapter with a discussion of "embodied rationality" that seeks to establish a break with standard desire and belief psychology. McCall's contribution on deliberation has the interesting feature, for an argument about deliberation and practical reasoning, of seeking to ground his example of deliberation in a form of physicalism ("brain states"). Moreover, there are both supporters and critics of rational choice theory who link the theory more narrowly to instrumentalism rather than strictly to a desire-belief model of agency. Smith, for example, implies that motivating emotions such as hurt or humiliation are inconsistent with rational choice theory, because these emotions are non-calculative.

Belief-desire psychological models and dependence on intentional explanations are actually quite widespread in the social sciences. We do not believe that they are features unique to rational choice theory. This kind of shared ground may well increase the likelihood that rational choice theory and at least some of its rivals complement one another. While this possibility is taken up in the second section, we turn to a more direct discussion of the bifurcationist model and its relationship to instrumentalism in the final section of the chapter. We consider the distinctions among instrumental, moral and expressive actions from several different viewpoints.

We develop our arguments by distinguishing (conventionally, we believe), between two different types of rationality. Without wanting to inscribe these differences in stone, they are parametric and strategic rationality.[4] We distinguish them provisionally in the following manner.

In the first case, where rationality is parametric, independent actors "observe" parameters and their values, and optimize within them. In the second case, rationality is strategic. Actors' preferences over outcomes do not translate into preferences over possible decisions since outcomes also depend on the decisions of other actors. In the first case, therefore, there are *parametric* structures, and individuals register (process) structural qualities in making decisions and acting. In the second case, however, the situation has a *strategic* structure and there is interdependent choice. In the first instance we need decision theory; game theory is needed in the second instance (Gates and Hume, 1997).

Hechter and Manfredi use rational choice theory in ways that illustrate some of these differences. Hechter's analysis is sociologically-centric and counsels us to explain the behavior of average, typical members of large populations. This advice has been part of the sociological mainstream since Durkheim; Hechter's innovation is his argument that rational choice theory is a better way into this issue than its sociological competitors. Manfredi presents an argument about politics in a small setting. His analysis ends when he has developed a causally adequate interpretation of the strategic choices of specific judges.

Parametric and strategic rationality set up differently, at least in theory. The former is more amenable to Millian models[5] of explanation and statistical inference, whether the data is qualitative or quantitative. Observations on outcomes are recorded and considered against variations in antecedent conditions. The general goal is unbiased and robust estimates of effects. Econometrics is the most sophisticated expression of this method of making valid inferences in the social sciences, but what it describes at a high level of abstraction also underpins much of quasi-experimental research design, even when the laws of large numbers cannot be satisfied. Parametric rationality is consistent with this model of inference because, under the assumption of parametric rationality, individuals are registers of parametric values (antecedent conditions) in chains of efficient causes[6] and intentional states. Typically, econometric analysis distinguishes exogenous and endogenous variables (and this feature is compatible with the model of an agent optimizing within exogenous parameters), and also places a positive value on exogenous variables. The latter allow models to be identified,[7] and thus estimated with as little bias as possible. By contrast, game theory is to strategic structures what econometrics is to parametric structures—a method—in this case, a method for analyzing strategic interaction (Cox. 1999: 159). Further, there is a strong tendency in game theory towards endogenizing variables, as we discuss in the next section.

Although both econometrics and game theory find their fullest development in contemporary economics, they are not economic *theories* and to use them, formally or informally, is not to apply economic theory. There are good reasons, therefore, to consider parametric and strategic rationality within an economic context, to start with here, and to consider how economic theory and more general method might be disentangled.

Rationality and Economics

Game theory in fact was not essential to the formal solutions to the problem that dominated twentieth century economic theory through the 1950s—the existence of competitive equilibrium. The neoclassical heart of economic theory assumed parametric rationality by a large number of agents in a perfectly competitive, private goods economy. An economy is competitive, in other words, if it has many agents, each of whom has too small an endowment to have a significant effect. There are prices for all goods that each agent takes as given. When in equilibrium, the price system coordinates the independent decisions of agents, each of whom is optimizing in a passive environment. Competitive equilibrium is the outcome of parametric rationality, and agents engage in independent choice. The problems for this model that arose from work on rational expectations point to assumptions about the information contained in the price system. One purpose of this work was to reconcile (a) aggregate states of the economy (the existence of business cycles) with (b) the efficiency properties of the price system and (c) the theory of optimizing behavior by individuals.

Competitive equilibrium, however, is also a limiting case of strategic rationality. As the number of agents tends to infinity, the "core" of a cooperative game (all those allocations in the economy that no coalition of agents can improve upon) tends to the set of competitive allocations (Aumann, 1964; Shubik, 1984: 378-92). That is, as the number of agents increases, the core 'shrinks' to a set of economic agents in which there are no coalitions, only independent agents. A similar result is obtained using non-cooperative game theory. The non-cooperative equilibrium converges to competitive equilibrium as the number of agents tends toward infinity (Gale, 2000: 11).

These results for economic exchange vary with the number of agents, the size of agents and the properties of goods. Roughly speaking, there are (1) few or many agents of (2) equal or unequal size in a (3) private goods or public goods economy. All else equal, for example, the fewer the number of agents, the more strategic interaction in a private goods economy. All else equal, the larger the number of agents, the higher the likelihood of strategic misrepresentation of preferences in a public goods economy (the free-rider problem).

This perspective on economic exchange under varying characteristics of agents and goods relegated game theory to a class of special cases or deviations, related to market imperfections or failures. The neoclassical analysis of general equilibrium was about parametric rationality—optimizing behavior by independent agents —from its foundations in the late nineteenth and early twentieth centuries to the formal work of Arrow and Debreu in the 1950s.

With the progressive development of game theory, however, it has become increasingly difficult to restrict the use of game theory to "special cases" of economic exchange associated with market imperfections or failure. There is now a research program aimed at providing strategic foundations for the theory of competitive equilibrium (see Gale, 2000). This program illustrates the power and ambition of game theory, and raises some issues that have implications both for the relationship of economic theory to other social sciences, and the role of game theory in other social sciences.

There are two key steps in this research program. The first step is to make endogenous as many variables as possible. The second step is to specify that all endogenous variables are chosen by players in the game (Gale, 2000: 3ff).[8] It is this second step that is the distinguishing mark of the research program, since models of market equilibrium that are not game-theoretic have endogenous variables that are not chosen by the agents (Gale, 2000: 3). This second step is the contribution of game theory qua method. A variable that is not chosen by agents, by implication, is not endogenous.

The second step does not *strictly* imply the first. However, variables that are not chosen by players are beyond the purview of game theory. So the second step tends to imply the first because, otherwise, the range of the application of game theory is limited. The more variables which are included as endogenous, the greater the range of game theory, as long as we also specify that endogenous variables are chosen by players. Hence the two steps work together in this research program. However, they are analytically separable. The tendency in this research program is to make endogenous as much as possible, while also specifying that everything endogenous is chosen.

Recall, however, that this is a program in economics; game theory is a set of methodological tools. This point can be overlooked because of the ways in which game theory and economic theory are intertwined in work in this area. In making everything endogenous in order to satisfy a methodological desideratum associated with game theory, however, what also happens is that everything is made endogenous according to economic criteria. So there is nothing that is endogenous that is not economic. But this is a *theoretical* specification, and it is not derived from the methods of game theory. The latter only specifies that everything endogenous is chosen, not that everything that is endogenous (and chosen) is economic.

However, when this methodological desideratum—that everything endogenous is chosen—is set within economic theory, what is maximized is not only the range of application of game theory but also the range of application of economic theory. Not only is everything that is endogenous chosen; further, everything endogenous is at the same time an economic phenomenon. There is something that is begged in all of this, when you are not a practicing economist. The relationship of economic exchange to other political, social and cultural activities and institutions falls out of the picture.

A sociologist, for example, might wonder if the economic exchanges that we associate with the modern market do not presuppose generalized trust among participants, and question whether generalized trust can be endogenously generated by those very exchanges that it underpins, as Smith has done in this volume. The *function* of trust in these economic exchanges may be to lower the transaction costs of exchanges. Whether this is enough to account for the emergence or presence of trust is another question altogether. To invoke "function" and to leave it at that, is to use a functionalist explanation rather than efficient causation or an intentional explanation. The sociological point of view thus asks whether generalized trust can be an endogenous variable chosen by players, in just the same way as those variables that endogenously produce competitive equilibrium are chosen. If generalized trust is required for competitive equilibrium but cannot be endogenously generated, this research program in economics fails, not strictly because of failure to meet the standards of game theory, but because it has been unable to identify the "embedded" nature of economic exchange.[9]

A political scientist might ask a very similar question about the relationship of authority structures to economic exchange. This issue is most apparent of course for the provision of public goods, and quasi-public goods where exclusion mechanisms are imposed on a public good (Snidal, 1979). It does not follow, however, that private goods economies are immune from the general problem of exclusion. The price system is not an exclusionary mechanism. So as long as there are exclusion costs in a private goods economy, a price system that reflects only production costs does have fully efficient properties (Millward, 1970). If control over exclusion is achieved through a system of property rights (Snidal, 1979: 546), the strategic foundations of competitive equilibrium must generate a system of property rights at the same time as they generate the required properties of the economy.[10] Otherwise, there are endogenous variables that have not been chosen by the players, and this result is inconsistent with game theory.

There are several possibilities at this point. One option would be to simultaneously specify what economic exchange implies as its necessary underpinnings—authority structures and property relations[11] on the one hand and generalized trust on the other, as well as the usual economic variables (cf. Hettich and Winter, 1999: 39). Another would be to demonstrate that these features are actually not necessary underpinnings and so do not need to be specified. Third, however, failure to accomplish either of these two options acknowledges spheres of activity that economic theory cannot take on board.

This research program in economics draws on game theory to establish the strategic foundations for market equilibrium. From this program, however, it is possible to see what underpins the ambitions of game theorists, independent of the application of game theory in economics. That ambition is to make as much as possible endogenous to the game and to make everything that is endogenous chosen by the players. Such a program is a pretty thoroughgoing alternative to much of conventional social science. It points out how much of the latter has depended on notions of parametric rationality. Much of social science is bound up in Millian methods of difference and similarity, quasi-experimental design and statistical inference that depend on the causal importance of unchosen exogenous variables, such that it can be difficult to see how radical is the challenge implicit in game theory.

While we can appreciate the ambitions of game theory, however, we also have to ask whether a program that makes everything endogenous is achievable. While it is too early to tell whether this program can be pulled off in a full-blown version, there are reasons to be doubtful. First of all, there is some evidence to suggest that a complete research program of this type cannot be consistently completed. Such a strong game theoretic research program might be vulnerable to the results of Gödel's incompleteness theorem. This theorem was in fact a response to the axiomatization of mathematics at the turn of the twentieth century that so influenced the development of mathematical economics (as described by Grantham in this volume). By taking advantage of the structure of self-referential paradoxes, Gödel demonstrated that the development of a contradiction-free synactic (content-free) framework for all mathematics was impossible (Godel [1931] in van Heijenoort [1967]). "[F]or every consistent formal system M, there is at least one statement G that cannot be proved or disproved in M" (Casti and Depauli, 2000: 37, see also Nagel and Newman, 2001).

Secondly, from a different point of view, the problem is one of bootstrapping. This problem within game theory is similar to the problem of under-determination in causal inference. This issue has already emerged within game theory. The problem is that there are too many equilibria and no way to choose among them (Morton, 1999: 164-208; Kreps, 1990: 95-127). There are "games that have many equilibria, and the theory [game theory] is of no help in sorting out whether any one is the 'solution' and, if one is, which one is" (Kreps, 1990:97). Moreover, it appears as if this problem arises, not at the limit, that is, just as the game theoretic research program is about to be completed, but relatively early in the program.

Two common solutions to this problem work by externally limiting the range of game theory. One solution is to admit endogenous variables that are not chosen; the other is to directly acknowledge the existence of exogenous variables. From a strict game theoretic point of view, however, these solutions are inconsistent because they bring into analysis something other than game theory. There are, however, also resources internal to game theory with which to deal with the problem of multiple equilibria. This type of solution generally depends on invoking a stronger notion of equilibrium (Kreps, 1990: 108). A prominent solution, for example, requires that a Nash equilibrium not involve an incredible threat (or promise) (Kreps, 1990: 126)[12] and this refinement is associated with the related game theoretic notions of subgame perfection and backward induction.[13] Manfredi's analysis in his chapter in fact lends itself to this type of refinement (Manfredi, 2002).

Two concepts have had some influence as external solutions to the problem of multiple equilibria: focal points (e.g., Schelling, 1960) and bounded rationality (e.g., Young, 1993 and the discussion by Grantham and Rowley in this volume). The first concept clearly brings into a game theoretic analysis something that is not endogenous. The second concept presents more complicated problems. The concept of bounded rationality is drawn from the literature on parametric rationality, which is about individual decision-making under uncertainty and risk. How it can be extended to strategic interaction is still an issue. On the one hand, bounded rationality might be interpreted as optimization under constraints—in this instance, constraints associated with cognitive processes.[14] If it is interpreted in this way, however, as a version of parametric optimization under special conditions, it must still be made explicitly strategic to be reconciled with choice in interdependent settings.

On the other hand, bounded rationality can be interpreted as implying heuristic choice that does not optimize. If it is interpreted in *this* way, however, there is evidence that individuals use different heuristics depending on whether their choice situations are parametric or strategic (Gigerenzer, 1996; Gigerenzer and Todd, 1999). In other words, even non-optimizing heuristic choice may vary systematically according to the type of situation—strategic or parametric.

What we have just described is the strong game theoretic research program, which rests on the two steps identified earlier. A weaker version of the program still depends on interdependent choice and strategic interaction, but it does not insist that everything that is endogenous is chosen (otherwise put, the weaker version admits the presence of exogenous variables). The weaker version of the program is still powerful.

The general conjecture of the weak game theoretic program is that human action is often strategic. Even in this weaker version, it is a challenge to assumptions that individual rationality in human activity is simply parametric. When strategic rationality is present (surely an empirical question), models based exclusively on parametric rationality may be first approximations, justified by the unavailability of information on actors and structures, or "reduced forms" of more general models based on strategic rationality.[15] Such models, however, may be adequate for many empirical problems. More strongly still, if a fully specified model of strategic interaction in which everything is endogenous is, in principle, unachievable, then these models will continue to be essential.

Indeed, this is where much of the debate about rational choice has been joined. That is, most debate has not been about game theory and strategic interaction, but about the mechanisms that link individuals and their choices, independent of the structure of the situation. Whether the structure is parametric or strategic, the mechanism is the same in rational choice theory: egocentric instrumental rationality. Strategic choice and parametric rationality alike are the result of egocentric instrumental rationality. While we consider the issue of instrumentalism more directly in the final section, we now look at the issue of theoretical rivalry and complementarity.

Rivals, Substitutes, or Complements?

Alternatives to rational choice theory are rivals according to how they specify mechanisms that link causes and action. "Institutional" or "structural" challenges to rational choice theory are thoroughgoing *external* challenges when they rest on non-individualist premises, and do not specify any individual-level mechanism at all that links causes and action[16]. This kind of argument would likely be drawn to some form of evolutionary theory.

An institutional or structural theory is a challenge to rational choice, and is *internal* to a form of *methodological* individualism, if it specifies a psychological mechanism different from rational choice mechanisms. And it is no challenge if it relies on mechanisms to link causes and action that are variations of those mechanisms that are consistent with rational choice theory.[17] For example, one of the strongest versions of an "objective, structuralist, non-voluntarist" macro theory in political sociology—Skocpol's (1979) theory of social revolution —can be recast in the language of rational action so easily that one suspects that it always depended on unstated assumptions about rational action. Skocpol (1994: 324-325) inadvertently admits as much when she claims that Taylor's (1993[1989]; 1988) rational choice criticisms are merely a gloss on her structuralist theory of revolution. Some "structuralists," such as Skocpol (1995), now see themselves as institutionalists, but much of this new institutionalism, when pushed, is dependent on assumptions about rationality and individual psychology. As we argued in the Introduction, rational choice theory is far less vulnerable to the charge that it presupposes atomised individuals than some of its critics realise. It is not inconsistent for a rational choice theorist, for example, to argue that processes of political mobilization are interactive over relations, rather than additive over individuals. Further, rational choice theory can specify models of mobilization or collective behavior more generally that are time-dependent ("cascade" models or "tipping" models), as is done, for instance, by Coleman (1990, ch. 9).

However, the key term in some of the current alternatives to rational choice theory, as Taylor and Hall (1996) have noted, despite the ostensible interest in *institutions,* is *culture.* Institutions are cultures; that is, they are repositories of intersubjective social meanings, pre-existing, unchosen (and learned)[18] by actors. To paraphrase an intellectual historian writing about related issues (Baker, 1982), they are fields of action symbolically constituted, each subject to elaboration and development through the activities of agents whose purposes they define. The role of individual agency, independent of cultural givens, is actually rather limited in these arguments; this is the point of emphasizing the importance of roles and socialization—the hallmarks of the types of institutionalism that we are referring to here. Culture is constitutive of meaning in these accounts and individuals are treated as carriers of cultural practices, and their action is treated as instantiations of cultural practices. Individuals are defined by their location(s) in culture(s) and individual purposes are little more than these locations. In other words, these fields of discourse or cultures are *endogenously* maintained and reproduced by carriers of culture, much as in strong versions of contemporary social constructivism.

This is an ambitious research program, as ambitious in its own way as the game theoretic research program we discussed earlier. It is, however, not obvious that it can be completed without contradiction. To the extent that these arguments depend on individual agency to account for cultural/institutional reproduction and change, they will be incoherent since they will have been shown to presuppose what they have claimed to reject. And without independently specified agents, who are more than structural locations, these types of accounts may be vulnerable in other ways.

Without *independently* specified agents, they are relying, implausibly in our judgement, on counterfactuals that do not imply individualist premises. A theoretical principle other than the systemic qualities of cultures, is required—an agent-principle that links the comparative implications of different discourses to the agent's dispositions. Still, a weaker (more sensible) version of such a research program is very plausible. Choice is not the free play of signifiers. We do not write on a blank slate when we act.

There is some reason to think, therefore, that some rival arguments are complements, rather than substitutes for rational choice theory. Rational choice theorists and at least some of their critics are actually writing on the same page. A really radical alternative to rational choice theory, as we have just noted, should be able to specify counterfactuals that do not imply individualist premises (James, 1985: 143-145; on counterfactual reasoning in the social sciences, see Elster 1978; Tetlock and Belkin, 1996; Ferguson, 2000; Przeworski, 1996). Alternatives to rational choice that specify counterfactuals that imply individualist premises share something with rational choice. This feature may help to account for the success of some of the dialogue across theories and, as such, the terrain shared by rational choice theory and some rivals is not trivial.

The debate about institutions and rationality thus is a debate internal to methodological individualism whenever institutional analysis implies counterfactuals that have individualist premises. Sociological and historical institutionalism sometimes look like more radical alternatives in the debate but they rarely are thoroughgoing rivals. Rational choice institutionalism is certainly methodologically individualist, but the "thin" version of parametric rationality on which much of it rests actually requires context, which is precisely what attention to society, history and institutions provide. As we noted in the Introduction, recent work on analytical narratives is designed to join rational choice theory and historical narrative (although, not surprisingly, not without some debate). So these varieties of institutional analysis are complements more than they are rivals or substitutes.

Instrumentalism, Beliefs, and Desires

In effect, the discussion in the preceding sections concedes ground to the critics of rational choice. Yet the ground conceded may not be enough for some of them. To suggest, for example, that theories are partial complements rather that pure rivals implies some degree of compatibility between theories and more radical critics will be inclined to challenge this implication.

There is a stronger type of criticism of rational choice, inconsistent with complementarity, that we therefore need to consider. It is that there are classes of action that are incompatible with instrumentalism. Hechter's separation of value-oriented action from instrumentally-oriented action (central to Weberian political sociology) and emotional action is one version of such an argument, and note that it comes from someone who is typically taken to be a proponent of rational choice theory. The distinction between instrumental behavior and normative and expressive behavior (e.g., Taylor, 1996) is another example. And another is the theory of action proposed by Habermas which rests on a fundamental distinction between communicative and strategic action (e.g., Habermas, 1984).

One basic intuition here is that the 'perfectly principled act" (moral action) and the "spontaneous release of feeling" (expressive action) share something that separates them from instrumental acts. "Moral action threaten[s] to prove an exception... because the reasons for it seemed to go too deep. Expressive action is supposed to pose a problem because the reasons don't go deep enough." (Vogler, 2002: 233-234). Moral and expressive actions are "essentially non-calculative" (Vogler, 2002: 230, cf. Hechter, this volume, and Michael Smith's emphasis on the importance of calculation in distinguishing different types of trust), according to this point of view. Since these classes of action have this essential feature, they are inconsistent with rational choice. Thus no rational choice account can coherently invoke them.

The criteria invoked within this point of view for distinguishing these types of actions, however, are still not fully convincing. These classifications are vulnerable to challenges from two different perspectives—causal and non-causal theories of action. Whichever of these two theories is true, and for present purposes we are indifferent between them, problems arise for these standard classifications of action. That they are vulnerable in this way, however, that is, across very different theories of action, suggests that these ways of distinguishing types of action need more detailed justification or even reformulation. There are serious difficulties for these classifications whichever of these theories of action is the superior one.

One influential causal theory of action (Davidson, 1980[1963], but see also Vogler's discussion of Davidson, 2002: 213-22) proposes that intentional actions are explicable in terms of agents' reasons. The notion of acting on a reason is built on two ideas: "the idea of cause and the idea of rationality. A reason is a rational cause. One way rationality is built in is transparent: the cause must be a belief and desire in light of which the action is reasonable" (Davidson, 1980[1963]: 9). And in Davidson's work, explanations by reasons are descriptions of instrumentally rational courses of action. (Mele, 2003: 71). This argument cuts rather a wide swath: for every action that can be assigned a reason explanation, that action is instrumentally rational. So the critics of instrumentalism who, let us recall, want to limit the extension of instrumentalism so that expressive and moral actions are not contaminated by it would have to argue these actions are either not actions at all, or are actions without causes, or have causes but these causes are not reasons, or provide a different account of reason explanations that did not depend on instrumental rationality in the way that Davidson's account does.[19]

There are non-causal theories of action as well, however. Is the standard way of distinguishing action (moral, expressive, instrumental) more defensible under a non-causal theory of action (such as Anscombe, 2000[1957])? Recent work by Vogler (2002) suggests that a non-causal theory raises similar problems. She examines what she calls the "standard picture" of practical reason, which is linked, in her view, to instrumentalism. She understands the latter as the doctrine (much as in Davidson above) that action derives from psychological states in which reason is instrumental to desires. She rejects this view. Vogler makes the case that the "calculative form" is characteristic of intentional action, including moral and expressive action. The rational structure in intentional action is calculative where the latter is understood as "the business of figuring out how to attain some end you want to attain" (Vogler, 2002: 231). The claim that practical reason is primarily calculative is not a claim about the psychological antecedents of rational action (as in Davidson). It is a claim that every action has a means-end structure. That is, calculation is not a cause but more like a constitutive feature of action.

Is it the case that calculation is essential only to instrumental action and, if it is common to all types of action, is it simply trivial because it is common? If common, it is hard to see that it would be trivial, given the importance of calculation as the activity that marks the instrumental off from other actions according to the critics.

If a means-end relationship, and the matching of means to ends (calculation), structures action in general, the price of preserving the distinctiveness of expressive and moral 'acts' by arguing that they are essentially non-calculative is to deny that they are actions at all. If we move in this direction, the odds are that the relationship of rationality to action will be quite different than it is in *both* contemporary rational choice theory and other forms of political and social theory. The most fundamental distinction might not be between rational action and its contrast class ('not-rational' action), but between action and its contrast (awkwardly, 'not-actions'). Calculation might stand in a conceptual rather than empirical relation to action, and 'rational' might be a strictly evaluative rather than an empirical term.

So the case of the critics would be strengthened if they could show that their definition of calculation has positive theoretical qualities that Volger's definition does not have. If they cannot do this, then they need either to give up a large part of their criticism (that certain types of action have incompatible qualities), or find another marker (other than calculation) by which to set instrumental action off from expressive and moral action. And if they cannot defend their version of calculation or find an alternative marker, then the claim of incompatibility is not valid. Notice that this is an exercise in providing criteria by which to identify instances of different types of action. To claim that the exercise is tautological would be to miss the point. The exercise is conceptual rather than empirical, explanatory or evaluative. And the problem for the critics is that the criterion used to differentiate types of action does not do the work they require it to do. If calculation is constitutive of intentional action, it does not distinguish different *types* of intentional action.

A response from the critics perhaps might argue that we have shown no more than expressive and moral actions are "rationalizable" and that rationalizability precludes relatively little. If almost everything social is rationalizable, what have we said that is theoretically useful? Recall, however, that these are the very same critics who claimed that these types of action could not be "rationalized" in terms of instrumentalism or calculation. When this claim is shown not to go through, they then claim that nothing important has been said, despite the fact that they have been shown to be mistaken. In other words, they claim that instrumentalism or calculation is so dangerous that expressive and moral action must be protected from their influence (claiming that essential features of these types of action provide the necessary immunization). When these types of action are shown not to be immune—when it is argued for example that moral and expressive action have a calculative form—they then claim that the influence of calculation is actually unimportant.

In responding in this fashion to some of the critics, we are not committed to the position that distinctions cannot be made between different types of actions and of explanations. However, if all reason-explanations are rationalizable, a criterion based on some kind of instrumentalism or calculation does not provide the basis of differentiation. One possible way to go here would be to argue that the necessary distinction(s) can be provided by separating weak and strong notions of rationality. Another way to get at differences in reason-explanations would be to focus on the types of ends motivating action under the assumption that actions are intentional under different descriptions. Then the debate is much less about rationality per se but about what ends are operative in particular instances. From this point of view, theories are different according to the restrictions they place on allowable ends within their theoretical schemas, thereby avoiding much of the muddle about calculation and instrumentalism.[20] It may actually be the case that the critics have something like this in mind when they distinguish these different types of actions, but their emphasis on instrumentalism and calculation obscures it.[21] We do not deny the deep-seated intuition that moral acts or expressive acts have unusual qualities. Rather, from two very different points of view about action—one causal (Davidson) and another non-causal (Vogler), standard ways of distinguishing acts are not completely successful. Moreover, our doubts are reinforced by the presence of similar problems in the work of Habermas, whose theory of action is probably more influential and better known in the social sciences than Davidson or Vogler.

In Habermas' case, the argument distinguishes strategic action, which is success-oriented, from communicative action, which is oriented toward reaching understanding. Social actions can be distinguished along these lines according to whether participants adopt either of these attitudes. Habermas uses Austin's (1962) speech act theory to make his argument about the relationship between understanding and strategic action. Habermas claims that illocutionary and perlocutionary speech acts map onto the distinction between communicative and strategic action. Skinner's (Tully, 1988) work, however, can be used to show that Habermas's claim is not valid. For Skinner, illocutionary acts can be strategic and still fulfill the constitutive condition of an illocution. Intentions in illocutionary acts thus are non-causal (hence constitutive of action), standing in neither a contingent nor antecedent relationship to an act, yet illocutions can still be strategic. Habermas, on the other hand, argues that intentions in illocutions are not causes but he does not admit that illocutions can be strategic. Acts that fulfill the constitutive condition of an illocution cannot be strategic. Skinner shows that this is mistaken and thereby provides a general argument about how conventions can be strategically manipulated by exploiting the illocutionary forces of language (Meadwell, 1994). While the region of pure communicative action does not shrink to nothing as a consequence of this problem in Habermas's argument, his difficulty is similar to the difficulties in identifying types of action already discussed.

Moreover, the strategic possibilities inherent in the illocutionary force of language provide in effect a theoretical foundation for work on the strategy of political rhetoric involving actors who have commitments[22]. Such actors may have commitments to prescriptive beliefs or to non-instrumental cognitive beliefs; they may be principled actors with political identities for example. Still, if they want to engage in politics, they have to think instrumentally; they have to try to assess the probable consequences for maximizing support and minimizing opposition of various alternative political strategies,[23] including rhetorical strategies. And thinking instrumentally in these contexts implies strategic thinking because of the interdependence of choice in political contexts. A discriminating activist may even mix tactics, according to the heterogeneity of the group in question. These tactics may involve the use of material incentives; however, agenda-setting and issue-framing and other rhetorical strategies aimed at persuasion are also relevant and consistent with strategic rationality.

This perspective on rational action seems able to meet some of those concerns that motivate the critics of rational choice theory, such as the relevance of identities, principles and ideologies—in short, the importance of commitments. It is often the case that a forced choice is expected between two positions: strategy without commitments or commitments without strategy. It is a false choice.

This forced choice insists on restricting rational choice theory to economic and material incentives, to agents who engage in economistic calculations of costs and benefits and who are radically undersocialized, having internalized no prescriptive beliefs or non-instrumental cognitive beliefs whatsoever (Barry, 1970). From this starting point, any theoretical attempt to allow agents some degree of socialization, or to think of calculation in terms other than dollars or cents or costs or benefits is considered to be post-hoc, ad-hoc or tautological. The charge of tautology surely works both ways, however, since it is the prior restriction placed on rational choice theory by its critics which makes good their criticism (virtually by definition, that is).[24]

Conclusion

The problem of rationality is at the core of the human and social sciences. Whatever one's position in the debates about rationality, it is hard to imagine a more fertile intellectual puzzle nor a more splendid object of controversy. The debate has produced some of the most powerful, and most sharply contested, work in social science.

If the debate about rationality has a long lineage, the contributors to this volume have taken up one important contemporary variant—rational choice theory. Despite their different disciplinary backgrounds, their chapters have provided an unusually coherent whole. As a way of concluding the discussion, we have returned to several themes raised by our contributors. They are themes of importance in the larger debate in the social sciences about rational choice: the influence of economic theory and method in theories of rational choice and action, the possibility of theoretical complementarity across rival theories and the issue of instrumentalism.

In a debate that is both long-lived and still highly topical, we have no illusions that controversy has now ended. The debate continues, improved, we believe, by the efforts of our contributors.

Notes

1. On this score, compare Lazear (2000) and Zafirovski (2000).
2. A key issue in this field, whenever an economic theory or model is used, is whether government activity is endogenous to economics, or is specified separately. We do not address the literature on political economy directly here, nor have our contributors, so we do not take up this issue directly, although our discussion in the first section of this Conclusion could in other circumstances be brought to bear on it.
3. Note that the follow-up to Green and Shapiro's *Pathologies of Rational Choice* (1994), which is an influential contemporary critical analysis of rational choice theory, is subtitled "economic models of politics reconsidered" Friedman (1996).
4. Examples from a large literature include Schick (1997) and Elster (1986).
5. For one illustration of this method, which is important in macro-level cross-national analysis, see for example, Skocpol (1979). On the relationship of Mill's method of difference to quasi-experimental and experimental research design, see King (1994). For some critical discussion, see Ragin (1987) and Brady and Collier (2001).
6. Recall that many of the foundations of quasi-experimental design came out of work in genetics research and agricultural field stations (e.g., Fisher, Wright) in which causes rather than intentions loom large.
7. A model or system of equations in which all variables are endogenous in not identified.
8. We note as well that this specification of the game theoretic foundations of competitive equilibrium also depends on modifications to standard assumptions about rationality in economics (Gale, 2000: 157-166).
9. The theme of embedded economic activity in the discipline of sociology goes back at least to Durkheim and thence to Parson's "problem of social order." It continues to be important in various forms ranging from the work of Granovetter (1985) to "socioeconomics" (Etzioni et. al., 2001) to Fligstein's (2001) work. More generally, see Guillén et. al. (2002).
10. The new economics of organization works in the interstices of these overlapping perspectives. See for example, Williamson (1996); Milgrom and Roberts (1992).
11. We note that this move would put politics in the service of the economy by privileging economic production and exchange, for example, treating political institutions as solutions to problems of positive transaction costs in that production and exchange (e.g., North, 1990; 1981 and the classic work of Coase).
12. The notion of an incredible threat is actually rather tricky. See Kavka (1983) and the literature that this piece produced.
13. For the uninitiated, these concepts can be found in any contemporary textbook on game theory.
14. On this theme, see Lupia, McCubbins and Popkin (2000).
15. Incorporating strategic choice into models of interaction has consequences for statistical estimation. See for example Signorino (1999) who draws on the work of econometricans such as McKelvey and Palfrey.

16.   A macro theory that rests on non-individualist premises probably cannot coherently talk about "action" at all. An interesting case would be the arguments of Satz and Ferejohn (1994) who develop an "external" interpretation of rational choice theory, but who do so by using almost exclusively neoclassical price theory as the exemplar of rational choice theory. See also the comments by Hausman (1995).

17.   There is an ongoing debate in political sociology about the strengths and weaknesses of varieties of institutional analysis. For discussion, see for example, Thelen (1999); Steinmo, Thelen and Longstreth (1992); Taylor and Hall (1996); Immergut (1998); Pontusson (1995); Ostrom (1995); Knight and Sened (1995).

18.   Without this latter proviso, we might not be able to distinguish culture and biology.

19.   For a discussion of intrinsic motivation, often also used as a counter to rational choice theory (e.g., Taylor, 1996) from a Davidsonian perspective, see Mele (2003: 73-74).

20.   The assumptive frameworks of different social and political theories may predispose them towards particular types of ends, for example. Let us note as well that we focus on ends here for the purpose at hand—which is to consider objections to rational choice that rest on distinctions between types of action: expressive, moral and instrumental. Talking about a theory in terms of ends will not exhaust the relevant content of that theory.

21.   Differentiating action according to degree of rationality ("weak" versus "strong") is strictly different from differentiating according to types of ends only if (1) strong can be distinguished from weak rationality without referring to ends and (2) if strong (or weak) rationality is not correlated with types of ends. (If 'strongly' rational actions, for example, tend to be in pursuit of particular types of ends, then strength of rationality and types of ends are correlated).

22.   Some of these possibilities can be seen in Skinner's contextual approach to political philosophy.

23.   De Nardo's *reductio* (1987: 53), aimed at the theoretical literature on free-riding, is revealing: "[S]ocialists will gladly participate in fascist demonstrations, and vice versa, if the organizers simply provide coffee and doughnuts to the marchers." This might look like a comment from a critic of rational choice, but De Nardo then proceeded to develop a rationalist theory of radical political activism while taking theoretically on board ideological beliefs. Green and Shapiro (1994: 79) use a similar example but draw different conclusions: "A Christian fundamentalist walking through a park in which two demonstrations are going simultaneously—pro-choice rally to her left and pro-life rally to her right—might easily join the former if the refreshments provided were sufficiently enticing."

24.   There may be examples of work in rational choice that have these features, but they will tend to be economistic, and economism is best seen as a limiting case rather than a core exemplar of rational choice or, if this is too strong, at least as only a subset of the latter.

References

Anscombe, G. E. M. 2000 (1958). *Intention*. Cambridge, MA: Harvard University Press.

Aumann, Robert J. 1964. Markets with a continuum of traders, *Econometrica* 32: 39-50.

Austin, John L. 1975 [1962]. *How To Do Things with Words*. 2nd. edition. Cambridge, MA: Harvard University Press.

Baker, Keith M. 1982. On the problem of the ideological origins of the French revolution, in Dominick Lacapra and Steven A. Kaplan (eds.) *Modern European Intellectual History: Reappraisals and New Perspectives*. Ithaca, NY: Cornell University Press.

Barry, Brian. 1970. *Sociologists, Economists and Democracy*. Chicago and London: University of Chicago Press.

Bates, Robert, Avner Greif, Margaret Levi, Jean-Laurent Rosenthal and Barry M. Weingast. 1998. *Analytic Narratives*. Princeton, NJ: Princeton University Press.

Blais, André. 2001. *To Vote Or Not To Vote? The Merits and Limits of Rational Choice*. Pittsburgh, PA: University of Pittsburgh Press.

Brady, Henry E. and David Collier (eds.) *Rethinking Social Inquiry: Diverse Tools, Shared Standards*. Lanham, MD.: Rowman and Littlefield.

Casti, John L. and Werner DePauli. 2000. *Gödel. A Life of Logic*. Cambridge, MA: Perseus Publishing.

Coleman, James C. 1990. *Foundations of Social Theory*. Cambridge, MA: Harvard University Press.

Cox, Gary. 1999. The empirical content of rational choice theory: A reply to Green and Shapiro, *Journal of Theoretical Politics* 11: 147-170.

Davidson, Donald. 2000[1963]. Actions, reasons and causes, in Donald Davidson, *Essays on Actions and Events*. Oxford and New York: Clarendon Press.

De Nardo, James. 1987. *Power in Numbers: The Political Strategy of Protest and Rebellion*. Princeton, NJ: Princeton University Press.

Elster, Jon. (ed.). 1986. *Rational Choice*. New York: New York University Press.

Elster, Jon. 1978. *Logic and Society: Contradictions and possible worlds*. Chicester and New York: Wiley.

Etzioni, Amitai, R. Fuerder and G. Wuebker (eds.) *Essays in Socio-Economics*. New York: Springer-Verlag.

Ferguson, Niall (ed.). 2000. *Virtual History: Alternatives and Counterfactuals*. New York; Basic Books.

Fligstein, Neil. 2001. *The Architecture of Markets*. Princeton, NJ: Princeton University Press.

Friedman, Jeffrey (ed.). 1996. *The Rational Choice Controversy: Economic Models of Politics Reconsidered*. New Haven, CT and London: Yale University Press.

Gale, Douglas. 2000. *Strategic Foundations of General Equilibrium*. Cambridge and New York: Cambridge University Press.

Gates, Scott and Brian D. Humes. 1997. *Games, Information and Politics*. Ann Arbor, MI.: University of Michigan Press.

Gigerenzer, Gerd. 1996. Rationality: why social context matters, in Peter B. Baltes and Ursula M. Standinger (eds.) *Interactive Minds*. Cambridge: Cambridge University Press.

Gigerenzer, Gerd and Peter M. Todd. 1999. Fast and frugal heuristics: the adaptive toolbox, in Gerd Gigerenzer and Peter M. Todd (eds.) *Simple Heuristics That Make Us Smart*. Oxford: Oxford University Press.

Gödel, Kurt. 1967[1931]. On formally undecidable propositions of *Principia Mathematica* and related systems, in Jean van Heijenoort (ed.) *Frege and Gödel. Two Fundamental Texts in Mathematical Logic*. Cambridge, MA: Harvard University Press.

Granovetter, Mark. 1985. Economic action and social structure: the problem of embeddness, *American Sociological Review* 26: 481-510.

Green, Donald P. and Ian Shapiro. 1996. *Pathologies of Rational Choice Theory: A Critique of Applications in Political Science*. New Haven, CT and London: Yale University Press.

Guillén, Mauro, Randall Collins, Paula England, and Marshall Meyer (eds.). 2002. *The New Economic Sociology: Developments in an Emerging Field*. New York: Russell Sage.

Habermas, Jürgen. 1984[1981]. *The Theory of Communicative Action*. Volume I Thomas McCarthy (trans.) Boston: Beacon Press.

Harsanyi, John C. 1995. Games with incomplete information, *American Economic Review* 85: 291-303.

Hausman, Daniel. 1995. Rational choice and social theory: a critique, *Journal of Philosophy* 92: 96-102.

Hettich, Walter and Stanley L. Winer. 1999. *Democratic Choice and Taxation: A Theoretical and Empirical Analysis*. Cambridge and New York: Cambridge University Press.

Immergut, Ellen, 1998. The theoretical core of the new institutionalism, *Politics and Society* 26: 5-34.

James, Susan. 1985. *The Social Content of Explanation*. Cambridge and New York: Cambridge University Press.

Kavka, Gregory S. 1983. The toxin puzzle. *Analysis* 43: 33-36.

King, Gary, Robert Keohane and Sidney Verba. 1994. *Desiging Social Inquiry*. Princeton, NJ: Princeton University Press.

Knight, Jack and Itai Sened (eds.) *Explaining Social Institutions*. Ann Arbor: University of Michigan Press.

Kreps, David M. 1990. *Game Theory and Economic Modelling*. Oxford: Clarendon Press.

Lazear, Edward P. 2000. Economic imperialism, *Quarterly Journal of Economics* 115: 99-146.

Lupia. Arthur, Mathew D. McCubbins and Samuel L. Popkin (eds). 2000. *Elements of Reason*. Cambridge and New York: Cambridge University Press.

Manfredi, Christopher. 2002. Strategic behavior and the Canadian Charter of Rights and Freedoms, in Patrick James, Donald E. Abelson and Michael Lusztig (eds.) *The Myth of the Sacred*. Montreal and Kingston: McGill-Queen's University Press.

Meadwell, Hudson. 1994. The foundations of Habermas's universal pragmatics, *Theory and Society* 23: 711-727.

Mele, Alfred R. 2003. Philosophy of action, in Kirk Ludwig (ed.) *Donald Davidson*. Cambridge and New York: Cambridge University Press.

Milgrom, Paul and John Roberts. 1992. *Economics, Organization and Management*. New York: Harper and Row.

Millward, R. 1970. Exclusion costs, external economies and market failure," *Oxford Economics Papers* 22:24-37.

Morton, Rebecca. B. 1999. *Methods and Models*. Cambridge and New York: Cambridge University Press.

Nagel Ernest and James R. Newman. 2001. *Gödel's Proof*. rev. ed. New York and London: New York University Press.

North, Douglass C. 1990. *Institutions, Institutional Change and Economic Performance*. Cambridge: Cambridge University Press.

North, Douglass. C. 1981. *Structure and Change in Economic History*. New York: W. W. Norton.

Ostrom, Elinor. 1995. New horizons in institutional analysis, *American Political Science Review* 89: 174-178.

Pontusson, Jonas. 1995. From comparative public policy to political economy: Putting political institutions in their proper place, *Comparative Political Studies* 28: 117-147.

Przeworski, Adam. 1996. The role of theory in comparative politics, *World Politics* 48: 16-21.

Ragin, Charles. 1987. *The Comparative Method. Moving Beyond Qualitative and Quantitative Strategies*. Berkeley and Los Angeles: University of California Press.

Satz, Sarah and John Ferejohn. 1994. Rational choice and social theory, *Journal of Philosophy* 91: 71-87.

Schelling, Thomas. 1960. *The Strategy of Conflict*. Cambridge, MA: Harvard University Press.

Schick, Frederic. 1997. *Making Choices: A Recasting of Decision Theory*. Cambridge and New York: Cambridge University Press.

Shubik, Martin. 1984. *Game Theory in the Social Sciences*. Cambridge, MA: MIT Press.

Signorino, Curtis. 1999. Strategic interaction and the statistical analysis of international conflict, *American Political Science Review*. 32: 279-298.

Skocpol, Theda, 1995. Why I am an historical institutionalist, *Polity* 38: 103-106.

Skocpol, Theda. 1994. *Social Revolutions in the Modern World*. Cambridge and New York: Cambridge University Press.

Skocpol, Theda. 1979. *States and Social Revolutions: A comparative analysis of France, Russia and China*. Cambridge and New York: Cambridge University Press.

Snidal, Duncan. 1979. Public goods, property rights and political organizations", *International Studies Quarterly* 23: 532-566.

Steinmo, Sven, Kathleen Thelen and Frank Longstreth (eds.) 1992. *Structuring Politics: Historical Institutionalism in Comparative Analysis*. Cambridge and New York: Cambridge University Press.

Taylor, Michael. 1996. When rationality fails, in Jeffrey Friedman (ed.) *The Rational Choice Controversy. Economic Models of Politics Reconsidered*. New Haven, CT and London: Yale University Press.

Taylor, Michael. 1993[1989]. Structure, culture and action in the explanation of social change, in William James Booth, Patrick James and Hudson Meadwell (eds.) *Politics and Rationality*. Cambridge and New York: Cambridge University Press.

Taylor, Michael. 1988. Rationality and revolutionary collective action, in Michael Taylor (ed.) *Rationality and Revolution*. Cambridge and New York: Cambridge University Press.

Taylor, Rosemary and Peter Hall. 1996. Political science and the three new institutionalisms, *Political Studies* 44: 936-957.

Tetlock, Philip and Aaron Belkin (eds.) 1996. *Counterfactual Thought Experiments in World Politics: Logical, Methodological and Psychological Perspectives*. Princeton, NJ: Princeton University Press.

Thelen, Kathleen. 1999. Historical institutionalism in comparative perspective, *Annual Review of Political Science*.

Tully, James. (ed.). 1988. *Meaning and Context*. Oxford: Polity Press.

Vogler, Candace. 2002. *Reasonably Vicious*. Cambridge, MA and London: Harvard University Press.

Williamson, Oliver. 1996. (ed.) *The Mechanisms of Governance*. New York: Oxford University Press.

Young, H. Peyton. 1993. The evolution of conventions, *Econometrica* 61: 57-84.

Zafirovski, Milan. 2000. The rational choice generalization of neoclassical economics reconsidered: any theoretical legitimation for economic imperialism? *Sociological Theory* 18: 448-471.

Contributors

Mario Bunge is the Frothingham Professor of Logic and Metaphysics at McGill University. He has published widely in various languages, on physics, metaphysics, epistemology, philosophy of science, and ethics. His current research includes philosophy of the social sciences and scientific realism. His latest books are *Emergence and Convergence: Qualitative Novelty and the Unity of Knowledge* (2003), *Philosophical Dictionary* (2003), and *Mito, realidad y razon* (2004).

George Grantham is associate professor of economics at McGill University. His research areas are economic history, especially the development of the French economy in the eighteenth and nineteenth centuries.

John A. Hall is James McGill Professor of Sociology and dean of the Faculty of Arts at McGill University. He has published widely about sociological theory, modernity, the state, the rise of capitalism, war, nationalism and civil society. His next book, about Ernest Gellner, is forthcoming in 2005.

Michael Hechter is professor of sociology at the University of Washington. His most recent books are *Theories of Social* Order, with Christine Horne (2003), *Social Norms*, with Karl-Dieter Opp (2001), and *Containing Nationalism* (2000).

Christopher P. Manfredi is a professor and chair of the Department of Political Science of McGill University. His research focuses on Canadian public law, constitutional law and the judicial process. His book *Judicial Power and the Charter: Canada and the Paradox of Liberal Constitutionalism* was published in a second edition in 2001.

Storrs McCall is professor of philosophy at McGill University. His interest is in logic and the philosophy of time. He has published widely about quantum theory, decision theory, probability and choice. He is the author of *A Model of the Universe* (1994).

Hudson Meadwell is associate professor of political science at McGill University. He co-edited *Politics and Rationality* (1993).

Robin Rowley is professor of economics at McGill University. He has numerous publications both in applied economics and economic theory, including probability and econometric methodology. With Omar Hamouda he is the editor of *Foundations of Probability, Econometrics and Economic Games* (1997) and co-author of *Probability in Economics* (1996).

Ian Shapiro is William R. Kenan, Jr., Professor and Chair of the Political Science Department at Yale University. His research interests include the methodologies of the social sciences, theories of justice and democracy, the relations between democracy and the distribution of income and wealth. His most recent books are *The Moral Foundations of Politics* (2003) and *The State of Democratic Theory* (2003).

Michael R. Smith is professor of sociology at McGill University. He has published widely about organizational structures, industrial disputes, macroeconomic policy and labor markets. He is the author of *Power, Norms, and Inflation: A Skeptical Treatment* (1992).

Axel van den Berg is professor of sociology at McGill University in Montreal. He is the author of *The Immanent Utopia: From Marxism on the State to the State of Marxism*, available from Transaction.

Index